P9-ASK-063

Gramley Library
Salem College
Winston-Salem, NC 27108

Writing and Technique

89-1875

PE
1404
.D63
1989

Writing and Technique

David N. Dobrin

National Council of Teachers of English
1111 Kenyon Road, Urbana, Illinois 61801

Gramley Library
Salem College
Winston-Salem, NC 27108

NCTE Editorial Board: Donald R. Gallo, Richard Lloyd-Jones, Raymond J. Rodrigues, Dorothy S. Strickland, Brooke Workman, L. Jane Christensen, *ex officio*, John Lansingh Bennett, *ex officio*

Staff Editor: Robert A. Heister

Cover and Interior Design: Tom Kovacs for TGK Design

NCTE Stock Number 58927

© 1989 by the National Council of Teachers of English. All rights reserved. Printed in the United States of America.

It is the policy of NCTE in its journals and other publications to provide a forum for the open discussion of ideas concerning the content and the teaching of English and the language arts. Publicity accorded to any particular point of view does not imply endorsement by the Executive Committee, the Board of Directors, or the membership at large, except in announcements of policy, where such endorsement is clearly specified.

Library of Congress Cataloging-in-Publication Data

Dobrin, David N.
    Writing and technique / David N. Dobrin.
       p. cm.
    Bibliography: p.
    ISBN 0–8141–5892–7
      1. English language—Rhetoric—Study and teaching. I. Title.
PE1404.D63   1989   88–38562
808'.042—dc19   CIP

Contents

Acknowledgments

Without the help of many people, this book would not have been written. My greatest debt is to John Searle and Bert Dreyfus, who taught me philosophy, and to Paul Anderson, who taught me technical writing. Long conversations with Christine Skarda, Corby Collins, and Jerry Wakefield helped me understand what they had to teach.

Charles Sides, Steven Strang, and Beth Soll closely read drafts of the manuscript. Bob Heister of NCTE and Elizabeth Rehfeld read what I thought was the final draft, helping me to correct many errors and suggesting many felicities. Michael Sullivan, president of DesignSystems in Cambridge, Massachusetts, did the diagrams in chapters 3 and 4.

Barbara Dobrin managed the references, for which work I am very grateful. Bachman Information Systems and MIT's Project Athena provided generous technical (!) support. A 1981 summer seminar in Foucault and Heidegger sponsored by the National Endowment for the Humanities gave me a chance to learn about Heidegger, and a 1982-1983 leave from MIT gave me a start on the first draft.

Numerous publishers have been generous in their permission for me to reprint and reproduce materials in this book: Addison-Wesley Publishers for Robert Rathbone's diagrams; Bayside Publishing Company, Inc., for materials in chapter 3; the Institute of Electrical and Electronics Engineers, Inc., for materials in chapter 2; Random House, Inc., for materials in chapter 9; and the University of Illinois Press for Shannon's and Weaver's diagram.

Many other people, too many to name, were generous with their advice and counsel, and I am grateful. Without them, this book would have many more faults. The faults that remain, of course, are entirely my own.

Preface

This book is about writing and tools. It begins with writing about tools (technical writing), considers writing itself as a tool, and concludes with tools that aid writing. The aim is to study the interpenetration of writing and technology: in particular, how technology has affected writing. It asks, for instance, whether writing about technology must be molded to its subject matter and also whether writing can be made into a technology.

The book cheerfully allies itself with a tradition of opposition to technology, a tradition that includes Thoreau and the Luddites, William Morris and the generals who prolonged World War I, Heidegger and the hippies. To belong to this tradition has always been somewhat impractical. One is forced either to decry something one enjoys the fruits of (pronouncing oneself a hypocrite) or to renounce it altogether and pronounce oneself irrelevant.

The sober-minded among the opposition adopt a hedge. They object not to technology itself, but to technology uncontrolled, technology that supplants the human. The trouble with this hedge is that technology is insidious; the notion of controlling it is already a technological one, leading us to discussion of methods of control, optimizing control techniques, and so forth. Yet, to take more extreme positions is to risk sounding shrill and to give up on any chance of having a real effect. Whether I have ended up sounding sober or shrill, I shall let the reader judge.

To join is to sail against a wind that sprang up in the Renaissance (some say with Descartes) and has continued unabated. Many different tacks can be taken against a wind; some even oppose each other. Yet, ultimately, it is the same wind.

"The essence of technology is nothing technological," says Martin Heidegger (1977). The essence of technology is, rather, a way of abstracting things so as to gain control over them and put them to use. Studying the effect of technology on writing, then, is not studying the increasing use of word processors. Rather, it is studying the way people in technical writing try to put writing at the service of technology; studying the descriptions of writing technique and the conversion of those descriptions into advice; and studying the conceptions of writing that make possible the development of writing tools.

The heart of the position I hold is simple. The mind (and hence language and meaning) works in a way that permits the kinds of abstractions that technology demands. All experience and all expression is grounded in the specific situation of a specific human being (I am talking to you right now) and abstractions of that situation always risk losing something essential. Therefore, generalization of such abstractions can never be reliable.

The merits and faults of this position can only be appreciated when they are applied to specific situations. This book is not, therefore, broad and sweeping in its method, however much it may be in its aims. Each chapter takes up a specific idea, or even a phrase expressive of an idea, and examines it closely. The examination is conducted so as to bring out the themes of the book but not to lead seamlessly into the next chapter.

The choice of ideas (or phrases) is actually somewhat arbitrary. Each chapter began as an article, and each article began when I ran across some statement that struck me as, shall we say, not the best that has been known and said. The computer article began when a developer at IBM said in a lecture that, to write his grammar analysis program, he went through every textbook and style guide on writing, looking for rules. "The stricter the rule, the better," he said, "because more precision meant that it was easier to computerize." Other articles were reactions to some statement in a textbook or to offhand remarks in long-forgotten articles. I resurrect these remarks not in order to have straw men, but because, in each case, the fact that somebody actually said them betrays habits of thinking within the community that are the real targets of my study.

When I began writing the articles, I had been hired by MIT to write articles about technical writing. As I wrote, the range of my interests expanded. As a result the first part of the book has material that is of specific interest to teachers of and researchers into technical writing. I have retained this material because it is integral to the argument. Those of you who have no interest in technical writing should feel free to skip what you want, but some of the force of the later chapters will be lost if you do.

In many cases, I hope that what I say will appear to be plain common sense. The main messages of the book are nothing more. The book says, for instance, that writing is very difficult to do and also very difficult to teach. It says that criticism of writing must come from a deep understanding of what the writer is trying to say. It says that systems and methods for doing or teaching writing are good up to a point, but only up to a point. At the same time, the consequences of commonsense assertions, however, can often be radical, and in this book such consequences are explored and often defended.

I believe, for instance, that the main thrust of composition research for the past ten years has been entirely in the wrong direction. If we are going to improve, we will have to abandon the "consensus" that Maxine Hairston described a few years ago (Hairston 1982). This research is founded on a technological analysis of mind and language that the developers of the position I hold are trying to confound. In a sense, I am fighting a skirmish in a larger battle.

I also believe that the whole effort to gain systematic knowledge of writing, a goal that any scientific discipline implicitly takes up, is wrongheaded and, unless radically reunderstood, unlikely to succeed. Rather than modeling our work on the sciences, or even the social sciences, which build up a body of knowledge, we should model it more on professional disciplines, like the law, which attempt to inculcate practices.

In any case, we all have a great deal of work to do if writing is to be improved in this country. This book tries to set that work in a different and more fruitful direction. Whatever course is taken, though, the important thing is for us to buckle down and do it. If this book helps, it will have succeeded.

David N. Dobrin
Paris, 1987

1 The Technology of Writing

Instrumental Writing

The gala at Tanglewood starts in half an hour, and you are lost. You stop a man walking on the side of the road. To your request for directions, he responds as follows:

> Go north along this road two miles until you pass a church. You will get to an intersection with a big tree in the northeast corner. Turn right. The road goes around a curve and you take the first right after that. It's immediately on your left.

The striking thing about this response is its simplicity. The man produces it easily, and following the instructions seems equally easy. The place found, the response would be forgotten by both parties. Unfortunately, what happens next may well be this. You go down the road, and after a mile and a half, you pass a synagogue. The next intersection has a reasonably big tree on what you think is the northeast corner. You turn right and are lost again. The performance starts without you.

For that specific situation, it's easy to see what went wrong. The man should have been clearer about the church; he should have been more precise about the tree. It would be nice, however, to have some more general analysis. This little communication is, after all, paradigmatic of much communication that goes on in our society. Manuals for computers, instructions to technicians, even directions on the backs of boxes are equally straightforward, at least in intention, and they, too, often fail. A general analysis of how to prevent these failures would have no small value.

In this chapter, I want to describe some of the analyses that have been brought to bear on this problem. These analyses have in common that they treat a failure of communication as a failure of technique. This strategy, admittedly, seems commonsensical. Moreover, it makes the analyses fit nicely into the political and social structures where the analyses are advanced.

To make some failure into a failure of technique, you have to look at what created and authorized the technique. Either the technique has been established by some (technical) discipline, which itself is part of some larger group of disciplines, like science or technology, or the technique is some everyday skill, which we all have learned, that can be understood by some technical discipline whose special focus is human nature. The first situates the technique within a technology. The second seeks a technical understanding of the technique.

I will not go into depth here; my purpose is merely to present the types of analyses and to describe the reasons for using them. Subsequent chapters will treat the analyses more fully.

Writing as Technology

What makes the failure of that man's directions so frustrating is that the action they were designed to facilitate apparently consists of a few discrete steps. The road takes you directly to the corner; turning right is one of the few possibilities, and so on. This is not accidental. A huge set of tools are at work regulating and limiting the choices that you can make. The road itself is designed to carry a car that is designed to roll only on the road and only in one of two directions. Numerous conventions about road size, gates, pavement techniques, and so forth guide the car and determine that side roads, driveways, or farm roads are not to be counted as possible choices, whereas other roads of similar size will. Technologies of land use, house building, flood control, and property management indirectly keep you on the path and have even been responsible, long ago, for setting up the signposts you will be using.

It is not at all unreasonable, then, to see finding your way to the gala as using a tool, or perhaps, since there are many tools interconnected, a technology. (A technology is a system of tools and techniques that provides us with means toward an end.) The instructions might well be seen as part of the overall technology, one more tool that enables you to reach your ends. In fact, since they do have their own identity, we might well call instructions a separate technology. There is an end, if the writing is a reliable means to the end, and making that writing itself requires a complex of tools and techniques; ergo, it is a technology.

Theoretical accounts of writing as a technology go back as far as Aristotle. In these accounts, writing is described as an instrument for instilling certain beliefs, causing people to take some definite action, or guiding people to some destination. As complete accounts of writing, they have never been entirely satisfactory for two reasons. First, certain kinds of writing—notably expressive writing—don't seem to be instrumental. For example, when William Wordsworth wrote "Resolution and Independence," he surely had in mind no definite beliefs he wanted others to have and no definite actions he wanted them to take. Second, even when it is instrumental, writing often seems to do much more than is intended. A flier urging someone to vote a certain way might carry information, arouse anger, inspire envy, suggest new ideas, or renew conviction, as well as produce the desired action.

Characterizing directions, or, generally, writing that helps us to use tools as a technology, does not, however, seem open to either of these objections. There is, moreover, an immediate, though subtle, advantage to this characterization because writing then plugs easily into the technological network.

Take the computer manual. Treating it as an instrument, a tool, may or may not be plausible. As soon as we make it plausible however, it can easily be located within the system. The computer is a means to some end (recording information, making calculations), and that end is itself an intermediate means to yet other ends. So is the manual: it helps the user use the computer. Like the computer, it is a product; the product has a value, can be marketed, and must be produced.

Producing the product are specialists: the printer, the designer, and, of course, the technical writer. They make up a production chain much like any other. Each link in the chain has specific skills and performs specific tasks; each falls into a separate job category. In large organizations, where manuals (reports, proposals) may require a team of forty or fifty people, the tasks involved in producing the manual are identified and enumerated. Performance is monitored and evaluated. When the manual is finished, its effectiveness is tested. So, treating writing as a technology also locates it within another network, the technology of production. And it legitimates the deployment of administrative strategies which are effective within that network.

Within the technological apparatus, these strategies are normal and reasonable. But notice that they would rapidly become unreasonable if the manual itself were not thought of as instrumental. How, for instance, could effectiveness be tested if the effect were not well defined? How could we know whether the tasks enumerated were the proper ones if the job itself were not delimited? Would the separation of job categories really make sense?

Such questions, naturally, do not come up in industry; nor have they appeared in the academic literature. The academic field most closely concerned with computer manuals or with faulty directions is technical writing. People in technical writing have largely assumed that writing is a technology; they try to describe the distinctive features of technical writing that make its assimilation possible.

In 1973, the Society for Technical Communication asked Tom Pearsall, a noted expert in the teaching of technical writing, to write a booklet for new teachers in the same field. He begins that book with the following description of technical writing:

> Technical writing may be defined as the presentation in written form of scientific information with clarity and precision on a level suitable to the intended audience. (Pearsall 1975, 1)

As Pearsall points out, except for the subject matter, by this definition technical writing "seems to differ little . . . from any successful writing." But there are some salient differences "caused by the requirements in technical writing for objectivity, formats and report design, graphics, and audience awareness" (p. 1).

For Pearsall, this first differentiating requirement, objectivity, is particularly important. "Technical writing is expected to be objective, scientifically impartial, utterly clear, and unemotional" (p. 1). The language is quite different from the "persuasive, emotional" language that the teacher of composition is familiar with, the kind of language used in the "novel" or even the "freshman essay." On the contrary, "technical writing is concerned with facts and the careful, honest interpretation of those facts."

Although "the concern for objectivity" can "show up in trivial ways," (for instance, when the first person is "proscribed in technical reports"), most "people realize that objectivity is measured more by the amount of factual information present and the honesty of the interpretation than by the kinds of pronouns used." There is, moreover, at least one "advantage in technical writing's objective style. Generally, objective writing is easier to evaluate than subjective writing." Technical writing is "functional." "If the audience can understand it and use it, it's good writing" (Pearsall 1975, 2).

For Pearsall, then, what makes technical writing functional is a combination of three things: the fact that the writing is about technical subjects, the fact that the presentation is objective, and the fact that the writing contains information. Other writing might be functional, but it would not be technical writing.

Nor, without these features, would technical writing be a technology. Unless the subject matter is technical, obviously, the writing can't be plugged in. Objectivity, too, is a necessary feature because a technology is always available to any qualified user. Consider, for example, the technology of roads and conventions that was described earlier. That technology is available to you and to the person giving directions and to anyone else who happens to come along. The objectivity of technical writing is what makes it available; writing with excess emotion or even excess identification with a single person would make it less available. And finally, functionality is a necessary feature of any technology; technologies must do something.

But does Pearsall's definition make it plausible to treat technical writing (but not medical or legal or literary writing) as a technological instrument? In a way it does. Writing such as those instructions consists of definite descriptions of definite actions; other kinds of technical writing consist, as Pearsall says, of facts and honest interpretations. It seems that the writing itself constrains the user in the same way as the technology it explains.

Once you accept the fact that the writing constrains the user, just as the road technology does, then diagnosis of any particular case becomes very simple. Why did these directions fail? Obviously, they failed to be clear. Such words as "church" or "two miles" were not adequately defined, or such clarifications as "not a synagogue," and "exactly two miles" should have been offered.

There is a problem, however, with diagnoses of this form, a problem that goes to the heart of this book. They are not principled. Receiving the instructions, you would not see any problems with what the words mean; nor would the man giving them sense any problem. Only afterwards can you see that the communication was not functional. But to make them principled is not easy. You would need, for one thing, to assume that, in every such communication, the meaning could be determined with absolute accuracy; only then would it be reasonable to say, as in the preceding case, that a failure indicated inaccurate or incomplete definition. But if one can't make that assumption, the whole plausibility of describing technical writing as instrumental suffers greatly because the writing technology would not be constraining the reader the way the road constrains the car.

We have pursued this strand as far as we need to in this chapter. I have been describing the notion that certain kinds of writing are technological because they are solely instrumental. Their function is to transfer technical information; they can do this because they present information objectively, in words that admit unambiguous definition. In the next four chapters, I am going to examine each of these four key ideas (*technical, definition, information transfer,* and *objectivity*) in far more detail. The first of these chapters presents some ideas that will be needed in the next three, at the same time presenting another example of failed technical communication. The next one examines the question of definition by looking at definitions of technical writing. The third looks at one characterization of technical writing as information transfer. And the last chapter examines the criterion of objectivity.

Writing as Technique

Even if describing a type of writing as a technology because it is instrumental turns out not to be fruitful, one might still describe the writing as a collection of techniques. The diagnosis of the preceding example would be that one technique or another wasn't used correctly. The description would not permit us to wear the mantle of technology, but it would permit us to situate the analysis itself within a large and powerful context, that of cognitive science.

Cognitive science is a branch of research conducted by philosophers, psychologists, linguists, and computer scientists. These people all share the assumption that mental functioning is a rule-governed procedure, exactly like the rule-governed procedures used by a computer. This assumption is a natural consequence of physicalism, the idea that any physical phenomenon must be caused. Cognitive science is on this account simply an attempt to describe systematically the causes of mental functioning.

The problems that cognitive science addresses are, in fact, quite far removed from the problems posed by the failure of the directions. They include the problem of how people parse sentences, the problem of creating machines that replicate human vision capabilities, and the problem of defining the theoretical constraints exerted by their governing assumption. Nevertheless, the findings of cognitive science have strongly influenced the study of writing; indeed, Maxine Hairston recently urged that our current "paradigm" of research is and should be founded on it (Hairston 1982).

It is important to realize that if cognitive science were successful, it would be able to describe the functioning of the mind and of language as nothing more than a set of techniques (or rules—I will use the words interchangeably). Similarly, if the current paradigm were successful, it would be able to describe the techniques that make up writing. This is a strong claim. It does not mean simply that people use techniques when they write (who could deny that?); it means that writing is nothing more than a collection of techniques, a complex one, admittedly, but still nothing but technique.

Without such a claim, of course, the results obtained by research would have no scientific standing. Observations of techniques would be like the zoological observations published in the *Proceedings of the Royal Society* during the eighteenth century: meaningless, because no zoological system permitted the observers to distinguish between salient and accidental features.

The current paradigm could include the so-called techniques of rhetoric, the strategies whereby writing influences the reader. But it doesn't. Rather, since investigators have been inspired by cognitive psychology and linguistics, the two foci of interest have been on the mental techniques used to produce the writing (the so-called writing process) and on formal properties of writing.

The strongest and most self-consciously cognitive description of the writing process as technique has been Linda Flower's (Flower and Hayes, "A Cognitive Process Theory," 1981). She describes writing as a "problem-solving process"; the techniques of writing are the techniques of solving the problems posed by the writing situation. The task of research into writing is to identify those problems and describe the techniques. Again, notice that, if writing were only partially a problem-solving process, this would be a completely uninteresting assertion. It would offer us no way of performing an analysis based on it because we would be unable to distinguish between inspiration, knee-jerk responses, and problem-solving. "Problem-solving process" would be reduced to a metaphor, and at that, an unsurprising and unilluminating one.

Flower's work is not so detailed that one can confidently imagine her diagnosis of those earlier, miserable directions. But the following description might be attributed to her. One problem that a writer faces is the problem of meeting the constraints imposed by characteristics of the audience. A cognitive account has it that the writer knows a certain number of facts about the audience and has some rules for evaluating those facts. For example, when choosing whether to say "bar" or "saloon," the fact that "my audience prefers short words" emerges for the writer, and the rule, "follow audience preferences," is applied. Accordingly, the shorter word is chosen. The cognitivist might well have discovered this empirically; the writer would have reported this during an experimental procedure called "protocol analysis."

In the earlier direction, the fact might be, "My audience is prone to error," and the rule might be, "Overspecify when audiences are prone to error." Strict adherence to this rule, however, would produce a much longer and more confusing set of instructions, so other rules, as yet undetermined, would have to lead the writer to specify "exactly two miles," and so on.

For this diagnosis to be an explanation, however, there must also be an account of how facts are known, brought to bear, and used. Cognitivism offers such an account, which I will describe in subsequent chapters. As it turns out, this account, too, relies on a belief that meanings can be made definite. So when I get to the cognitivist account of audience in chapter 6, material from the previous four chapters will be used again.

Those who investigate the formal properties of writing are working by analogy with linguistics. Linguistic studies describe the properties that sentences must have if they are to be intelligible: for example, that they have nouns and verbs. To put this into the terminology previously used, you could say that one technique for constructing a proper sentence is to use a noun and a verb. In the teaching of writing, the focus is usually on linguistic units larger than the sentence, like the paragraph or even the essay. As I will show in chapter 8, investigations into these units have been influenced by the feeling that some sort of structure ought to be there, a feeling which goes back to cognitive assumptions about technique and to physicalism. I will show that, in fact, there is no technique for writing paragraphs.

All such investigations have had a heavily prescriptive side to them. The formal features of paragraphs are discovered so that they can be taught and so that problems of failed communication can be diagnosed. No apparently formal problems are more vexing than the problems of a longer piece that is disordered or has not been planned properly, and thus nowhere would it be more desirable to have a list of formal features of a paper or techniques for producing one. In chapter 7, I look at one such planning method, and from that, I show why it's implausible to believe that any planning technique exists.

Again, investigation into formal properties might be able to provide a diagnosis of the failed communication. However, in constructing the example, I have deliberately given it the formal property that is most often stipulated for instructions: for example, make them step-by-step. The aim of formal analysis is, of course, to be able to identify the formal properties that this communication lacks, or, to put it another way, to give infallible instructions for creating infallible directions.

Writing Tools

If techniques for producing writing or lists of formal features (techniques of writing) existed, and if cognitivism were right, much of the work of writing could be given to a computer. It is not surprising, therefore, that some people have been working backwards, trying to find techniques of writing that the computer can test or even implement. In the last chapter, I look at how well they have succeeded.

I regard the advent of computer tools for writing as an empirical test of the theories I am advancing. If writing is indeed a technology because it is instrumental, there is no reason to believe that similar or better technologies, probably computerized, would not produce better effects. If writing is, in fact, a collection of techniques, there is no reason that the computer can't reproduce those techniques or substitute better ones. Indeed, even if I am right, and writing cannot be effectively understood as a collection of formal techniques, the computer ought to be able to test the extent to which writing is formal, again by substituting computerized processes for human ones or by checking for the existence of the formal features. So far, computer aids for writing are severely limited. I argue, in chapter 9, that the limitation is a principled one: in essence, the limitation is the lack of formal features in writing. So that the argument is not circular, but empirical, I include some predictions, the confounding of which would severely compromise my overall argument.

Why Isn't Writing a Technology?

Even if we cannot get any analytical purchase on the problems of writing by treating it as a technology, there are two reasons for wanting to do so. The first is a residue of the physicalism mentioned earlier. If we believe in science, and if we also believe that any phenomenon can be explained scientifically, it is hard to believe that writing cannot be subjected to a fruitful scientific (formal) analysis. The second is that the current academic system valorizes the results of scientific analysis. The picture we all have is that scholarly work, for which we are all rewarded, is the construction of a great house of knowledge devoted to a particular subject. The knowledge that wins the most esteem is the kind that fits easily into the structure, namely scientific knowledge of abstract (formal) features and their function (technique). If knowledge of writing were ineluctably local, purely a matter of how an individual should respond in a unique situation, it would be very hard to build an academic discipline from it, and publication would become even more difficult.

In this book, I argue that technical analysis is not fruitful and that it is much more fruitful to seek out local knowledge. Just so you know where I'm going, let me give a synopsis here of why I think so.

In a technical analysis, one attempts to isolate features that all instances of the analysand (the thing being analyzed) share. (The analysand can be any phenomenon.) Correct technical analysis isolates the features that matter; in controlling those features, one controls the analysand. Proper technical analysis of paragraphs finds us the crucial features of paragraphs; inclusion of those features in paragraphs makes for good ones. Proper technical analysis of the information content of a manual allows us to determine whether the information is transmitted efficiently and teaches ways of improving this efficiency. Proper technical analysis of spelling, style, or grammar shows us the features of good style, spelling, and grammar and permits us to program computers to look for those features.

Any proper technical analysis requires that you be able to abstract the crucial features from the rest of the situation. My argument is that the very nature of meaning does not permit accurate abstraction. Meaning, you see, is always situation- or context-dependent: at any time, anything about the situation or context can affect the meaning crucially. Abstractions have no principled way of detecting changes in context or situation, so no accurate, principled statements involving these abstractions are possible. Furthermore, no method of diagnosis or control and no prescriptions that depend on this analysis can be accurate.

Worse than being inaccurate, technical analysis leads us astray. It leads us to expect that certain kinds of communications will work when they actually won't, and it leads us in the wrong directions when we're looking for a solution. We end up missing the gala. If we realize that the success of all communication depends on our ability, as human beings, to find a way of communicating—not on our ability to apply techniques—we can often find our way.

To return to those directions, they fail because both you and the farmer meant different things by the words (more on this later), but there is no principled way to discover this in advance. But we can use our common sense and a certain amount of study of similar situations to discover better ways of giving directions ("in this countryside," "among these people").

In my experience, for instance, the following kind of communication might well work better:

> You see that hill in the distance [pointing]? Tanglewood is right behind it. The road heads straight toward the hill now, but just before it gets there, it veers away. You have to get off the road and then go around the right side of the hill. Just before the road veers away, there's an intersection; it's the only one with a big, tall tree on the far right side. (And so on . . . .)

As long as you can see the hill, this version helps you orient yourself while you are following the instructions; that's why it's better. This observation, however, is not principled; it might not help you orient yourself, and orientation might not be better. Could I publish this claim in an academic journal? If not, I want to argue it in this book; so much the worse for the academic journal.

Remember, nothing about writing intrinsically demands that it be treated as a technology, as something that must be investigated, or as a subject of analytical academic articles. Writing is a skill; many skills that we use every day have never been subjected to analysis and require no specialists to teach them.

We could, of course, subject other skills to similar treatment. Imagine, for instance, that for some odd reason everybody decided that bad manners were impeding our productivity. In our corporations, we would start sequestering the louts and make specialists— you make up a job category for them—responsible for their interface with the outside world. We would make managers responsible for the manners of their employees. We would add the category of manners to evaluation forms. Complaints about graduates' manners would soon flood deans' offices, and people in academic departments (history? psychology? social work?) would be deputized to develop courses. If they failed, we might have to spin off a new academic department staffed by people with graduate degrees in manners. Their academic journals would, of course, be filled with the same cries of triumph, proclamations of new paradigms, and incomprehensible statistics that ours are.

But would making manners into a technology do any good? No. The reason, of course, is that our manners are tied up with our entire being. Proper manners, in any situation, depend on the person

Gramley Library
Salem College
Winston-Salem, NC 27108

we're talking to, our view of the situation, our sense of ourselves as moral agents, our sensitivity to others, our knowledge of others, our sense of our own purposes in the situation, our ingenuity, and, of course, our upbringing. In any situation, all these things interact in complex ways. Teaching people to have good manners, therefore, is tantamount to changing their view of the world.

Of course, manners are actually taught. At some private high schools and a few American and British universities, people learn manners and keep them for the rest of their lives. But these people are taught by being immersed in a world where everyone has the requisite manners. They are taught by changing the student's way of life. Everybody, notice, is responsible for this teaching, and it goes on all the time. No one requires technical analysis of the factors involved, and specialization would be a positive liability, though, of course (tipping my hat to dear Mrs. Martin), some may be more expert in the area than others.

"Perhaps," you might say, "the analogy is getting a little strained. Sure, it would be nice if good writing were demanded as a matter of course. But what do manners, something deeply tied up with ordinary human relations, have to do with straightforward writing, like instructions, which are simply a matter of getting the right words in the right order?"

The answer is that instructions are also a matter of ordinary human relations. Expertise comes from knowledge and experience, not from specialized research. Skill comes from steady practice and frequent failure. Improvement comes from constant work in an environment that simply demands it. And teaching is mostly a matter of listening carefully and correcting gently.

2 Do Not Grind Armadillo Armor in This Mill

In this chapter, I want to show you a concrete example of what I mean when I say that writing successful instructions is primarily a matter of human relations. I also want to show you how important common sense is in communications and how easy it is to forget about it. And I want to bring up some theoretical ideas that will be used throughout the book. Before you read further, look carefully at the instructions for a coffee mill, which are presented in figure 2-1.

Some time ago I showed these instructions to an audience of technical writers. While they were reading, I heard titters all over the hall. Yet, when we began to discuss the instructions, no one could say what was wrong with them, and most people had to admit they were pretty ordinary—run of the mill, you might say. Certainly, nobody could see any reason to get exercised about them.

If the instructions are ordinary, and I agree they are, it's too bad. They are not good instructions. As a matter of fact, I'm going to argue that they're not instructions at all, even though they are called instructions and even though they have the linguistic form of instructions. Instructions must do more than be called instructions and sound like instructions; to be instructions, they have to satisfy some commonsense rules. These instructions violated those rules, and that is what caused the titters.

Those rules have been extensively studied in a branch of philosophy called "speech act theory." In this chapter, I am going to describe the rules and show you how these instructions fail to follow them. Before I go into detail, though, let me explain in intuitive terms what is wrong. Look at the instruction, "Do not use outdoors." This instruction, taken literally, makes no sense. Obviously, there is no reason on earth why I should not, if the mood strikes

An earlier version of this chapter first appeared in *IEEE Transactions on Professional Communication*, vol. PC-28, no. 4: 30–37. Copyright 1985 IEEE.

IMPORTANT SAFEGUARDS

When using electrical appliances, basic safety precautions should always be observed, including the following:

1. Read all instructions.
2. To protect against risk of electrical shock do not put unit in water or other liquid.
3. Close supervision is necessary when any appliance is used by or near children.
4. Unplug from outlet when not in use, before putting on or taking off parts, and before cleaning.
5. Avoid contacting moving parts.
6. Do not operate any appliance with a damaged cord or plug or after the appliance malfunctions, has been dropped or damaged in any manner. Return appliance to the nearest authorized service facility for examination, repair or electrical or mechanical adjustment.
7. The use of attachments not recommended or sold by the appliance manufacturer may cause fire, electric shock or injury.
8. Do not use outdoors.
9. Do not let cord hang over edge of table or counter, or touch hot surfaces.
10. Do not use appliance for other than intended use.
11. Check hopper for presence of foreign objects before using.
12. This appliance is for household use. Any servicing other than cleaning and user maintenance should be performed by an authorized service representative.

INSTRUCTIONS FOR USE

Check voltage-for AC supply only
Make sure that the voltage indicated on the appliance is the same as indicated on your voltage supply.

Capacity up to 1.5 ozs.
Grinding period: about 20–30 seconds.

Capacity up to 2 ozs.
Grinding period: about 20–30 seconds.

Capacity up to 3 ozs.
Grinding period: about 30–40 seconds.

How to grind your coffee.
The mill can only be operated with the cover closed. The hand which holds the mill at the same time pushes the switch thus guaranteeing utmost safety.
You may choose the grain size of the coffee by prolonging or shortening the grinding period.
How to clean your coffee mill.
Unplug the appliance.
Remove all coffee after each grinding. Clean the housing with a cloth.

SAVE THESE INSTRUCTIONS

Fig. 2-1. Instructions for a coffee mill.

me, go out on my patio and grind coffee while I'm watching the sun rise. Nor, for that matter, is there any reason why I should not take the coffee mill along on a backpacking trip, plug it into the nearest redwood, and grind away. Certainly, in some situations, using it outdoors might be dangerous. If I fell in my swimming pool while I was grinding on the patio or if I let a pinecone fall in while I loaded the beans, I might have a problem. However, those situations are not really covered by this instruction, just as the problem of traffic accidents is not covered by the instruction, "Do not drive."

Look at the process I just went through. At first, the instruction seemed silly because it violated common sense. Then, applying my common sense, I could see how it would be sensible if only it said, "Do not use in (certain) situations outdoors." There is a funny dynamic at work here. If I have common sense, it seems silly, yet it takes common sense to distinguish between the dangerous and the safe situations that the instructions refer to. I need common sense to figure out the instructions, but if I have that much common sense, I don't need them. I understand the situation more precisely than the instructions do. A similar dynamic is at work with several other instructions. Consider "Check hopper for presence of foreign objects before using." If we take this literally, then we must not grind things that we obviously can grind, like pistachios. If we do not, then we need so much common sense that we do not need the instructions.

One way of solving the problem would be to start specifying the dangerous situations. But a writer who decided to do so would still have a problem. In order to reach that segment of the audience that has no common sense, the writer must specify every conceivable dangerous outdoor situation or every conceivable foreign object. Not only should the writer say, "Do not grind pebbles in this mill," the writer should also say, "Do not grind armadillo armor in this mill." In practice, of course, the writer was content with absurdities of a quieter kind, the original instructions.

But why would the writer address people with no common sense? Obviously, because the makers of the coffee mill want to protect themselves from the people with no common sense who damage themselves by falling into the swimming pool or by grinding armadillo armor. If the need for self-protection of this kind is a given, then the writer's solution is actually not so terrible. That is what the audience recognized when they refused to get exercised about these instructions.

But should the writer be addressing an audience with no common sense? Is doing that really protecting the company from liability? Is there some way we, the people who are likely to understand, can be addressed by the writer? I will answer these questions, but first, I must describe the speech act rules. Just so there are no surprises, let me say now that I think it's both costly and unnecessary to write silly instructions like this. It's better to write them in a different way, a way I will explain at the end of the chapter.

Speech Act Rules and Instructions

What is a speech act? A speech act is an utterance that has a point to it: an order, a statement, a request, an announcement, an instruction. The philosophy of speech acts asks how it is that an utterance (a group of noises, after all) can be made to have a point. Not all utterances, mind you, not even all grammatical English sentences, do. "Swim backwards through the concrete," when uttered, has no point, even though it is a grammatical English sentence with the linguistic structure of an order. Some utterances, moreover, can have more than one point: "Is your room clean?" may, for instance, be both a question and a threat. Speech act philosophy is not, therefore, a branch of linguistics; rather, it is the study of a certain branch of human relations, the relations we set up when we want our linguistic utterances to accomplish something, such as instructing people in the correct use of a coffee mill.

Those relations are, in part, constituted by a group of implicit rules, which speech act theory describes. These rules are structured very much like the rules of a game. In a game, a move only *counts as* a move because the (preset) rules of the game say so. These rules usually work by setting out *conditions* that must *obtain* if the move is to count as a move. (The italicized terms are technical terms in the theory of speech acts.) In football, for instance, a touchdown only counts as a touchdown if the ball has crossed the goal line in possession of the ball carrier, if the ball was in play, if no other member of the team had been caught violating the rules of the play, and so forth. The job of speech act theory is similarly to describe moves (the speech acts) and the conditions that must obtain if an utterance is to count as a speech act. In a game, if all the conditions do not obtain—if, for instance, somebody on the offensive team had held an opponent on the same play—the move does not count; it is called back. In speech act theory, when all the appropriate conditions do not obtain, the move cannot be called back; instead, speech act philosophers say, the speech act is *defective*. If the conditions do obtain, then the speech act has been *performed successfully* (Searle 1969).

The conditions for the successful performance of a speech act are even more complex than the conditions for the successful scoring of a touchdown. The most important, for our purposes, are two *universal* conditions for the successful performance of speech acts—conditions which must obtain for any speech act to be successful—and two *specific* conditions on the successful performance of instructions. The universal conditions are that a speech act must be "non-obvious" (the *non-obviousness* condition) and that a speech act must be relevant (the *relevance* condition).[1] The specific conditions on instructions (a member of the class of orders) are that the speaker must have the appropriate authority over the hearer (the *authority* condition) and that the speaker must specify something that the listener is capable of doing (the *propositional content* condition).

Imagine that I holler, whisper, or otherwise pronounce, "Shut the door." This counts as an order if it satisfies the speech act conditions. The non-obviousness condition is satisfied if it is not obvious to speaker and hearer that the condition referred to by the statement already obtains or will obtain. If there is a door, and it is open, and it doesn't shut by itself, then, probably, the condition is satisfied. If, on the other hand, there were a door, but the hearer was already shutting it, then the non-obviousness condition would not be satisfied, and the order would be defective. Or, if the door had just been shut, not only would the order be defective, but so would an assertion like, "The door is shut," or a question like "Is the door shut?"[2] The relevance condition is satisfied if the course of the conversation allows the speech act as a possible continuation. In ordinary conversation, "Shut the door" is usually an allowable continuation, but in intense conversations or in formal ones (a marriage ceremony, a court hearing), it is not. The authority condition is satisfied if I am allowed to order you to shut the door. If I am your superior officer, your employer, or your friend in a situation where it is easier for you to shut the door, then the authority condition is satisfied, and I can order you to shut the door. If I am your child or a social inferior, I cannot. The propositional content condition is satisfied if you can, in fact, shut the door. If, however, the door were made of plutonium or weighed ten tons, and we both knew that to be the case, then the order would be defective.

The first eleven coffee mill instructions on the left-hand side of the diagram are defective; they fail to satisfy one or more speech act conditions. Consider the first order. It is defective in precisely the same way that "Shut the door" is, when the hearer is already shutting it. It tells you to do something that you are obviously already doing.

"But is it obvious?" you might say. "We all know that people do not read instructions." True, they don't. But in any communication situation where an instruction to keep reading is to be taken seriously, both parties have already agreed implicitly that the reader will keep reading, and since the agreement has just been made (the reader has just started to read), the situation specified is already the case.

This implicit agreement comes from the relevance condition. Whenever it is satisfied (as it is, presumably, for the first instruction), the speaker and hearer (or writer and reader) are involved in a conversation. Conversations are a form of cooperative activity. In any cooperative activity, each party assumes that the other is acting in good faith, and each agrees to act in good faith as long as the other person does so or until the activity is accomplished. In this case the reader must read all the instructions and hear the writer out in order to act in good faith. By picking up the instructions, therefore, the reader already implicitly agrees to read all of them as long as the writer acts in good faith.[3] The writer, assuming the intent of good faith, must take it that the agreement is made. However, the reader may, in fact, be intending to renege on this agreement, but that makes no difference. The writer must still take it that the agreement holds. The first instruction, however, shows that the writer is not taking it that the agreement is made. The writer's reneging makes it a defective speech act. Ironically, as soon as the defective speech act is made, the writer has broken the good faith agreement, and the reader can feel free to stop reading.

I can imagine a response to this argument, which goes as follows. "Sure, if these were the good old days when instructions contained relevant material, then we would not need to remind people of what to do. But these are the bad new days. Most instructions are no good; and people know that, so they no longer engage themselves to read all the instructions. Today, we have to have an instruction at the beginning that says, in effect, 'These instructions are different; you really do need these.'"

Unfortunately, unless there is, in fact, some special, unusual reason for reading the instructions (not the case here), this is a no-win argument. The "hey-you-really-do-need-these" line indicates that, for some reason, you think the original agreement to cooperate may not be satisfied. But evidence of that suspicion is, in many circumstances, sufficient to abrogate the agreement. "Oh, the writer thinks I won't do my part? But that must be because the writer is thinking of doing the same thing," and so forth. Even in these sophisticated days, such a disclaimer has to be a strategic mistake because it calls into question all the rest of the instructions.

In any case, more than such subtle arguments are needed to defend these instructions because, as I have said, the next ten are defective, too. Instructions 2, 3, and 4 also violate the non-obviousness condition. Instruction 2 is just silly; what other liquid, benzene? Instructions 3 and 4 are pointless in the same way that "Do not use outdoors" was. If somebody is going to let children grind their fingers in the coffee mill or immerse the mill while the cord is plugged in, this instruction is not going to stop them. (It is, by the way, virtually impossible to operate the coffee mill without putting on the very close-fitting cap.) Not only is instruction 5 much like instruction 4, but it also violates the propositional content condition: it is impossible to contact the moving parts. Instruction 6 violates the authority condition. When one's authority comes from one's knowledge, one cannot order people to do patently unreasonable things. It is just plain unreasonable to ask a person to pick up a coffee mill each time it is dropped, put it in a box, mail it to the manufacturer, while leaving coffee beans to spoil in the refrigerator, and not even to try it out once in order to see whether or not it is damaged. Anyway, you are getting the idea. The first eleven instructions violate one or more of the speech act conditions. (The twelfth is not, strictly speaking, an instruction at all. As a statement, it does not obviously violate the speech act rules.)

Let me hasten to point out that "obvious" is a relative term, and so, therefore, is "defective." An order is defective when it instructs someone to do something that person would obviously do anyway. And, of course, what is obvious to you may not be obvious to me. Nevertheless, you should not try to defend the instructions on something like the following grounds: "People should be warned about relatively unlikely possibilities on the off chance that the reader did not happen to know about them or had not thought about them. After all, every one of us has been known to accidentally catch a cord that was hanging over the edge of a counter and to fling the small electric appliance to which it was attached to the ground and desuetude. Wouldn't it be nice to remind us not to do it, as in instruction 9?"

This reasoning does justify casual, if silly, warnings in conversation. You say, "Look out for the cord," even though it's very unlikely the person will catch it. But in written instructions, the reasoning doesn't hold. You see, we have all lived for several years, and during that time, we have all discovered that electric appliances are rather cantankerous when their cords are pulled. We already have the knowledge that the instructions are trying to give us. Our problem is that, even having this knowledge, we still leave cords hanging over the edge. What we really need is to be reminded at the proper time. The instructions, however, cannot possibly tell us at the appropriate time. We read the instructions when we want to learn how to use the coffee mill, not when we are about to destroy some small appliance. And when we want to learn how to use the coffee mill, this instruction is perfectly obvious and, thus, defective.

The Penalties for Violating the Speech Act Rules

"But," you might say, "why not include defective instructions? It does no harm." Ah, but it does. I have been comparing speech acts to moves in a game. When a move in a game is defective, the resulting situation is outside the game. When a speech act is defective, there is no outside to go to. This is as it should be. To the extent that the analogy works, the game is the communication activity, and being outside the game means being without communication. If human beings are to get along, this cannot happen too often; consequently, the communication situation is set up so that apparently defective speech acts do not wreck things. Thus, whenever we hear an apparently defective speech act, we take it that the person is still cooperating, and we try to reconstrue the speech act. Most commonly, we allow an apparently defective speech act to count as some other speech act, an *indirect speech act*. Less commonly, we misunderstand either the statement or the situation. In either case, the conversation continues.

When, however, both of these possibilities are exhausted, the defective speech act will be discovered, and the listener will feel warranted in ending the conversation because the speaker is not cooperating. The penalties, then, are of three kinds. First, and most likely, the direct speech act will be taken as an indirect speech act. Second, the direct speech act will be taken as saying something other than what was meant; it will be misunderstood. Third, the defective speech act will end the conversation.

The first two possibilities deserve some further description. The paradigm case of an indirect speech act is as follows.[4] You and I are sitting at a formal dinner, and I ask you, "Is that the salt over there?" This statement ostensibly does not satisfy the propositional content condition for questions: for example, a question doesn't count as a question when it's evident that the questioner already knows the answer. I probably know it is salt. You realize that I have probably made a defective, literal speech act, and rather than ending the conversation, you look around for some other speech act that I might be making instead (because you assume I'm cooperating). In this case, the possibility that I am making a request (another kind of speech act) leaps to mind. You pass me the salt.

Indirect speech acts are very common in our culture. We use them when we want to be polite, ironic, sarcastic, or, well, indirect. We can use them so frequently only because we have evolved the convention that apparently defective speech acts should be taken as indirect speech acts, if that is at all possible.

Many times, however, an apparently defective speech act cannot possibly be an indirect speech act. Your next step, according to the convention, is to take it that the condition apparently violated is not, in fact, violated and cast around for some interpretation of the situation that would make the violation acceptable. Let us say, for instance, that the non-obviousness condition is apparently violated. Your response is to look around for something about the situation that calls for the speech act. Take, for instance, that first instruction, "Read all instructions." You might read it as, "Read *all* instructions"—as saying that there are two sets of instructions, and it is important for you to read both. Your response would then be to look around for that other set of instructions. (Too outlandish? A friend of mine actually did it.)

Notice, by the way, that this is why pleonasms are so confusing. Take a sentence like, "Start the starter." The meaning itself does not confuse us. The fact that the speaker may be indirectly alerting us to the existence of an abnormal condition confuses us. It might be that the starter actually does require separate starting before it can be used to start the engine. It is while we consider and reject this possibility that we feel a moment of confusion.

How do we tell whether a speech act is direct, indirect, or a call for reinterpretation of the situation? It is very simple; we use our common sense. Common sense tells you I want the salt; common sense tells you there might be two sets of instructions. Notice, though, that we don't just invoke our common sense when we think a speech act might be defective. We use our common sense to tell whether any speech act is defective in the first place. We use our common sense, in other words, whenever we understand any speech act. Not only that, we assume that the other person also has common sense, since we assume that the other person is going through the same reasoning we are. Thus, the entire communication situation is built on our common sense. And the less common sense either party to the communication has, the less possible communication becomes.

The writer of these instructions is writing instructions that will either be misunderstood or taken as defective by anybody with common sense. The writer does this, as I have said, in an attempt to reach people who do not have any common sense. But my argument shows that people who have no common sense cannot understand the instructions anyway.

Legal Considerations

This extensive analysis makes the instructions seem pretty silly. Well then, why write them? A good guess is that the company is trying to protect itself. If a user, the reasoning goes, is on a camping trip and loads the hopper with coffee and a pinecone falls in and the blades break on the pinecone, breaking the top and sending a blade shooting out into the user's eye, the company wants to be able to say, "Well we told you not to use it outdoors." In court the user, not the company, is negligent, the argument runs, because the user did not read or pay any attention to the instructions. The instructions, then, are not meant to be part of a genuine conversation. They are put there simply to take care of silly cases. The legal department sits around and tries to think up every conceivable situation in which some foolish people could damage themselves with the coffee mill, and then for each situation, it puts in an instruction so the company will not have to pay.

My argument shows, however, that simply naming cases and putting them in the form of instructions ought to do nothing whatsoever about the company's liability. In order to prove that it has not been negligent, the company must show that it has warned people of the dangers. Warning is a speech act. For the warning to be a warning, the instructions must be successful speech acts, and they must be embedded in a successful conversation. Otherwise, no one needs to pay any attention to them. But in this case, as we have seen, these warnings cannot be successful because they have not been given in the right situation. One cannot, as I have said, warn people not to leave the cords hanging out over the edge by putting a warning to that effect in some instructions.[5]

Is the coffee mill company negligent if it does not include those instructions? Clearly not, since putting them in has no effect. At most, the only safety precaution of this kind that the company needs to put in is something general like, "Take the same safety precautions you would take with any electric appliance." It only needs to do that because it is conventional to put some warning in instructions, so putting nothing in might make the conversation defective. The company would have to do more, of course, if the mill were badly engineered or non-obviously dangerous in some way. But as it is, it's a pretty good coffee mill.

What Are the Costs of Writing Instructions like These

The goal of these instructions is to get people to use the coffee mill safely and correctly. If the goal is reached, the mill-maker benefits. If it isn't, the costs are of two kinds. First, the coffee mill could be harder to use. Second, the company could lose money or its reputation.

If I really did need instructions to operate the mill correctly, the worst the defective portions would do is confuse me, and that confusion would, in this case, be transitory and unimportant. Moreover, if I am inured to instructions like these, as most of us are, I will not even blame the company for wasting my time, especially since the mill was made in Korea, and the instructions were printed in Hong Kong.[6]

More likely, I will stop reading the instructions and work things out on my own. Remember, the very first instruction has announced that the writer is not going to cooperate, and each succeeding instruction saps my confidence. Of course, working things out is pretty easy. The coffee mill is designed well; just put the cap on and push down. Whirrrrr. If I am the same, normally sensible human being who did not want to read those instructions, I can manage just fine without reading them—until, of course, I try to figure out answers to questions like the following:

1. If I do not fill the hopper full, does that reduce the grinding time?

2. What grain size do I need for drip coffee?

3. Can I grind walnuts in the coffee mill?

Then again, the current instructions don't answer those questions either.

The costs, then, are not great. The bad instructions don't prevent me from using it, and they don't slow me down. I don't hold them against the company. The other costs are negligible, merely the costs of paying the writers, printing the instructions, and including them in the box.

But if the device were a little more complicated, the costs to the company would be more serious. I would certainly hold it against the company if I could not get the machine to work. I would also hold it against the company if the bad instructions led me wrong. Say, for instance, that the hopper were badly designed, and acid from the coffee beans were to corrode the hopper and the blades. It would be imperative to clean the hopper after every use, just as the instructions say. Frankly, I don't do that. I pay no attention to that instruction because these instructions are from the people who brought me, "Return the machine when you drop it." I trust the design more than the instructions. I would, moreover, feel justifiably angry if I were to discover a corroded hopper.

Notice, by the way, that the company's forcing me to trust their design could get them into legal hot water. On the outside of the box that the mill came in, I read, "Grinds nuts, spices, and grains," and the machine itself is clearly designed to do that sort of thing. But instruction 11 says, "Check hopper for presence of foreign objects before using." The combination leaves it up to me to work out what counts as a foreign object. This isn't all that easy. Surely, walnuts are acceptable, but what if I accidentally get some bits of walnut shell in there, or even a lot of walnut shell? What about cardamon pods? What about pine nuts? And if those work, what is a foreign object? Surely something softer than pebbles but harder than walnuts will screw up the mill and endanger my eyesight. But what? The instructions do not say, and if I get it wrong, I feel entitled, as I guess every American does these days, to sue.

A Better Way

There are two questions remaining. One, is there any logical way of writing instructions that ought to reduce legal liability? Two, how does one write instructions that address the concerns of the actual readers? (How much coffee? What is a foreign object?) We know how to start. Take the common sense of the readers seriously. But even doing that, the answer is not clear. Lists of instructions just cannot meet all the possible concerns of the sensible readers: most such concerns are irrelevant to the majority of readers, and so the writer still runs the risk of performing defective speech acts. This is a general problem with lists when the readers read with different interests. There is no simple way around it.

But there is a complex way, and it really is better. To see what it is, let me return to one of the defective speech acts: "Do not use this appliance for other than the intended use." Apart from the pleonasm (use for use), why is this defective? Because we all know that tools are meant to be used in certain ways and that they do not work well when they're not. We rely on this knowledge whenever we learn to operate a machine. I learned how to operate the coffee mill by ascertaining the intended use of the various parts of the mill. (Aha, the lid fits on that way! So, if you push this down, the mill goes . . . .) So with this instruction, our hands are already figuratively on the doorknob.

Notice, though, that this instruction subsumes all the rest. Using the mill outdoors is not an intended use. Grinding foreign objects, including armadillo armor, is not an intended use. If one construes "use" broadly enough, then even the caution about leaving the cord over the edge can be subsumed under the instruction, since "use" includes the way it's used. There is nothing wrong with that subsumption; indeed, I think it is the way to go. If people know how something is intended to be used, they can then work out how to use it; they can work out all the safety precautions mentioned here; and, as a big bonus, they can also work out the answer to all the natural questions they have.

I propose that these instructions can be replaced by one instruction, "Use as the mill is intended to be used," as long as the intentions are spelled out. Here is an example of what I mean:

1. Use the mill as it's intended to be used. It's meant primarily for coffee beans. If you grind nothing but coffee in it and clean it out fairly frequently, you will get years of useful life from it. It will also grind any small, dry object that is softer than coffee beans, including toasted grain, many spices, and nut meats.

2. If you do grind anything but coffee in it or if you never clean it out, two things could happen. First, although the hopper is tightly sealed, residue or oil can eventually filter through the shaft into the motor and gum up the works. Second, oil,

acid, or hard particles can damage the hopper or the blades. If you try to grind very hard spices, like cardamon pods, or very oily ones, like peanuts, you will probably reduce the useful life of the machine. When grinding nut meats, be sure to pick out all the bits of shell. Otherwise, the blades may break, and even though the hopper lid is strong, the flying blades could be dangerous.

3. The mill is emphatically not designed to grind up fingers, pebbles, earrings, or knife blades. One of our younger users tells us that it will not grind up small, plastic dinosaurs. Please, take that user's word for it.

At even a superficial level, something like this puts the writer way ahead of the game. The writer is providing useful information and being readable, if not positively entertaining. But even if the instructions weren't particularly readable or entertaining, they would still be better because they accomplish something at a deeper level. They get the user to think about the tool in the right way—to adopt the point of view of the designer. With this point of view, the user might even treat the tool with respect. With this point of view, the user might even read a sensible discussion of the mill's limitations:

4. The coffee mill is very sturdy, but if you drop it on a hard floor, it might break. Probably, only the casing would crack, and if that's all that happens, don't worry. But if part of the internal mechanism breaks, the mill could be very dangerous. [Note: This is not obvious, by the way. To say this with any authority, one must know how the mill works.] So if you drop it, use the following procedures:

- Inspect the casing and the hopper for stray bits of plastic. Look especially carefully around the blades. If you find any bits of plastic, remove them; otherwise, they might fall into the motor.

- Rotate the blades by hand. If they do not move freely, send the mill in for repair. Don't even try to start it.

- Shake it hard and listen for rattling. If it rattles, you have probably broken a spring, and any further use will burn up the motor. Send it in for repair. If nothing seems to be wrong, try grinding a little bit of coffee in the mill. If it works, don't worry. But if it makes funny noises, let the factory take care of it.

Even this has a little too much of the obvious about it. It might be improved by including more information that the reader does not know. One could say something like, "The casing is made of sturdy, shatterproof plastic, but the insides have a number of delicate parts. If you drop this from a counter onto a hard floor, probably nothing will happen. If anything does break, most likely. . . . " Nevertheless, the principle is clear: if you tell people how things ought to work by using information they do not know, then they can be relied upon to use their common sense—to send the mill in only when they should.

I must say that this version went against the grain for the technical writers. They didn't like the length or the relative complexity. Some of them, at least, believe that a reader only reads short instructions that are laid out in neat little steps. Many of them believe that readers need to have everything spelled out. Some thought they were too cute, which is probably right. I admit that these are legitimate considerations. Readers, especially readers in a hurry, are put off by lots of dense, black print. But my suggested version can be made to look neat, can have a pretty format, and can even have little pictures. It can also be shorter.

But really, their objections don't address the basic point. The original instructions, and most instructions like them, are defective. My suggested version, whatever its faults, is not. Always, my version subscribes to a basic principle: tell people, directly or indirectly, things they do not already know. Adhering to this principle is simply a matter of having respect for the other person. Failing to adhere to it, no matter how great one's fear of lawsuits and no matter how substantial the precedent, is simply failing to have this respect.

Addendum

Several readers of the original draft asked me to spell out the costs and benefits of doing instructions in the way I suggest. In a sense, I think this is the wrong way of thinking about it because the argument for doing things my way is, at bottom, moral. But here they are anyway. First of all, there are no costs; anyone with common sense does not read the original instructions. The benefits have mostly to do with the fact that people will use the coffee mill more effectively; the company sees few immediate advantages from that. At best, the repair department will be used more effectively. But the long-term advantages are significant: people who know exactly what the coffee mill can do and who get satisfaction from using it are more likely to buy other products manufactured by the company or more coffee mills for presents. Good documentation gives a company a good reputation. Perhaps this is due to people having respect for a company that clearly respects them.

3 What's Technical about Technical Writing?

We saw in the first chapter that one way of treating writing as a technology is to identify certain kinds of writing—called technical writing—as purely instrumental. If the directions with which I began the first chapter are seen as instrumental, then an immediate diagnosis of their failure leaps to mind: they didn't use clearly defined terms. This chapter begins a lengthy investigation into the plausibility of the identification, and it does so partly by way of looking at the diagnosis. As I will show, the intuition that certain kinds of writing are technical relies heavily on the intuition that it is possible to attach definite, invariable meanings to words.

The title question indicates one of my foci: what makes certain kinds of writing technical? Questions of this kind have been asked frequently by people in the field; I begin the chapter with some of their answers, which are, as it turns out, definitions of technical writing. I will first show the difficulties such definitions run into, and then I will turn the discussion on its head by showing that many of these difficulties occur whenever you try to come to some definite, invariable definition. Unfortunately definitions of technical writing rely particularly on the assumption that definite, invariable definition is possible, so the fact that these difficulties do occur vitiates the definitions.

I argue further that a certain view of language authorizes the attempts to define a specifically technical writing. I propose that this traditional view is mistaken, and propose an alternative derived partially from the theory of speech acts. With that alternate view, I conclude, perhaps ironically, with a new definition of technical writing, one that is less subject to the limitations I point out and one that does not treat technical writing as a technology.

The title question is framed as it is because I want to call attention to some peculiarities in the conjunction of the words "technical" and "writing." Similar questions of the same form (What's medical? What's legal?) would have a trivial answer (nothing) because the

29

words "medical" or "legal" designate a clearly defined discipline whose subject matter is not writing: medical writing is writing about medicine. There is, however, no discipline of "technics," so "technical" has more the force of an adjective; there is something about the writing itself that is technical. The phrase "technical writing," moreover, is somewhat ambiguous because "writing" is. Writing can be a thing (a piece of writing) or an activity (an act of writing). In the first case, "technical writing," the technicality is in the piece. In the second, the adjective shades off into an adverb: one doesn't write technics but "writes technically." Interestingly enough, the course that definers of technical writing have taken has largely depended on this ambiguity. Some definers chose to define "technical writing," some to define "writing technically."

Technical Writing

In our culture, a standard way of defining something is to assemble many instances of that something and describe their common features. The definition is then a list of these features (or "criteria" as they are sometimes called), and one tests whether something satisfies the definition by determining whether it has those features. We say, for instance, that a chair has a seat, legs, and back, and it serves to seat people; then we determine whether something is a chair by checking for those features.

We have already seen Tom Pearsall's definition. In his and in many others, the features cited fall into three categories: format, style, and content. (For some who choose only one of these, see Dandridge 1975; Hays 1975; Sparrow 1976.) According to John Walter (1977, 6–8) for instance, each piece of technical writing has the following features:

1. Specific rhetorical modes and formats that were pitched to specific readers (FORMAT).
2. A specialized vocabulary and an objective style (STYLE).
3. Primarily technical content (CONTENT).

Patrick Kelley and Roger Masse use the same categories but conflate them because they overlap:

> Technical writing is writing about a subject in the pure sciences or the applied sciences in which the writer informs the reader through an objective presentation of facts. (Kelley and Masse 1977)

This definition may seem to cover only content, but Kelley and Masse make clear elsewhere that "objective presentation" and "inform" refer to style and format.

The language is simple. The categories are familiar. But the definitions are by no means adequate. For one thing, they wouldn't decide problem cases. Without distortion, neither definition would count environmental impact statements as technical writing, because their subject is nonscientific and they are by law directed toward any reader, but both would count fraudulent scientific works such as Velikovsky's *Worlds in Collision*, which is highly technical, informative, and directed toward astronomers.

This problem is typical of a definition that works by describing features. Look back, for a moment, at the definition of chair. Some objects, like sofas, have all these features, yet are not chairs. Other objects don't have these features, and yet are chairs. Some armchairs have rollers (or even runners) instead of legs, and the new, back-saving chairs don't have backs, and people don't sit on them, but kneel.

When one is defining by enumerating features and needs to resolve problem cases (one doesn't with "chair"), the usual strategy is to elaborate on the features. In the preceding definitions, however, this strategy will, as we will see, run into serious problems. Already, words like "objective," "technical," "presentation" (as opposed to, say, "argumentation"), or "specialized" hover on the edge of needing clarification. Elaboration, far from getting rid of the undefined terms, will multiply them.

In a moment, we will see how this problem emerges with the words "technical" and "objective," but first, let us look at the other kind of definition.

Writing Technically

The definers of "technical writing" look at texts; the definers of "writing technically" look at the encounter that produces the texts. They seek the unique features of the way the mind grapples with a technical subject and then converts that grappling into writing. Encounters are not exactly a "thing"; so they don't have distinctive features. Consequently these definitions provide a way of taking hold of the subject, not a list of features.

Of the many definitions of "technical" (see, for example, Carter 1979; MacIntosh 1978; Rabinovich 1980), the most sweeping is John Harris's:

> Technical writing is the rhetoric of the scientific method. (Harris 1978, 135)

Whether or not a piece of writing is technical is determined by its way of handling a subject: "quantitatively rather than qualitatively, and objectively rather than subjectively" (Harris 1978, 135). As such, writing conveys "data." A closely related definition, Charles Stratton's, seizes on what happens as a result of the rhetoric:

> [A technical writer in] a particular art, science, discipline, or trade . . . helps audiences approach subjects. (Stratton 1979, 10)

A technical writer, he continues, renders his own act of writing invisible because technical writing is communication, not self-expression, and the information itself is far more important than the writer's attitude toward it.

A third definition of writing technically, W. Earl Britton's, makes the previous two conditions more stringent by adding one interesting criterion. Not only must writing technically be objective, it must be univocal:

> The primary, though certainly not the sole, characteristic of technical and scientific writing lies in the effort of the author to convey one meaning and only one meaning in what he says. (Britton 1975)

Thus, while both Stratton and Harris would admit as technical writing something that is linguistically dense, Britton would not. He explains why in an analogy that appears frequently in his writing. For Britton, writing is like music. If one wants complexity in a piece of music, one writes a symphony; if one wants to wake up soldiers, one plays reveille on a bugle. Literature is a symphony; technical writing is a bugle call.

Rhetoric, Science, and Technical Writing

The definitions of technical writing and of writing technically do not conflict, and the key notions, save Britton's univocality, seem to be the same. But in the definition of writing technically at least one interesting confusion has crept in. Harris has substituted the word "scientific" for the word "technical," and the word "rhetoric" has been used instead of the usual word, "inform." Showing why this has to be wrong can help clarify what all these definitions are trying to get at, and it will also help us get a handle on what the word "technical" means.

For analysts of science, ranging from Popper to Kuhn, the "rhetoric of the scientific method" already has a meaning, and it is not Harris's. For them, the aim of science is to get true descriptions of the physical world. These descriptions usually contain assertions about relationships among theoretical entities. $F = ma$, for instance, is a relationship among the entities force, mass, and acceleration. These descriptions are held to be good for all instances of the entity: every force, every mass, every acceleration. By placing several theoretical entities in a relationship that always holds, the descriptions are making what philosophers call "universal truth claims." Notice that, because the theoretical entities are always in several different relationships, these claims are woven in with each other. The whole fabric of claims constitutes the discourse of a discipline, like theoretical physics.

If a scientist within a discipline writes a new "universal truth claim," he or she is, in effect, asking that the new claim be made part of the fabric. Each such claim subtly, but unmistakably, affects the rest of the network. Any new constraints on how accelerations behave automatically also constrain how forces and masses behave. Once the statement is accepted, moreover, to prove it wrong also requires that the related statements about forces and masses be proven wrong. Science is a self-regulating discourse. The "rhetoric of the scientific method" must be the way scientists ask that the claim be admitted to the discourse.

So much for scientific writing. Technical writing consists of quite different sorts of statements. "You'll come to an intersection with a large tree," for instance, is just not a universal truth claim. It is, rather, an empirical statement. To prove this statement wrong requires only that the intersection happen not to be there, not a readjustment of the disciplinary discourse. Technical writing is merely empirical. If there is any rhetoric associated with technical writing, it is the rhetoric of empirical statements. "The rhetoric of empiricism" or "the rhetoric of technology," are not, however, satisfactory definitions. They would still be begging questions, and they lack that noble ring.

This does not mean that, to the extent that technical writing is special, the specialty is not partially determined by the subject matter. It surely is. But what is that specialty? What is "technical"? None of the preceding definitions is entirely satisfactory. Kelley and Masse conflate "technical" with the "pure and applied sciences," which we've seen is wrong. Stratton generalizes it to any "art, science, discipline, or trade," which would seem to include the law and yoga. The others just assume that we know what is meant.

Let me say right here what I mean by technical subject matter because I will be and have been using the word in a particular way. The observations recorded in technical writing help us to manage the things around us and bring them under control, not to make them the subject of a systematic discourse. The word "technical" in technical writing, for me, comes from the word "technique;" technical writing shows us how things fit together, how tools may be used, how goals may be reached. Technical writing places things at our disposal. Thus, for me, directions to the symphony are emphatically technical writing (though they might not be for other people), whereas certain scientific discourse is not.

My objection to treating technical writing as being itself a technology or a group of techniques is that it creates a rather odd picture of human relations. In it, the writer (the user of the technique) is thereby putting another person (the reader) at the writer's disposal. I just don't think human relations work that way. When I am asking for directions, I am at that person's disposal in the same sense that subjects of techniques are at the disposal of the wielder of the technique.

Have I now defined "technical" more satisfactorily than the others? Probably not; I, too, am counting on your already knowing what technique is. The point, though, is that this is all right. Definition always counts on your already knowing the meaning of key terms; definition is not meant for amnesiacs. I could go into some detail about what technology is, what technique is, and so on—detail possibly involving some excursions into the history of technology and the nature of everyday language. But unless you already had a pretty good idea of what I was talking about, it would be meaningless to you. More important, unless you were comparing my ideas to your ideas, you wouldn't be able to see whether I was right.

And this is true of all definition. In actual fact, the definition doesn't come first and the knowledge of meaning later. We don't see, for instance, whether something is a chair by seeing whether it has four legs, and so forth. We already know what a chair is, and if something counts as a chair for us, and it doesn't meet criteria advanced by a definition, so much the worse for the definition. Admittedly, there are cases when a definition can help us resolve a question. But those are cases where we are already unsure of the nature of the object.

You can now see why I am always concerned with definers' purposes. Definition does not so much set out criteria as it highlights features of the thing defined. The choice of features to highlight has to do with the rhetorical purposes of the definer. The purpose a definition like Walter's serves is fairly obvious, and the definition serves it well. For that purpose, there is no need to define "technical."

Formal Versus Epistemological Objectivity

I don't mean that definitions should not be undertaken. Careful examination of the meaning of words helps us clear up confusion and saves us from error. To show you what I mean, let me look further at the confusion surrounding the word "objectivity." Almost all the definers have used it; but no one has used it well.

In the definitions of technical writing, "objectivity" has referred to style. The definers are stipulating that the writing have what I call "formal" objectivity: that the writing use linguistic devices, such as impersonality, to indicate that a speaker is performing an objective role. The definers of writing technically want this, but they also seem to want what I will call "epistemological objectivity": that the speaker actually be objective. (In Harris's definition, handling information quantitatively is seen as a way of gaining objectivity.) None of the definers except Pearsall (see chapter 1) distinguishes between the two.

The relationship between the two is, as Pearsall points out, merely conventional. If I am objective, I don't have to use linguistic indicators of that objectivity (such as not using "I" or using the passive voice), though sometimes they can be useful. Not using "I" or the passive voice, moreover, doesn't confer objectivity, though it can be a shield.

Indeed, the whole stipulation of formal objectivity is puzzling. Surely objectivity doesn't, as Stratton suggests, "bring audiences closer to subjects." Its major function is simply to specify a point of view. Where the point of view is to be taken as general and shared, mentioning oneself is often unnecessary. Where point of view isn't, you should bring yourself in. (More on this in chapter 5.)

The interest in epistemological objectivity may be justified on better grounds. Techniques, as I have said, are available to anyone; so, presumably, are facts and information. But it is not clear why only facts, and not speculations, theories, remarks about the facts, or any other judgments that a skilled purveyor of techniques might make, should be proscribed.

For the moment, let me just make one further remark about definition. A danger inherent in taking up definition is that confusions which were minor in the way we use the original concept may be magnified by the definition. This happens most commonly when the definition is serving a vaguely illicit purpose.

Univocality

The definitions we have been looking at have had, let me remind you, two purposes: to justify the intuition that certain kinds of writing are instrumental (that the writing, in Pearsall's words, is "functional") and to make those kinds of writing resemble their subject, technology. The discussion, so far, has shown the second purpose in operation much more than the first.

If technical writing were univocal, however, it would, in fact, be functional. According to Britton, technical writing should be univocal; it should have "one meaning and only one meaning." You can see how that would make the writing instrumental; the meaning would dictate the course of the reader's response just as the road leads in only one direction. But from what we have seen of people's attempts to define the meaning of just one term—technical writing— and from what we have seen about how definition works, Britton's stipulation seems problematic.

You will recall that Britton gets around this problem by arguing that certain forms of expression, like symphonies or poetry, are complex; others, like bugle calls or technical writing, are simple. Alas, things are not that easy. The meaning of a symphony largely depends on its context. Reveille performed in a concert hall would probably be complex (in Britton's terms); Beethoven's Fifth played over loudspeakers at Fort Bragg would be simple. So if Britton's writer wishes to mean one and only one thing, this writer must specify the context; moreover, that specification must itself be unambiguous.

Now is that specification itself part of the meaning? Modern literary criticism would say "yes"; the meaning includes almost any related item that can be construed as affecting what is meant. Britton wouldn't like that idea (neither do I, but for different reasons). To counteract it, Britton extends his metaphor. Words, says Britton, have primary and secondary meanings, primary tones and harmonics. We know how to separate the two. We can identify and eliminate secondary meanings established by the speaker's experience ("rock" from a geologist doesn't mean quite the same thing as "rock" from a child), the cultural context ("rock" before 1953 has a different flavor from that of "rock" now), the philology of the word, or the sound of the word. The soldier at Fort Bragg, Britton would say, hears only the message, "Wake Up." The soldier does not hear the secondary meanings: the insistence that each listener is uniform with respect to the speaker; the affirmation of a continuing authority; the promise and provision of a visceral reward when individuality is ceded by the listener.

This picture of the way people understand language—and hence this picture of meaning—is phenomenologically rather implausible. No one is conscious of going through such an interpretive procedure. So it is well to look at why a commentator would choose to believe it. For Britton, I think, the picture comes from the dictionary. There, language is treated as if meanings come in discrete units. People presumably decode language units larger than the word by plugging in the appropriate units and applying some grammatical rules. This isn't as naive as it sounds. When computers first came into vogue, people thought that machine translation of other languages would work in precisely this way. They soon discovered they were wrong: that dictionary entries describe meaning, but do not determine it.

Still, Britton's idea is not completely implausible. It does seem possible that some things are simply univocal; a stop sign, for instance, might just say "STOP."

Unfortunately, intuition fails. Even here a stop sign is not univocal. If it were, then an accurate paraphrase of its meaning would also be univocal; the stop sign should amount to nothing more than "You stop." So let me try to paraphrase what a stop sign says, ignoring secondary meanings, overtones of authority, everything but what it obviously says. First of all, it's clear that the stop sign only applies to motorists who are coming from the direction directly facing the sign: "You motorists coming directly toward this sign, STOP." They are also supposed to stop just before the intersection or behind the line of cars stopped at the intersection, so consider that specification inserted as well. In various states, the meaning varies according to the laws and customs. In my home state of Massachusetts, "STOP" is merely a suggestion, not an order: "You motorists . . . please stop just before . . . if you find it convenient." And of course in all states, the instruction does not apply at certain times. "You motorists . . . please stop . . . if you find . . . unless there's an ambulance or police car behind you which can't get through." Thus, a "univocal" message.

Britton just makes a mistake when he says that technical writing should be univocal. He probably means that it should be so clear that readers will never mistake the meaning. This stipulation, of course, does not merely apply to technical writing, and so it's not a distinguishing feature. But it is what Britton means. I think.

The Cartesian Empiricist
View of Language

One possible response to my comments on univocality runs like this. Your "paraphrase" is a trick. The word "STOP" is univocal, but the paraphrases are less trustworthy and are not. Earl Britton might say this; so might Francis Bacon. This response relies on a certain idea of language that is shared by both. According to them, at least a few simple words reliably mean a few simple things, and all the rest of language as used by men is inaccurate and confusing. Between Britton and Bacon are many others: among them Descartes, Locke, Spencer, Russell, and the early Wittgenstein. Each of these men had a stake in believing that a language of plain, simple univocal words is possible and that the failure of language is merely a sign of our fallen state.

Each of these people has a theory of language and its decline, and though the theories themselves are often opposed, it is fair to say that underlying them is a common view of language. Carolyn Miller (1979) calls this view the "windowpane" theory of language and ascribes it to the logical positivists. George Steiner (1975), looking farther back, calls it the "universalist" view of language. I, following Hubert Dreyfus's suggestion, will call it the view of Cartesian empiricism.

Cartesian empiricists share the following beliefs:

1. The world is out there.
2. By properly applying our minds, we can know it.
3. There is a best way of knowing the world (a "privileged access") that the nature of the world dictates—the world is an open book; the world is decipherable.
4. This best way of knowing the world is available to any intelligence.
5. It is thus independent of language and human quirks.
6. Language is a way for us to fix and tell what we know of the world, a coding, if you will, of the world.

7. We are able, in principle, to distinguish between correct and incorrect (true and untrue) codings just by looking at the world without using language.

8. Distinguishing the correct from the incorrect is difficult and we often fail at it.

9. If we can purify language and our consciousness, we can formulate a perfectly correct language, a universal language, in which we would not make mistakes.

10. It is our responsibility to do so (this is often unstated).

Miller calls this a "windowpane" theory because the perfect or universal language would be transparent to things themselves. Steiner calls it a "universalist" view because the perfect language would be universal. The reasons for the suspicion of current language in this view are clear: language in its present state clouds the window and prevents us from seeing the truth. Bacon and Descartes took this view while they were in the course of suggesting new methods for knowing the truth; they thought the reason their "scientific method" had not suggested itself before was that people spoke too much and confused things.

Thus, it not surprising that scientists or empiricists (often unwittingly) espouse this view of language, nor surprising that writers about technical writing should inherit it. Science, today, has managed to preserve the Baconian/Cartesian ideology despite the fact that most philosophers of science no longer believe it. Indeed, the view has entered our culture. It is this view that Harris implicitly adapted when he used the extraordinary word "data" in his definition. It is this view that makes people think it's all right to speak about communication as a form of information transfer (something I discuss in the next chapter). Since this view is as much a moral as a philosophical position, it does not merely inform the ideas of the people I've been looking at; it gives their writing some of its tone. In the definitions you've seen, there is pride, pride that technical writers, like scientists, are part of a moral crusade, engaged in a lonely, often thankless struggle for precision and truth.

You can, perhaps, see more clearly now what is at stake in the earlier diagnosis of the failed directions. If language is a window on the world, then, obviously, that speaker failed to be clear, and that's why the writing wasn't functional. (Notice the moral superiority there.) If language is not a window, then perhaps all that happened was a failure of sympathy.

Wittgenstein on Language

Miller attributes the windowpane theory of language to the logical positivists, and in a sense, this is an apt choice. They were the last to hold it, and they prepared the ground for its destruction. One of the foremost positivists was Ludwig Wittgenstein who, in 1917, published a treatise on the possibility of grounding language in mathematics—a standard way, since Leibniz, of purifying language. In 1934 or thereabouts, while logical positivism was in its heyday, Wittgenstein changed his mind. The result was first a series of lectures, *The Blue and Brown Books*, and, then, in 1946 *Philosophical Investigations*, in which the later Wittgenstein attempted to rethink what language is. Wittgenstein is a careful, difficult thinker, but at least the outlines of his argument can be described here.

He begins with an observation that I have already used. Even so homely and familiar an object as a chair does not have any single distinguishing feature or group of features. There are chairs that don't have backs, legs, or seats; chairs that aren't person-sized; chairs that are made out of almost any material you name; and chairs that aren't used as chairs. If, therefore, we try to develop criteria for determining whether something is a chair, we will fail. One's determination of whether something counts as a chair is not made, says Wittgenstein, by consulting a list of criteria; rather, the correct identification of a chair, the "grammatical" usage of the word "chair," depends on one's "form of life," Wittgenstein's word for the totality of our shared experience. To put it another way, we already know what a chair is when we apply criteria, and that's why we can apply them, when we can, successfully.

Much of *Philosophical Investigations* is devoted to puzzling examples of situations where we clearly divine the correct use of a word without resorting to criteria; much of the rest is devoted to investigating the "grammar" of accounts of how we use words. There is only one knock-down argument for this position. It runs like this. Imagine that we have a rule for determining whether something is a chair. (A rule would consist of a set of criteria.) In any particular situation, we have to apply the rule. In order to apply it correctly, we need a rule for how to apply it. ("Is that couch over there a chair? It has four legs, a back, and a seat. Oh, no, those criteria don't apply when the seat is meant for more than one person.") But in order to apply the application rule correctly, we need a rule for how to apply it, and so on. Attempts at exhaustive definition, says Wittgenstein, always end in "infinite regress." (This is described more fully in chapter 5.)

For Wittgenstein, this observation severely limits the possibilities for analysis of language or analysis of mind. Linguistic analysis can never be confident that its substitutions for the word as spoken in context capture what the word actually means. Therefore, the substitutions are not, as we have seen, innocent; they are performed so as to serve some purpose.

Writing at almost the same time, a philosopher in quite a different vein of Anglo-American philosophy, W. V. O. Quine, came to some remarkably similar conclusions about scientific analysis in general. Quine's problem was what kind of foundation logic could provide for science. He decided, at the very least, that logic ought to determine when two sentences are synonymous. He showed in "Two Dogmas of Empiricism," however, that the criteria for synonymity depended upon the notion of synonymy and, thus, every definition of synonymy was circular (Quine 1953). Later in *Word and Object* (1960), he extended this notion to sentences that state empirical observations, showing essentially that the meaning of any such sentences depends on the meaning of other possible sentences in the speaker's repertoire. In a sense, Quine is saying that "chair" is no different from the force, mass, and acceleration in $F = ma$. All depend for their meaning on a huge network of relationships. *Network* from now on will be a technical term, referring to groups of interdependent Intentional states: to a totality of knowledge. The meaning of the word "chair" can't be determined by fixing criteria or even by gesturing toward some chair; it also depends on what other words in our language mean—chair, not sofa, object for sitting on, not object for standing on and so on and so forth. Quine's view, which has come to be called "holism," is now accepted by many, if not most, philosophers. Wittgenstein's, which is more radical, is therefore more controversial.

Neither Wittgenstein nor Quine are saying that we don't mean anything or that we don't know what we mean when we use words like "chair" or "technical writing." On the contrary. Both philosophers are talking about the claims one can make for the analysis of language. In the universalist view, defining a word fixes it; a word is a convenient shorthand for its definition. In Wittgenstein's view, the definition of a word cannot substitute for the word; definitions merely call attention to some aspect of the usage of a word. Definitions are most useful when something goes wrong. If, for instance, we see what appears to be a defective chair, we can use a list of features for discovering what is defective about it. Does it have four legs? Yes. Does it have a seat? Yes. Would a person fit into it? No, it's only three inches high. Aha! But that analysis neither replaces nor supersedes our knowledge of the chair; it merely comes out of our ordinary understanding of the chair. Thus, any kind of analysis, including the analysis in this book, must always begin and end with the phenomena, with our ordinary experience as we actually experience it.

Hubert Dreyfus and John Searle on Language and Thought

Wittgenstein's and Quine's are essentially linguistic theories. How do those theories fit into modern linguistics? Essentially, they don't. Linguists have not been deterred from analysis by the knowledge that language use arises out of our "form of life." Instead, they have either ignored the idea or relegated the "use" of language to a somewhat neglected category of linguistics. According to the theories that these people largely share, language performance, which is what Wittgenstein was talking about, can be explained by reference to three different kinds of rules: the syntactic, the semantic, and the pragmatic. Syntactic rules govern the construction of sentences and paragraphs; they apply no matter what the meaning of the sentences. Semantic rules apply to the meanings of the words; they are what give "context-free" utterances of sentences like "The cat is on the mat" their meaning. Pragmatic rules govern the actual use of sentences in situations; they are what allow us to apply "The cat is on the mat" to this cat, that mat, and so on. According to them, Wittgenstein's objections apply only to pragmatic rules and are irrelevant to them in the majority of cases.

According to Wittgenstein, such a response is perfectly possible. One can construct as many theories as one wants, and they will apply in many cases. But they won't accurately describe language as it's actually used. In my view, which will be argued in the next section of this book, this is what has happened, at least in the study of writing.

Another possible response to Wittgenstein is to try to evolve a psychology that accounts for his observations. If, in fact, we possess a grammar grounded in our form of life, and if it is this grammar and not sets of criteria that allow us to use words like "technical writing" or "chair," then it is sensible to try to describe this grammar. This kind of response has been taken up by two Berkeley philosophers, John Searle and Hubert L. Dreyfus, their colleagues, and their students. This loose confederation draws on Austin, Husserl, and Heidegger, as well as on Wittgenstein and Quine, to give an account of mind and language that both embraces and partially explains the difficulty of analysis (Heidegger 1962; Husserl 1973; Austin 1962). These people do not always agree, but the following description gives the essentials.

Searle and Dreyfus accept the fact that we do talk to each other and make ourselves understood; they recognize that, in common speech, we have a huge vocabulary for describing speech and comprehension, for example, "I said this," "I meant that," which should be taken seriously. For them, the basic unit of language—the thing we as writers or teachers of writing should be concerned with—is not the context-free sentence, but the speech act, a sentence uttered by somebody who means it. The speech act is, of course, what our common-speech way of describing language is concerned with.

In modern linguistics, a theory of speech acts is a linguistic theory; a speech act is governed by the syntactic, semantic, and (particularly) pragmatic rules. In the Searle account, though, a theory of speech acts is not simply a linguistic theory; it is also a psychological theory. Speech acts, you see, are always made by people. These people intend to make the speech act, and they intend to mean something by it. The meaning of the speech act is, in part, determined by those twin intentions. But, since intentions are psychological entities, a full explanation of speech acts requires some kind of psychology.

Fortunately, the psychology and the linguistics of speech acts dovetail together. Let's begin with a simple situation (figure 3-1). In figure 3-1, John has a certain mental state, namely perception P. (Here the term is used somewhat technically: it means a mental state—not what hits the eyes or is processed, but the thing we are conscious of.) This perception is a *representation* of the state of affairs out in the world, namely that the cat is on the mat. Thus, the perception may be said to have two parts, the mode (which in this case is perception) and the representation. These parts are independent; the mode can change while the representation stays the same, and vice versa. If John closed his eyes, for instance, only the mode would change (figure 3-2).The mode turns to belief. Or, if the cat got off the mat, against John's will, the mode would be desire (figure 3-3). Mental states with a mode (belief, desire, hope, fear, intention) and a representation (that the cat is on the mat, that Washington crossed the Delaware) are called, for historical reasons, *Intentional states*. (The "I" is capitalized.)

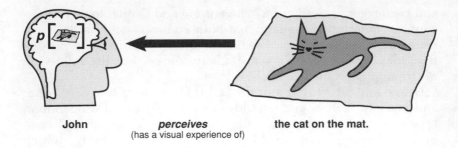

John   *perceives*   **the cat on the mat.**
                      (has a visual experience of)

Fig. 3-1. Representation of perceptual experience.

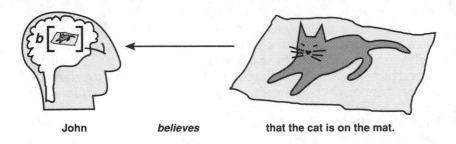

John   *believes*   **that the cat is on the mat.**

Fig. 3-2. Same representation with mode changed to belief.

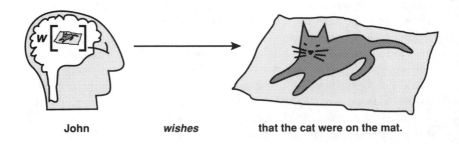

John   *wishes*   **that the cat were on the mat.**

Fig. 3-3. Same representation with mode changed to desire.

Speech acts express Intentional states. (There are a few exceptions.) If John, for instance, wanted to express belief that the cat is on the mat, he could simply say, "The cat is on the mat." The point of this speech act is to get you to recognize that John has a certain Intentional state, namely the representation that the cat is on the mat in the mode of belief. Speech acts that have similar points are called *assertions*. Notice that assertions have a structure corresponding to the structure of the belief itself. They have a representation of a state of affairs (that the cat is on the mat) in the mode of assertion. As with mental states, the mode of a speech act can change while the representation stays the same, and vice versa. "Is the cat on the mat?" expresses a desire to know about the same state of affairs; the same representation is in the mode of questioning.

So far, the discussion doesn't demand that psychological theories take priority. Everything could, moreover, be explained by purely linguistic, universalist theories. It could be, for instance, that, when we have a belief we want to express, we cast around for a sentence that happens to have exactly the meaning we want, and we recite it. The reason, then, that language fails us so often would be that frequently the right sentences don't exist, so our meaning isn't expressed clearly.

The problem is holism. We can't express something merely by seizing on the words that already mean the right thing because meaning the right thing depends on the entire network of intentions. The locus of meaning, therefore, is not in the words but in the head. The head "lends" the words their ability to represent: a speech act represents this cat and its relationship to that mat because the person uttering the speech act intends it to mean this cat, that mat. This being so, then the representational ability of the mind must also be holistic.

This sounds difficult, but it is actually completely commonsensical. It says that we know how to pick out (represent) a cat on a mat only because we already know a lot about animals, sleeping, pets, household goods, and so on. If we didn't have this knowledge, then we might well be unable to distinguish a cat on a mat from a hair ball, dog, or plastic model.

By putting meanings in the head, however, we make linguistics into a branch of psychology. Now descriptions of the meaning of sentences must presuppose psychological descriptions. Stating "rules" of syntax and semantics requires that one also describe the ways people follow those rules.

The Background

If meanings are in the head and meaning is holistic, then the preceding definitions of technical writing lose most of their grip. The "functionality" or "clarity" of technical writing, the way readers are brought closer to subjects, now depends on mental processes. Without a theory of those mental processes, little explanation is possible: to put it another way, one person's inability to find a concert hall on the basis of someone else's directions cannot be diagnosed without looking at the mental states (most crucially, the network of knowledge and beliefs) of both parties.

Many people in the field of writing do have psychological theories that are drawn from the vast field of cognitive science. How does this account bear on their positions? Many of these theories are not holistic. (We will see some in later chapters.) The idea is that the task we want to study (say, the way people use headings when they read) is separate from other mental processes and thus may be studied separately. Or else, the area of study can be located in the mind; then, the mental function we are interested in is accomplished by some specific module in the mind, and the functioning of that module may be studied separately. (The possibilities for doing this are examined at great length in Fodor 1983.) Since what is adduced from these theories is a set of techniques, the eventual idea, as we have seen, is to combine the techniques to make a technology.

Holism argues, however, that conclusions made on the basis of these theories are completely unsafe because, at any time, almost any belief (or skill) may affect the experimental results. Whether or not someone uses a heading in a particular document may depend on how well that person understands the structure of the material being discussed, on whether one thinks the author is being cooperative, on the physical location of the heading on the page, on the perceived relevance of the heading, and so on. These dependencies cannot be factored out because any or all of them may determine the end result.

Such studies certainly have some value, just as our commonsense intuitions, for example, about whether people use headings, have some value. But the value is limited because one can't safely abstract the results of one study and apply them in a different situation. A person's mental state (whether one is reading voluntarily, for instance) or an extra half-inch of margin may well completely change that person's reaction to the headings. The studies do not end up describing a technique; at most, they give insights into communication.

Some cognitive theories are holistic, however, and these turn out to look very much like the Searle-Dreyfus accounts (Fodor 1983). But there is a crucial difference. In cognitive accounts, any representation must be completely describable as satisfying a set of rules. (For something to match its definition, for instance, it must satisfy a set of criteria.) Searle and Dreyfus, following Wittgenstein, argue that there is no such complete set. Instead, along with rules that we do follow, we have what they call "Background skills" (the "B" is capitalized), skills which can't be fully described by explicit rules, but which we call upon for every activity.

Cognitivists, to put it another way, think that all "intelligent" activity can be described as resulting from beliefs (or other Intentional states) and rules for applying those beliefs. They believe that all human action can, in principle, be explained in terms of human knowledge and, conversely, that affecting action can always, in principle, be done by giving people new knowledge. Cognitivist explanations use words like "assume," "know," or "think," each of which indicates the possession of an Intentional state. (Searle and Dreyfus, by contrast, use words like "take it" that or "have a sense" that. The difference between the two will be the focus of chapter 6.)

The Searle-Dreyfus account has it that, in addition to knowledge, there is know-how. People have skills for dealing with the world; those skills are not reducible to knowledge, and they cannot be taught only by imparting knowledge. These skills are used whenever we perceive, think, or do anything, but unlike perceptions, thoughts, or actions, they are not Intentional.

Here are some examples of Background skills. Whenever we talk to somebody, we stand a certain distance away from them. That distance varies from culture to culture. We have no rule for determining that distance, and we don't think about it when we do it. We just do it. As we walk, we put our foot down with a certain force and at a certain angle. The way we do it depends on the kinds of soles we have, whether the ground is rough or smooth, what kind of material is there, whether we're on a slope, how we're feeling that day, and so on, yet we don't think about how we do it. We just do it.

One thing we don't do as we walk is to walk as if the ground is about to give way. Why not? The cognitivist explanation is that, as we walk, we "assume" (Intentionally) that the ground is solid. The Searle-Dreyfus account has it that we just "take it" (non-Intentionally) that the ground won't give way. There are two basic arguments for this account. First, assuming that the ground won't give way is not a phenomenologically accurate explanation; people don't consciously make such assumptions. Second, it puts the total number of Intentional states at an improbably high level. If we assume that the ground won't give way, there must be literally trillions of other possible assumptions that we would be making with each step we take.

The counter-objection is grounded, once more, in physicalism. If we don't make assumptions, then how is it that such clearly mental activities are undertaken? Surely we must be calculating the amount of pressure to put down because that's what mental functioning is. The answer is, "not necessarily." The need for calculation is often illusory. Consider an analogous situation often cited by Searle. Say we were asked to calculate the shortest route down a hill. After considerable pain, we could probably figure out the answer. But we could also just put a hose at the top of the hill and watch where the water went. The water finds the way down without making any calculations.

The picture of mental life that Searle and Dreyfus give us is something like this. At every moment of our lives, we are paying attention to something. We are worrying, thinking, analyzing, wishing, hoping, perceiving, or desiring some state of affairs that we are representing. (We have some Intentional state or other.) At the same time, in order to have that particular Intentional state, we are also deploying many other Intentional states and many other Background skills. We are not conscious of doing so, and, in fact, we are not capable of fully analyzing how we do it. Instead, the deployed Background skills are like our personal horizon: surrounding us, always there, but always at the edge, no matter how we move toward them.

We can think of the Background, if we want, as our sense of what normally happens. Normally, no pit gapes beyond the door. Normally, we mean the obvious cat and mat. This sense of normality is to a great extent the product of our experience with physical laws and our own capabilities with respect to them. It is normal to react to gravity by standing vertically, to use our legs as levers as we walk, and so on. But it is also a product of our cultural practices. We consider it normal to want salt on food served at dinner parties, and that is part of what allows us to understand when someone makes an indirect speech act like, "Is that the salt over there?"

We might also think of the Background as our capacity for determining what is relevant in any situation. It is this capacity which, when we walk, makes the light, the weather, our know-how about municipal repair strategies, and the state of the season available ("ready-to-hand" is the Heideggerian term) to us as bearing on the way we walk, and makes the current political situation or our hopes for promotion farther removed. Personally, I find this capacity somewhat amazing. Once, during orientation week at my university, I looked up and saw a small plane with what looked like some paper glistening just below it. Without thinking, I took the scene as an orientation prank—the plane was dropping some shiny, obnoxious something onto the campus. At any other time, I would have seen, immediately, that it was, in fact, two planes, the one below being much farther away and reflecting the sunlight.

The Background and the Use of Language

As we read or listen, the Background is constantly placing knowledge and skills ready to hand. One way of characterizing the preceding discussion of meaning is to say, as Searle does, that our literal meaning is always held against a Background of skills and a network of knowledge (Searle 1979). Even apparently similar meanings can carry with them vastly different Backgrounds and networks. This is not accidental, and it is not forgotten when we communicate. When we communicate an understanding of a meaning, we are also communicating part of the Background and network.

This is a terribly important point, and one I've always found easier to understand with the help of a metaphor. Look, for a moment, at the way two similar meanings are embedded in different Backgrounds and networks and the way we use those differences.

Let's take two different addresses: 12 Pinckney Street, Boston, and 15368 Ventura Boulevard, Los Angeles. Superficially, they're similar. Each locates a specific point within a network of streets. If we had a map, we would treat them as essentially the same kind of abstractions. But when we're in these cities, and we want to get to the addresses, we begin to see and use the fact that the two networks have very different organizations, and those organizations reveal quite different things about the territories where they are located.

Pinckney Street is a lane in Beacon Hill, a posh, labyrinthine, steep, historical, and small area of the city. To find a street or to park in Beacon Hill is practically impossible. When unfamiliar with the area, one should just park nearby, walk in, and ask for directions. On the other hand, 15368 Ventura Boulevard is one hundred and fifty-three blocks north of the City Center on Ventura Boulevard, which runs parallel to the Ventura Freeway. The name of the street and the number thus provide a location on an abstract grid. One proceeds there by following the freeways that (roughly) travel along major grid lines. In the process of finding the address, of course, one need not take into account any geographical or cultural facts about the city; indeed, as far as the person driving is concerned, the streets might have large, blank walls on either side.

Finding 12 Pinckney Street requires that I understand the neighborhood it's located in. The better I understand it, the easier it will be. Indeed, in Boston, generally, knowing the city well doesn't mean knowing the automobile routes. It means being oriented to the major landmarks, having some knowledge of Boston's commercial life, and even remembering a bit of the city's history. When I near the place, I have to take into account what the people there are like. Getting to 12 Pinckney Street requires that I organize enormous amounts of my experience.

The Los Angeles address is easier and faster to get to, but it leaves out much of the life of the city. You don't and needn't take into account the fact that you're going through a mountain range or a Korean neighborhood on the way. The Boston address is more difficult to get to, but once one gains the necessary knowledge, the Boston way of getting there is richer. It requires and simultaneously organizes a feeling for the life of the city located around that address.[7]

The metaphor shows that apparently similar sentences (for example, "Go to 12 Pickney Street" and "Go to 15368 Ventura Boulevard") can work by lighting up quite different areas of network and Background. Each address, in the anology, is meaningful by virtue of its place in a system for designating such addresses (a network). That network stands in some relation to the region around it (the Background). The same may be said of any two ways of describing a thing, any two sentences. Each has a different place in a network and exists against a different Background, providing a different understanding. Perhaps one way makes access harder but gives deeper understanding. Another way might make the Background invisible, though making access easier.

How does one locate and describe the Background and network in which an Intentional state is embedded? The problem is a vexed one, particularly in these post-modern, Derridean times. In this book, I use the terminology that Searle and Dreyfus use. The "meaning" of a speech act is the representation intended by the speaker in the appropriate mode. Myriad things may be "indicated" by the fact that the speech act was used. Depending on what they are and my interest in them, I may call them "implications," "involvements," "orientations," "overtones," "indications," or, of course, "Background skills deployed." For those of you who do not know Searle and Dreyfus, the distinction is roughly that which E. D. Hirsch made between "meaning" and "implication" (Hirsch 1967, 24–67). Hirsch was criticized because this distinction was never clear-cut in any particular case. But the previous discussion shows that the criticism of Hirsch was silly. You can't expect such distinctions to be clear-cut.

The Searle-Dreyfus account has it that when you express an Intentional state, you set up a way for people to understand the situation that the Intentional state represents. You organize their understanding for them. Thus, the adequacy of a way of speaking is not measured merely by seeing whether people gain access to the explicitly represented information (an assumption that any universalist would make). It is measured by looking at the kind of understanding (knowledge and know-how) that the way of speaking imparts.

This is not quibbling; it has an important consequence. In this terminology, one may express one's meaning perfectly well—be as clear as one wants—and yet not communicate that meaning because people do not have the Background and knowledge they need in order to pick out what you're talking about.

This way of putting it allows us to advance a more accurate diagnosis of what went wrong with the directions that began this book. The problem was a failure to share Background and network, a failure that meant you were unable to understand the speaker's meaning at a crucial point. The speaker lived in the area and knew (and took it that you knew) that all major roads were on section lines. The speaker also knew that you had just come through an intersection of section lines and therefore thought that two miles would mean "exactly two miles" to you because there wouldn't be any major roads in between. (So far this is mostly knowledge, but the last part is probably Background—a skill at distinguishing major and minor roads.) Once that intersection was located, the speaker tried to remember distinctive features of the landscape. The church and the tree were sufficiently unusual that they seemed to serve the purpose. (Picking out "unusual" features is a Background skill.) The synagogue might have counted as a church, but since the speaker considered only places of Christian worship to be churches, the synagogue became irrelevant to the directions. You, on the other hand, knew little about how the speaker's understanding was being organized; you didn't know about the major roads and section lines; and you weren't sufficiently confident about the speaker's use of the language (Background skill) to the extent that you could afford to ignore the synagogue.

We are now able to see why one would want to think about holistic issues, the Background and the network, and the mental processes that occur as we write or read. First of all, thinking this way makes us better able to diagnose mistakes. At the same time, it helps prevent mistakes. For now, instead of focusing on the facts, the information to be conveyed, we can focus on presenting the facts so as to organize the reader's Background and network properly. Second, it suggests that Background skills (as well as techniques) are used when we write. Third, whether we are teaching writing or instructing people in the use of something, we can now realize that the activity they will perform requires Background skills. Unfortunately, Background skills cannot be imparted by relating facts. So, whether teaching or writing directions, we must structure the way we present facts (or any Intentional states) in a manner that permits the reader to develop any missing Background skills.

The instructions for the coffee mill, for instance, can be thought of as a means for trying to teach Background skills in the safe use of small electric kitchen appliances. However, this doesn't work. We must count on the existence of common sense (which is both Background and network) if we wish to be understood. Instead of trying to teach Background skills, the instructions should convey information that can be used by people with the right Background skills.

Of course it's not quite that easy. The information has to be conveyed so that the right Background skills can be deployed. An instruction can always be couched in a manner or vehicle that prevents people from understanding its force or its applicability. When reading, the audience might not be deploying the right Background skills, and so, when the time comes, they won't understand whether or not nutshells count as a foreign object.

A New Definition of Technical Writing

The objection, finally, to the definitions we have seen is that they are calling attention to the wrong things. By concentrating on language when what is important is the understanding that language expresses and produces, the definitions make it easy to think of technical writing as performing some definite function, but they make it very hard to understand what technical writing does. This is particularly unfortunate because technical writing, then, seems much easier than it is. If technical writing is a matter of making facts explicit, and if the human act that produces technical writing is a matter of coding (see the next chapter), then writing is in principle very easy, and people really are culpable if they can't do it. If, however, hanging on any speech act are the ways people interact with each other, their knowledge, and their skills, and if a writer must translate one set of practices into another whenever communicating across groups, then even straightforward writing is a mighty hard thing to do well.

At the same time, the definitions make technical writing much less important than it is. If all that matters in writing a manual or a scientific paper is being explicit in the optimal way, then writing is merely a recording process, a necessary chore, perhaps, but not work we value. If, however, the writing of a manual or a scientific paper is what makes one's work valuable to other people, if the value depends on the way in which people understand the work, and if the understanding is produced by the writing, then writing matters deeply. Because writing does more than make the facts explicit, and because it reveals the territory around the facts (the way the facts hang together), bad writing may do more than just confuse; it may make the understanding sere, like one's understanding of a grid city. Good writing, by contrast, may bring the territory into sharp relief.

And finally, though the definitions are hard on people who don't do technical writing well, they implicitly encourage a certain slackness in much technical writing. As I said, it's a common belief that technical writing should be invisible, that it should get people to the spot as fast as possible without being noticed, like a Saab. If, however, that way of understanding the material isn't the best way, only the writer, not the reader, will know it. It is easy to write instructions that seem to say something but that actually leave out the reader. It is harder, particularly given the current view of technical writing, to obtrude oneself and make the reader work,[8] yet an honest appraisal of the reader's needs and the writer's responsibilities may make that the right thing to do. It's easy, in other words, to write a step-by-step manual that does not show the reader how the process works and then to blame any problems on the reader when things don't work out. And it's also easy to write instructions like those for the coffee mill; the definitions implicitly authorize that kind of behavior.

I am not suggesting that we abandon clarity and precision in our writing, nor that we become whimsical or precious. I am not suggesting that we abandon lists of parts or make every scientific paper an essay. What I am suggesting is something both simpler and more difficult. I am suggesting that the intuition we began with, that certain kinds of writing are instrumental, must be radically reorganized. Whatever makes this kind of writing different from Wordsworth's "Resolution and Independence" must have more to do with the way people experience things than with particular formal features of the writing or even any particular subject matter; or, for that matter, with any instrumental or technological character of the writing itself. If there is anything technical about technical writing, it must have to do with particular structures that technologies give to experience, with particular Background skills and practices shared by people who use technologies or who are in technological groups, and with a means that technology gives us for understanding ourselves and what we do.

With that in mind, I suggest the following definition of technical writing, a definition that calls attention to the experience of technology, rather than to the technology of writing. I should add that this definition does not isolate any essential characteristic of technical writing; instead, it is descriptive. It describes what technical writing is like today; with changes in our society, this definition could change or become irrelevant.

> Technical writing is writing that accommodates technology to the user.

"Writing" should be understood as one kind of speech act. (Verbal directions like the ones we began with also count.) The ambiguity in the word "writing" is welcomed; writing is either a way of expressing a person's thoughts which constitutes an act (writing as act) or the physical relic of that expression (writing as thing). "Accommodate" suggests the invasive quality of technology (even to technologists) and the self-effacing role technical writing often plays. (This word is the closest I get to the stylistic stipulations of earlier definers or to the idea that "audiences are brought closer to subjects.") "Accommodate," curiously, allows its indirect and direct objects to be inverted with only a flick of the eye; in an invasion, who is accommodating whom—invader or invaded, technology or user—depends on the power of each. "User" is appropriate rather than "reader" because technology is meant to be used; moreover, "user" reflects the fact that technical writing exists within a system that measures actions, people, and things by the criterion of use. "Technology" is more than an array of tools or procedures. It extends to the way human beings deploy themselves in the use and production of material goods and services. One may speak profitably of an economic strategy or an administrative formation as being a technology (Heidegger 1977). In the first chapter, I began using the term "technology" in that sense. But since that sense of the word is somewhat strange, let me offer a brief explanation here. (A longer discussion of technology is given in chapter 5.)

Let me begin with common speech. In the sentence, "Computer technology has improved productivity in the industry enormously," the word "technology" signifies not only the machines, but also the way they are designed, hooked together, and used. The word "technology," as I have said, refers to a network of machines and uses. This network implicitly includes various models of the way human beings work with machines, models of what human tasks are like, models of responsibility for performing those tasks, and the like. Installing a computer technology is not merely installing machines; it is installing a set of designs for human behavior and machine behavior that makes both useful.

In modern Continental philosophy, so heavily influenced by Hegel and Marx, thinking of technology not as a collection of things but as a way of being is quite common; in American thought, it is not. That's why my earlier use of the term may have occasionally sounded strained. The Continental philosopher I am following is Martin Heidegger, who in *The Question Concerning Technology* says that technology has no intrinsic connection with machines, per se. "The essence of technology is nothing technological." Instead, technology is a way treating anything or anybody: specifically, treating anything or anybody as useful (Heidegger 1977, 4).

I object to the previous definitions because they try to situate technical writing within technology—make it into something instrumental, functional, or useful. I have said earlier that the major thing accomplished by doing this is to give the writing protective coloration. Treating technical writing as useful legitimates the evaluation of its effectiveness, the productivity of technical writers, or the cost of the writing component of a project.

Heidegger would see such an attempt, not as an isolated move by people who are trying to gain some respect, but as an aggrandizement that is inherent in technology itself. (This is why I take the motivations so seriously.) For Heidegger, the peculiar characteristic of technology is that it is invasive. The vast network of things understood as using and being used is always growing. We might agree that the world is more technologized these days because there are more machines and these machines do more for us. But that's not what Heidegger means. For him, the aggrandizement of technology is an aggrandizement of understanding. Technology has its own ways of modeling the activities of human beings, its special categorizations of experience, its particular modes of responsibility, its particular ideas of control. Something has been "technologized" when those ideas get applied to it.

Let me give an example. Most of this chapter was written while I was sitting in a Steelcase desk chair; the rest in an old-fashioned swivel desk chair that was made years ago by a chairmaker. The Steelcase one came with a manual. The old chair, which has much the same design, did not. The two chairs have identical functions, but, as the presence of a manual indicates, one is a technology, and the other is not. The manual and the chair and Steelcase define a particular relationship with me and project a particular power over my experience. They define the relationship as one of control: Not that they control me—rather, the control is apportioned among me, the design of the chair, and the manufacturer. Consider, for instance, what should happen if I have trouble with the chair. The manufacturer assumes responsibility for my trouble and gives me a way of getting around it. I don't have to and shouldn't have to just go next door and ask somebody for help. Moreover, the manufacturer defines the kinds of troubles (and uses, therefore) I should have and defines the limited responsibility that Steelcase has for those troubles. With the craftsman's chair—much the same chair—these things are not even an issue.

This description of what happens to the chair would seem pushy or exaggerated if similar descriptions had not been advanced by many others since Heidegger. Marcuse is particularly illuminating on what happens when something is suddenly included into a technology (Marcuse 1964). According to him, something begins to be understood as a technology when people claim a scientific basis for its operation; when its operation is treated with a value-free objectivity; when the world in which it finds itself is composed of quantifiable and interchangeable things, qualities, and relationships (positivities); and when the positivities are described in operational or instrumental terms. All these events are seen as means for control or, as Marcuse puts it, "domination." Marcuse calls the set of ideas (and Background skills) that make up this world "the logic of domination."

Clearly, the Steelcase chair has become subject to the logic of domination. Clearly, too, technical writing, in these definitions, is in the same way of being taken over. I don't necessarily think it's bad for chairs to be taken over (though it seems a bit silly), but I don't think it's good for communication to be taken over in the same way.

You might think that the very inutility of treating technical writing as an instrument would save it from being taken over. But, as Marcuse says, the logic of domination is scarcely monolithic; it is as riddled with inconsistencies and confusions as any other logic. Making something into a technology may do very bad things to it: witness what would happen if justice or counseling were turned into technologies. But according to Marcuse, technology is very successful at hiding its failures. Something can be technologized and thereby made "costly"—the term itself is technological—but the technology would be unable to discover that.

What, then, is the difference between "accommodate" and "use," and why is the second so costly? When a technological idea is created, it moves outward—from designer to millwright, from engineer to manager, from distributor to customer. At each point, this idea, or else the physical realization of the idea, must be made useful to somebody. Very often, it is technical writing that makes it useful. It takes something initially strange, invasive, and expensive, and accommodates people to it—turns it into something familiar and useful. Much more, however, is involved in making technology useful than simple factual statements about the technological idea. The technology must be accommodated to the way people actually are. It must accommodate the idea to such things as the way the company is organized, the way people work with related products, the way the idea is being produced, the goals of all the people involved, and many more—precisely what depends on the Background and knowledge of the user. The word "accommodate" reminds us that integrating a technology is setting up a human relationship, with all the attendant feints.

When technical writing is treated as useful in modern industry, its use is to transfer objective technical information. This information consist of facts or step-by-step instructions; it is created by technical writers whose job it is to write down those facts or instructions. When this is done, however, not much gets accommodated. The word "use" hides the fact that what is at stake is understanding, not facts. The result is writing that is flattened—writing that gives access without understanding, like the address in Los Angeles.

The Implications of This Definition
for Teachers of Technical Writing

My definition suggests that research into technical writing should tack a completely different course. In this new research, the piece of technical writing or the act of writing technically would be only two of several foci. Others would include the practices of the groups the writer is writing to, writing for, and writing from, as well as the practices of the group in which the writer has located himself. An examination of technical writing should, in effect, be a natural history of technical writing. It looks at each thing in its domain both as an organism (which has a history) and as an entity (which is simply there).

The examination would begin where someone conceives the need to accommodate, adducing the relationships of power and perception that caused this conception. The examination would end where the accommodation is completed. Along the way, the examination would follow the traces of the accommodations left in human relationships. This kind of research is very difficult, for penetrating groups of which you are not a member requires learning a new way of thinking. It is likely that this new way of thinking will not be easy to generalize. The way they handle technical writing at Kodak is very different from the way they do it at Corning, and each way is tied up with the corporation's organization, its self-image, its decisions about what is acceptable behavior, its valuations of judgment and knowledge, and so on. But this research would address itself more directly to an understanding of technical writing in its quiddity.

[*A historical note. This definition was written some seven years ago and subsequently published some five years ago. Since that time, I have noticed a definite swing towards the kind of research I suggest. I claim no credit for this progress. Such swings are the products of independent decisions by researchers, editors, proposers of conferences, and so on, many of whom expressed emphatic disagreement with the original article, and more of whom ignored it completely. Nevertheless, I applaud the swing, and hope it continues. When this research begins to have its effect in industry, we will have fewer manuals that are a disgrace and more that are worthy of admiration.*]

4 Information Transfer

A Simple Mistake

If definition does not determine the meaning, but instead calls attention to features of the defined, two new problems arise. First, we can no longer rely on definition to keep word usage in line. Second, the misuse of a word is more perilous than we might have thought. Since the meaning of a word helps organize the way we encounter an entire situation, misusing a word encourages false perceptions, occludes possibilities, and gives us bad habits.

One such bad habit I mentioned in the last chapter: the habit of referring to technical writing as "information transfer." In this chapter, I want to look at the valences of this usage, the set of ideas it encourages in us. Doing so will not only serve to remind us of how complicated and difficult it is to understand language usage, but will also allow me to treat the themes of the last chapter more concretely. In the last chapter, I asserted that the meaning of an utterance depends on the Background and network of the speaker and that a meaningful utterance is always a speech act. This chapter will show you how those dependencies work.

If you've read the textbooks, you've seen technical writing described as "information transfer." Thus, Deborah Andrews and Margaret Blickle, in *Technical Writing: Principles and Forms*, say that "this book is about communicating scientific and technical information"—communication that is described as a design process which "parallels the process for designing an appropriate cooling system" (Andrews and Blickle 1982, 1). Robert W. Bly and Gary Blake say, "The primary goal of technical communication is to *accurately transmit technical information* [italics theirs]," and thus, where necessary, "style, grace, and technique" must be sacrificed to "clarity, precision, and organization" (Bly and Blake 1982, 2). And John Lannon, inspired by Kelley and Masse (1977), says, "In technical writing, you report factual information objectively for the practical use of your readers." To give the point some force, he contrasts Tennyson's poem, "The Eagle" and an encyclopedia entry for "eagle"; the latter, it turns out, is more objective and factual (Lannon 1982, 4–5).

And, finally, in the definition I will discuss at length, Robert Rathbone, in *Communicating Technical Information* (1966), describes the "simple communication situation" (figure 4-1). Rathbone is trying to show that "all man-to-man communication is susceptible to noise," but none more so than writing." The noise enters in because "the English language itself is so irrational and because the originator and receiver have no feedback channel of any kind between them" (p. 52).

If these definitions are grating, you should realize that the actual audience does not find them so. The audience and the authors share a view of how communication works that makes sense of the definitions. They believe, as I said in the last chapter, that a body of information, of objective facts, is just lying out there waiting to be communicated. When the communication is successful, the receiver is put in possession of those facts. The facts determine the communication, unless the originator interferes. The job of the originator is to move the facts from one place to another, handling them as little as possible so as not to tarnish them.

Within this valence, the content of a communication is information; the function of technical writing is to "transmit," "report," "communicate," or "transfer" information. Of the four verbs, "transfer" is the most illuminating for my purposes because of its history, which shows us simultaneously how the usage came to make sense and also what's wrong with it.

Claude Shannon and Mathematical Information Transfer

The term, "information transfer," and Rathbone's visual rendering of the process are both drawn from Claude Shannon, who in the early 1950s invented something he called "the mathematical theory of communication" (Shannon and Weaver 1949). Shannon worked for Bell Telephone, as it used to be called. His job was to figure out whether there is any theoretical limit to the amount of electronic information that a telephone wire could carry. It turns out that there is. When a piece of information is coded, as when a telephone turns a sonic signal into an electrical signal, or when we convert a sequence of letters into a sequence of Morse code signals, there is always a certain degradation of the signal. (The equation, perhaps significantly, is formally similar to the basic equation for entropy.)

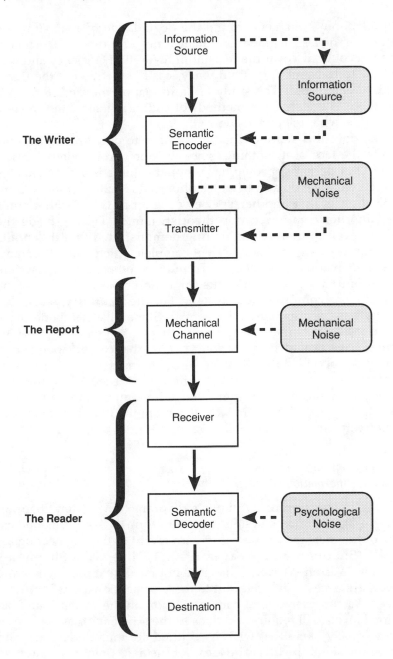

Fig. 4-1. Rathbone's simple communication system.
(Source: Rathbone 1966, 52. Reprinted with permission.)

In telephony, one gets around the degradation of a signal by repeating it. The less degradation, the less need for repetition. Thus, if Shannon could discover the maximum theoretical efficiency and find out how to transmit at that efficiency, costly repetition of the signal could be eliminated. The study of "information transfer" for Shannon, then, is the study of methods of coding signals. "Information transfer" is what telephones do.

What does this sense of the phrase have to do with what people do? On the face of it, nothing, since we don't emit coded electrical signals. But perhaps, people have thought, there is a close analogy between what we do and what telephones do. Perhaps human communication is just another species of coding. During Shannon's time, another communication theorist, named Turing, made the analogy even more forceful. Turing demonstrated that the inputs and outputs of any physical system completely determine the transformations made by the system. To put it another way, any system with definite inputs and outputs (digestion, rocket ships) may be modeled as a computational system. For the last thirty years, this analogy has been extremely influential. Some, like Rathbone, have treated it as a useful analogy. Many others, as in modern cognitive science, have extended the notion to argue that computation is precisely what people do when they think; the model, in other words, is completely accurate. And yet others have tried to explore the analogy by building computers that mimic human thought processes. In the next two sections I will explore the first two responses. A full treatment of the last will have to wait until chapter 9.

Human Communication is like
Telephone Information Transfer

The original version of Rathbone's diagram comes from Shannon (figure 4-2). Shannon's system is purely formal: "The semantic aspects of the message are necessarily irrelevant to the engineering aspects" (Shannon and Weaver 1949, 1). But, says Shannon's coauthor, Warren Weaver, "this does not mean that the engineering aspects are necessarily irrelevant to these semantic aspects" (p. 100). Indeed, "a consideration of communication on the semantic and behavioral levels will require additions to the schematic diagram, but it seems equally likely that what is required are minor additions, and no real revision" (p. 101). The idea, for instance, might be simply to add more boxes to the diagrams or to analyze the mode of transfer more closely.

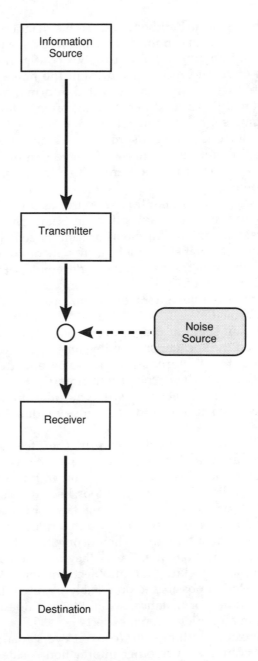

Fig. 4-2. Shannon's communication system.
(Based on Shannon and Weaver 1949, 7.
Used with permission.)

That is what Rathbone did. In his diagram (figure 4-1), each box represents a collection of data. The arrows between the boxes represent coding steps. The arrow-box configurations below the main lines of communication represent the noise that enters in during coding, which distorts the coded information. Rathbone has indicated that there are different kinds of noise for each coding step, but in doing so, he misunderstands the nature of the theory. For Shannon, noise is noise: disorder inside an orderly thing. "Semantic noise," therefore, is "noise that enters in during the semantic coding step"[9] but it is no different from the noise that enters in during any other step.

If we want to take this seriously as a model, we need to make some of the same assumptions as Shannon. A message in a box is discrete; it contains all the information needed to make the transformation. The transformation itself is made by following a set of distinct, unvarying, formal rules, for example, "Every 's' is three dots." The message itself, then, can be broken up into a set of units called bits, for example, letters, or, in our case, words, which are the items transformed.

We can see that there have to be at least three different coding steps on the speaker side and symmetrical decoding steps on the listener side: (1) perceptions must be encoded into thoughts; (2) thoughts must be encoded into language; and (3) language must be encoded into speech acts. If you take the model seriously, the Rathbone picture would have to be modified to something like the figure 4-3.

Let's look at each step in turn. The first is the most mysterious. Light waves impinging on the eye are converted into electrical signals and, then, even before we know it, into a thought. This process is fairly reliable—every time I look I see the same thing—so it might seem to be susceptible to straightforward analysis. Unfortunately, there don't seem to be purely formal rules for converting eye signal bits into bits of thought. When people have tried to find the rules by building computers that "see," they discovered that even something as simple as picking out an object *qua* object is exceptionally difficult—even impossible to do reliably. A robot that picks up parts has a hard time, for instance, when the part doesn't have precisely the position and orientation it expects.

We can pick things out (convert eye signal bits to thought signal bits) because we use other information besides that which is taken in by our eyes. Let's say that I'm looking at a hammer. True, every time I look, I see a hammer. But it isn't just the light waves that are

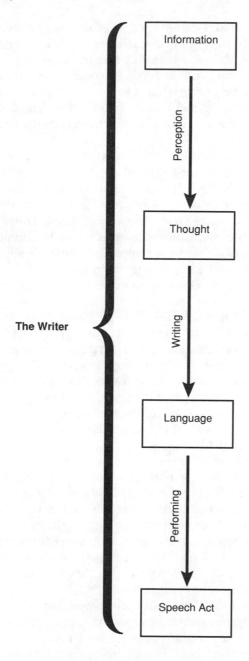

Fig. 4-3. The writer's coding system.

producing the visual experience. It is also my knowledge of what hammers are, of how they are used, of tools, and so on, as well as my Background skills for handling hammers, for placing tools within my environment, and so forth. If I didn't have those things, the hammer would be to me what it is to the computer, or what it is to an infant: a brown splotch. Or, if I had a different Background and network, if I were an aborigine, for instance, it might be a badly made boomerang.

This presents a problem for the analogy. If I need Background and knowledge in order to transform the visual message, but the Background and knowledge aren't part of the original message and they aren't used in a formal way, then I am not transforming a message unit according to strict, unvarying rules. There are only two ways to save the Shannon account. One is to consider the Background and network as noise, since, in Shannon's system, anything that comes from outside the original message is noise. (This is silly because the noise is necessary to make the message come out right, but people say this anyway.) Just to get a handle on it, I call this "epistemological noise." The other way is to do what the computer scientists do and try to incorporate the Background and network into the coding system as a set of formal rules. There are three problems with this. First, the rules aren't formal; they depend on an evaluation of the situation, they change from person to person, and so forth. Second, a complete treatment would require an infinite regress, in the manner of Wittgenstein. And third, the Background can't be described as a set of rules. (The second is, of course, an argument for the third.)

The same kind of problem comes up when we try to code thought into language. Either systematic noise gets added in, or else new formal rules have to be added. The picture of language coding we have from the universalists is that, for each thing, there's a word. Let's look again at some of the problems with this notion. First of all, for almost any thought, we have many different words; each word represents the same thing that the thought represents under a slightly different *aspect* (Searle 1983). "My brother-in-law," for instance, might also be "John Jones," "that guy over there," or "Shirley's husband." The particular aspect that's selected depends largely on things outside the original thought—one's rhetorical purposes, for instance, or one's sense of audience.

If one is a universalist, the selection depends, too, on what other words are available. (This is why Rathbone thinks that English is inexact.) Thus, to return to the original example, if there were only one word for "house of worship," then the speaker might have had to say "Baptist church"; but since there is one word for church and another for synagogue, "church" would be sufficiently precise. Part of the meaning, then, of the choice of "church" is "not synagogue." This meaning is not part of the original message. It is semantic noise.

The other choice is to assume that formal criteria exist for selecting the right aspect and to start writing rules. That's what people did when they first tried to develop machines that translated. They immediately ran into the problems that Quine had pointed out. They couldn't find a formal rule for when something counted as synonymous, and without such a rule, defining particular conditions for synonymy became onerous. "Bachelor," for instance, is not the same as "unmarried male" when the unmarried male is a priest, divorced, less than ten years old, of another species, and so forth. To test whether such a translation would be legitimate—or which would be more appropriate as a translation from thought into word—would necessitate searching the entire world of available information to find out which of those conditions are satisfied. Such a test, of course, is subject to the results of other tests, and so on; it's the same infinite regress.

At the last step, language into speech acts, the same dilemma occurs. A speech act, remember, is an utterance that has a point to it, a representation in a mode. The problem of determining the representation was already taken care of in the previous step; the problem, now, is to determine the mode. The sentence itself does not determine the mode; the same sentence can have several different modes, depending on the context. Take, for instance, the sentence, "The cat is on the mat." If the point of the statement were to tell you something you need to know, it would be an assertion. If the statement were inflected in a slightly different way or even uttered as an echo to someone else's assertion, it might be a question. If you were one of my many servants, and if it were well known that the master doesn't like cat hair on the mat, it would be an order. Again, correct coding of the sentence into the speech act requires a good deal of knowledge about the situation that wasn't part of the original thought or perception. One must know about conventions of speech, lines of authority, the previous parts of the conversation, cats, and hair before the last speech act can be coded correctly. Again, this is either noise—called "illocutionary noise" because, in speech act theory, the point of a speech act is its "illocutionary force" (Austin 1962; Searle 1969)—or the transformation into speech act must be governed by a host of formal rules.

An updated and corrected Rathbone diagram would now have to look like figure 4-4. The boxes are either "noise," which is a bit silly but truer to the original Rathbone idea, or a black box full of formal rules that automatically handle the conversion. In either case, the analogy has simply become too unwieldy. Perhaps there was an original message in the sense impressions, but it has gone through so many transformations that the message on the other end no longer looks at all the same. Shannon's idea—the whole idea of calling this "information transfer"—was neat because it was simple. But this is no longer simple. It is no longer neat.

One way of putting this point is to say that a communication never contains naked facts. It contains a person's understanding of the facts—the facts held against the speaker's Background and knowledge, as communicated in a particular vocabulary, within a particular communication situation. It contains facts that the speaker believes to be true (for stated or unstated reasons), that the speaker is taking responsibility for, and that the speaker believes to be relevant—facts stated in terms that are meant to be useful and understandable, for reasons known to speaker and hearer.

Strict Computational Models of Thought

It may be possible to characterize any physical process as a form of information transfer, but the previous argument shows that, unless there is some motivation for it, such a characterization is unlikely to prove useful. It's just plain too difficult to build such a model. Turing's conclusion has, however, led many people to believe that it is possible in principle, however difficult it has been so far. Their assumption, which is called "strict cognitivism," is that mental processes are nothing more than computational processes. If this assumption is right, then all writing is information transfer because the processes that perform it are those which transfer information.

There is a simple argument against this assumption; it is John Searle's "Chinese Room Argument" (Searle 1983, 28–41). The idea of the argument is to show that even a computer, which behaved perfectly like a human being, would not be thinking; it would only be simulating thinking. The argument works by comparing the simulation to the real thing and by showing that the real thing has something which the simulation doesn't.

A computer is nothing but a device that takes symbolic input, ma-

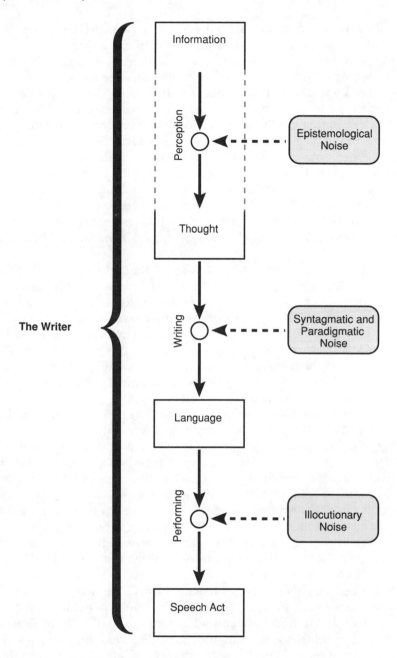

Fig. 4-4. The writer's coding system, complete.

nipulates it according to a set of instructions, and produces symbolic output. Usually, such devices are electronic, but logically, everything they do could be done by a little-man-in-a-room. He could take the input, consult a rule book, and then generate the output. Imagine, then, that we had this man-in-a-room device, which was programmed to answer Chinese questions correctly and thus could accurately simulate what a real Chinese person does. In actuality, of course, the little man takes in Chinese characters, looks up what to do next in books of rules, and performs what the rules say to do. The rules could be written in English, and if they were, the man-in-the-room could do all this without understanding any Chinese. The little man would thus be simulating the behavior of a person who understands Chinese, without actually understanding Chinese himself. You could have, in other words, all the behavior, without any of the understanding.

What does a Chinese person have that the little-man-in-the-room does not? Essentially, in understanding Chinese, the Chinese person's mental states *represent* or are about something outside the states themselves. The man-in-the-room's responses, on the other hand, do not represent. They are not about anything. This ability to represent is the irreducibly mental aspect of the mental. Computational states, which consist of formal counters (meaningless symbols manipulated by formal rules), have only formal relationships with other counters. None of these represent anything.

The reason we think the man-in-the-room is representing is that we attribute to the device the ability to represent. We do the same thing when we think of an adding machine as adding the number 2 and the number 2. In fact, the machine is only manipulating electrical signals, which are structured so that we can treat the input and output as representations of the numbers 2 and 4. By contrast, we don't merely attribute the ability to represent to our own mental states; our own mental states are, intrinsically, representations.

If, however, computational states are not identical to mental states, then there is no a priori reason to think that what they do is a form of information transfer.

Let's put all this in commonsense terms. The Rathbone model and similar uses of the term "information transfer" obliterate a commonsense distinction between what two kinds of communicators do. Used in reference to human beings, "information" (in uses like "tourist information" or "new number information") denotes information about something—places to go or people's phone numbers. Used in reference to telephones, "information" (as in "the rate of information transfer") just denotes raw data. The information that the telephone transfers could be nonsense syllables, random numbers, anything; it doesn't make any difference as far as the telephone is concerned. The information that we get about tourist attractions, on the other hand, does matter to both parties. To see the difference, consider what is happening with this article. As I type it, I am communicating information to you in the ordinary sense. I understand what I'm typing; I know it's about something; I think it matters to you; and if you've gotten this far, so do you. I am also, simultaneously, communicating information to this word processor in the technical sense; it is taking my keystrokes and converting them into electronic signals in a reliable way. But as far as it's concerned, the symbols are meaningless; it neither understands them nor cares about them.

Not "Decode," but "Understand"

Human communication is not telephone communication, then, because human beings understand what they're communicating. When we take in information, we don't just change its form, the way an information transfer device does; we place the information in relation to all sorts of things we already know. This "placing in relation" is understanding. Our understanding it, moreover, is not just an ancillary fact about a message we communicate; it is the essential fact. We can't even say what a message is, unless we first think of it as understood.

In the Rathbone model, the content of the message is obviously governed by the information being coded. Information may be transformed by the relatively simple coding steps, but it remains the same information. When we give up on the Rathbone model, we also give up on the idea that the original content is the governor. When we think of what's being expressed as an understanding, as a representation held against an entire network of knowledge plus a Background of skills, it's hard to pin down exactly what is being communicated.

Nevertheless, I'm happy to drop the Rathbone model. I don't like to think of myself as a telephone, and I'm glad that what's important about my communication is my knowledge of the world, of language, and of institutions and situations. I'm glad that my knowledge goes into my writing. But if you are beginning to agree with me and think it is a pretty good thing, let me caution you. If you are in technical communication, you've just created some problems for yourself.

More Consequences for Teachers
of Technical Communication

The trouble is that we can no longer see how well a piece of specifically technical communication is working. Under the information
transfer model, the obvious test of a manual is behavioral. If we give
a manual for the coffee mill to a person and that person can use the
coffee mill, it's a good manual because it has communicated the
facts.

Once we abandon the information transfer model, this formulation is not so simple. For one thing, it may not be just the manual
that is doing the work; it may be the good design of the coffee mill.
Now the relationship between the two becomes more problematic.
More important, the behavioral test may or may not be a good indication of the person's understanding, which is really what is at
issue. The test of understanding may only come when the person
tries to grind chick-peas or when the person drops the coffee mill on
the floor.

If the behavioral test is one side of the coin, then step-by-step instructions are the other. They, too, are praised by the Rathbone
model and by the textbooks I mention. You can see why. In the valence of the Rathbone model is the notion that information is transmitted mechanically, in small bits, in code; step-by-step instructions
look like this kind of information transfer. These instructions, of
course, fit nicely with behavioral tests because you can see which instructions were followed and which were not.

Unfortunately, the real test of step-by-step instructions occurs
when the machine breaks in some obscure way. If the person then
knows approximately what to do, the instructions have succeeded.
If, however, the user becomes stuck just by following directions,
then the instructions have failed to give understanding. Because
step-by-step instructions neglect global explanations of what is
going on, and because conditional statements about what to do
when things go wrong interfere too much with the flow, step-by-
step instructions usually give very little understanding. They make a
machine into a kind of safe that can be cracked by punching in the
right numbers, and they leave us entirely helpless if just one of the
numbers turns out to be even slightly wrong.

Step-by-step instructions do, on the other hand, make it easy to
treat writing as a technology. They make it easy for the company to
sell a product whose performance is measurable. They make it easy
for the purchaser to determine how well the users are doing (until

something goes wrong). They make it easy for the technical writing department to justify itself. They just don't make it easy for the reader.

My proposal that we abandon this system has been met with real unhappiness from readers. Nevertheless, I don't think it's so bad to think of technical documents as having an uncertain fate out in the world. Many other things are created and released with more riding on them and even more doubt about their success. Think of technical writing as being in the same boat with the television industry or the advertising industry. They test and test and test, but they still can't tell whether the public will like a television show or whether an advertisement will sell. Think of manuals as marketing documents, not repositories of facts.

Conclusion

If we speak of technical communication as transferring information (reporting information, transmitting information, or communicating facts), we suggest to ourselves that we are like the telephone, which takes input and turns it into output almost invisibly. It encourages us in believing that, like the telephone receiver, the transmitter must function invisibly and that the success of the transmission can be measured by looking at what shape the facts are in when they arrive. Speaking this way obscures the fact that understanding, not facts, is being communicated.

A better model is the one described in the previous chapter. One reason it's better is that it more accurately accounts for why things go wrong. If we think that information is being transferred, then failures are either culpable or mysterious, depending on what we think of the communicator. But if we think of understanding as being conveyed, then failures are misunderstandings. The source of most misunderstandings is the fact that people have different Backgrounds, different knowledge, different practices. To anticipate or to remedy misunderstandings requires immense sympathy and painstaking work, for one has to explore, assimilate, and reconcile the practices of two different groups. If this is the goal of technical writing, then the technical writer is a kind of translator—taking an understanding couched in the terms of one culture and converting it to an understanding couched in the terms of another. This is not easy.

5 Is Technical Writing Particularly Objective?

We saw earlier that every definer of technical writing had insisted that it is particularly "objective." We also distinguished between two kinds of "objectivity," the formal, which refers to features of text, and "epistemological," which refers to features of the mental state. Different definers insist on different kinds of objectivity, though only one (Pearsall) distinguishes between the two. We saw, too, that this insistence on objectivity, like some symptoms of neuroses, is held on to with more tenacity than circumstances warrant. Why, after all, shouldn't the instructions we began the book with be spoken with the word "I" or contain a purely subjective intuition about the best way to get there?

The intuition with which we began the book is that certain kinds of writing—ranging from the instructions to environmental impact statements—are instrumental. We have since shifted; we now call most members of that class "technical writing" and added that its defining characteristic is that it accommodated technology to the user. In making the shift, I have implied that technical writing goes on in technological communities and is partly structured by the practices of those communities. The best, viable reason for clinging to objectivity is now that the community practices require it. Being (formally or epistemologically) objective provides protective coloration.

But how does objectivity provide protective coloration? And where is the gain for the community as a whole in demanding it? Is there anything else to be said for objectivity in writing? And if there isn't, should language teachers (not just technical writing teachers) respond? Should we try to change community practices?

In this chapter, I will answer these questions. I will also use the notion of objectivity as a tool for digging still deeper into the matters that have concerned me in the previous chapters: technology and understanding. If you are a holist, I shall argue, it's just silly to think that any genre of writing is "particularly" objective, but it may well be that particular groups practice objectivity in particular ways. People who create, produce, write about, manage, or use technology do, in fact, have such particular practices. I will then describe those practices (as they relate to the use of language) and the consequences of those practices for people who are concerned professionally with writing, in particular, technical writing.

What Is Objectivity?

I am concerned, here, with the adjective "objective" when it is predicated of states of mind or expressions of states of mind. "Objective" can also be predicated of objects: cats, mats, or sealing wax. I am not concerned, however, with this second sense of the word.

The word "objective" is used in the first sense in the following examples:

1. I have objectively determined the size of the leaf.
2. The umpire was objective in ruling it a home run.
3. The arbitrator made the decision with great objectivity.
4. The scientist based the theory on an objective assessment of the facts.

In examples 1, 3, and 4, determining, deciding, and assessing are states of mind; in example 2, ruling can either be a state of mind or an expression of a state of mind.

These uses of the word have a number of things in common:

1. Those states of mind that can be objective are directed towards some (often external) state of affairs that is not the state of mind itself. They are about something, like leaf size or scientific facts.

2. Objective states of mind have what John Searle calls "mind-to-world direction of fit" (Searle 1983). If the states of mind do not "fit" the world, we change the state of mind. (With states of mind that have "world-to-mind" direction of fit, like hopes, we try to change the world to fit them.) Thus we can only speak of objective judgments or predictions; we cannot speak of objective fears or desires.

3. Perceptions are neither objective nor subjective. Objective states of mind may use perceptions, but they also have recourse to memory, knowledge or feelings. The umpire doesn't see, but rules that it's a home run.

Taken together, these observations tell us that we predicate objectivity of a judgment or a prediction. What makes such a judgment objective? In common speech, we have a number of different descriptions. Objective judgments, we feel, are *fair-minded*, *rational*, and *uninvolved* (in the sense that the judge does not side with either party in a controversy). Being fair-minded, and so forth, the objective person comes to a judgment, feeling confident it could be repeated; the judgment is *repeatable*. The objective person can also offer reasons for coming to the judgment; the judgment is *justifiable*. Another person can evaluate those reasons and see whether they make sense; the judgment is *checkable*. Generally speaking, we feel that another person would come to the same conclusion by following the same reasoning and using the same information, so objective judgments are repeatable by someone else or (to prevent confusion, I use an uncommon word) *interchangeable*. And perhaps because objective judgments are those that several people can come to, we count on them; they are *reliable*.

By contrast, a subjective judgment is biased, emotional, or involved. Such a judgment is often idiosyncratic; we don't feel the person making it could come to the same conclusion over and over again. When a person offers a justification for a subjective judgment, we often don't buy it or we feel it's incomplete. We can't check a subjective judgment, nor can we reliably come to the same one ourselves. Hence, we trust a subjective judgment less than an objective one and find it unreliable.

Objectivity, Reliability, and Truth

By virtue of what is an objective judgment *objective*? And why should whatever it is make us think that objective judgments are more reliable?

The answer propounded since Bacon and Descartes has been that an objective judgment is objective because it is reached by using a method. The reason the judgments are fair-minded and rational is that the method is; they are repeatable and checkable because the method can be followed over and over again. Consider, for instance, a judgment about which of two leaves is bigger. I could just look at the leaves and decide. Or, I could use a method such as the following:

1. Put each leaf down on separate parts of a piece of paper.
2. Draw an outline around each leaf.

   3. Cut out the two outlined areas.
   4. Weigh each cutout and compare the weights. The cutout
      with the larger weight will have come from the bigger leaf.

This latter judgment seems more careful than the subjective judgment and also seems subject to fewer accidents. Each little step is so
small that no accidental subjectivity can creep in and affect the judgment.

Indeed, both Bacon's and Descartes's idea in proposing that we
use methods such as this was eventually to make them so reliable
that they would guarantee us the right answer. Since each step in
the method consisted in ascertaining some fact—a self-evident one
in Descartes's case or one that is perceived in Bacon's—and since inexorable logic led us from step to step, we would certainly reach the
truth.

We've seen, though, that Bacon and Descartes can't be right. Observations are made against a background of practices, skills, and
prior knowledge and are inseparable from them (Quine 1953). Bacon
and Descartes (and later universalists) would have it that somewhere there is a direct, consistent, and unambiguous connection between the impingement of the outside world—"sense data" is one
term for this—and some mental events. But as we've seen, the same
"sense data" can cause many different mental events (a hammer or
a brown blob) depending upon our knowledge, and the same mental event (for example, seeing a leaf) can be caused by a quite different set of sense data. (The experience doesn't change when a shadow falls across the leaf, nor when the leaf is turned.) So there can't
be any such connection.

According to Wittgenstein's infinite regress argument, moreover,
the "inexorable" logic that would bring us to the right conclusion is
inevitably lacking sufficient metalogic for us to be sure it's leading
us aright. In the earlier description of the procedure for weighing
leaves, for instance, there are immediate problems with how to
draw the lines, what kind of scale to use, and even what is meant by
"larger." (This method, for instance, gives us the larger projected
area.) To resolve these problems, we would have to introduce still
other problems—ways of building precision instruments for sharp-
ening pencils, and so on—and the resolution of those problems
would create still more (Wittgenstein 1946).

If Bacon and Descartes were right, an objective judgment would
establish a causal chain between sense data and judgment. If Wittgenstein is right, there can never be such a causal chain. Without

such a causal chain, there is no a priori reason for thinking that objective judgments reached by following a method are true.

Although Bacon and Descartes do not adduce this, there is a second reason to believe that methodical judgments are more reliable. Not only does following a method prevent us from fooling ourselves, but it also makes our judgment available to other people. The idea is that breaking the judgment into a series of small steps makes it easier to share what you've done. Another person can, presumably, check your work by checking each step or even by repeating each step. Following a method leaves you open to correction, and this is more likely to make your observations true. Notice, though, that just following a method does not in itself give a judgment objectivity. It presupposes, moreover, that people's evaluation of each step and their metaevaluation of the overall method are consistent, otherwise the choice of method, the way of following it, or the method itself would be subjective. The objectivity, then, of this procedure depends on the objectivity of the evaluation of that procedure. That objectivity, in turn, depends on the objectivity of the evaluation of the evaluation. There is no escape from the infinite regress.

How Objective Judgments Are Made

The infinite regress argument would be less forceful if people actually did make (and share) objective judgments by rigorously following a method. But the idea that they do is, phenomenologically speaking, nonsense. The belief that we have followed a procedure in any instance rests on the fact that, when we do make (objective) judgments and we happen to disagree with someone else, we have myriad ways of justifying ourselves, one of which is to reconstruct our judgment by describing the "steps" we took in making it. But this description is merely a narrative strategy.

Radiologists, for instance, are pretty consistent in their judgments of X rays. When they see things in X rays, surgeons usually find what they see. But radiologists don't consciously follow a method in making their judgments; they just see whatever it is they see. This seeing is certainly educated; when I look at the same X rays, I see nothing. But even the education was not in a method. Radiologists learn to read X rays by occupying a place in a community of radiologists—treating patients, learning medicine, discussing cases with other doctors, and reading a lot of X rays. In the process, they assimilate a huge collection of practices, habits, and bits of knowledge. That entire collection goes into each of their judgments. (Which is why, of course, it's unreasonable to think of them as following a method. A method that systematically consulted each facet of their entire professional experience would take forever to follow.) Radiologists don't agree because they're comparing notes on how they follow each step in an explicit method; they agree because they've assimilated the practices of their group.

Notice, by the way, that on this account, following a method doesn't necessarily gain anything. It won't necessarily make the judgment more reliable, more true, or even more objective. To see why, consider what would happen if somebody developed a method for judging X rays and required all radiologists to follow it. The infinite regress would still take hold. The radiologists would soon develop shared practices for determining what counts as following the method. Agreement would be reached in the same way as before (by sharing practices), but that way would be far more circuitous and difficult.

The same problem arises for anybody making a subtle professional judgment about something. When we English teachers try to guarantee that judgments of papers are objective by defining criteria for good papers and getting everybody to use those criteria, we fail for the same reasons that the radiologists would fail. People disagree on how to apply the criteria and on how well a paper meets them. A better way to get objective judgments of papers would be to do it the same way the radiologists do: have everybody get lots of practice making judgments and check with the surgeons from time to time to see if they are right.

If you are a holist, then, you believe that we learn to make objective judgments by becoming a member of the group that makes those judgments, learning the knowledge and the practices of the group. As members, we make the same judgment everybody else does. There's nothing subjective about that judgment; holists are not subjectivists. They do believe that facts are what we make of them; or that we create the world in our minds. Holists just believe that what we know and how we see depend on what we already know and see.[10]

So what about objectivity and technical writing? If you are a follower of Bacon and Descartes (a universalist), technical writing is terribly important because it is the means by which the steps are shared. For a holist, writing is one way of describing and justifying a judgment, but there's nothing special about it. There is, moreover, nothing particularly objective about technical writing. The objectivity expressed in technical writing is the objectivity of the group of people who make technological judgments, just as the objectivity expressed in legal writing is the objectivity of lawyers. There is no standard of objectivity that could make one more or less objective than the other. The objectivity of technical writing can only be different in kind, not in degree, from other kinds of objectivity.

If one wants to say anything, therefore, about objectivity and technical writing, one must discover the special features of objectivity in the group that makes technological judgments. The objectivity referred to pertains, of course, to the mental state, and, as we've seen, it's not a mental state we have much access to. The radiologist simply experiences the X ray and makes a judgment. If there is anything special, therefore, about technological judgments, it must be what is special about experience in technological contexts, or, as I shall put it, about experiencing things technologically.

Objectivity and Technology

What is that special thing? Properly speaking, this question has nothing to do with what has gone before. To answer it, I will have to return to Heidegger and technology.

Heidegger's first description of technology is straightforward and, at this point, familiar (Heidegger 1977). Technology is the system of tools and tasks that are the means for achieving our ends in the physical world.[11]

When we experience things technologically, we experience them as things to be used, things that help us reach our ends. Toasters are things that heat bread; subways are things that transport us; X ray machines are things that allow us to detect tumors. Any object can be so experienced. As I write this, it's snowing outside. The unfortunate people in the Cambridge Public Works Department are experiencing the snow as an obstacle, something to be removed. (I, on the other hand, am not experiencing it technologically; to me, it's just pretty.) Even people can be experienced technologically. Tomorrow, when I go outside, the snow will be an obstacle, and the people in the CPWD will be obstacle-removers, just as their machines are. We even experience ourselves technologically, for when we experience something as useful, we also experience ourselves as users. We understand ourselves functionally, technologically. Tomorrow, when I go down the stairs into the subway, I will be experienced by the subway designers, operators, and fare collectors as a traversing mechanism, and that's also how I'll experience myself. When I get to the token booth, I'll be a paying mechanism. At the slot, I'll be an inserting mechanism. At the turnstile, I'll be a turning mechanism. And toward the seat (if I can find one), I'll be an occupying mechanism. Actually, given how ill-adapted the seats are to the mechanism, I'll be an uncomfortable occupying mechanism.

When I experience myself technologically, I am simultaneously fitting myself to a technology and being fitted to it so that I am interchangeable with anyone else. With respect to that activity, I am anyone. I am a physical body; I touch things, see things, vote, and so on; but I am that body just as everyone else is their own, respective body. I experience myself and am experienced as anyone, as using and being used. As Heidegger says, I am a resource, a resource engaged in drawing forth and utilizing other resources. These resources, too, are so engaged with still others. The whole is a vast net of using and being used.

Put abstractly, this way sounds apocalyptic; plus, in the abstract, the subtlety of the process is lost. So let me clothe the point in an example. Let us look, for example, at how a mountain may be drawn into the net. The nontechnological experience of it may be simply letting it lend a certain structure to the quotidian (living on the mountain, you have to walk down to get food) or it may be religious ("I will lift up mine eyes unto the hills, from whence cometh my help."—Psalms 121:1). The technological experience may be, by contrast, to look for places in it where minerals might be buried, to look for routes around the mountain where one might put in a highway, or, suspecting it's volcanic, to assess the dangers it poses to nearby housing development. It's very easy, of course, for the technological experience to swallow up the others. The slope can easily be seen merely as an impediment, which a new road would overcome. And, of course, when it is experienced technologically, previous ways of experiencing (letting the slope be) seem curiously passive.

It's important to realize that anything can be taken over. The one experience of the mountain we would think cannot be technological is the aesthetic. But of course the aesthetic experience can be measured, controlled, and made useful, just like anything else. If, for instance, my lack of mental health were interfering with my productivity, and if it was thought that spending a certain amount of time viewing aesthetic objects would restore my health, then the mountain would become a resource for improving mental health, and looking at the mountain would be a way of utilizing this resource.

This resource would be plugged easily into the network. We could grade it, perhaps by developing criteria for the beauty of mountains, and then by inventorying the beautiful mountains, complete with rankings. We might want to set aside particularly highly ranked mountains, build roads to the best viewing sites, add comfort facilities to the sites, and so on. Or, part of the mountain's value might be its inaccessibility, so we would make it a wilderness area and prevent roads from being built. In any case, by doing this, we are converting the nontechnological aesthetic experience of the mountain into the experience of anyone—a controlled, monitored, evaluated, and flattened experience. There is nothing false about this; the mountain would actually be beneficial to my mental health.[12]

One way of describing this special feature of technological experiencing is to say that technological experiencing objectifies things because it makes them interchangeable. (I'm going to call this characteristic "technological objectification.") Thus, the special feature of technological objectivity (what makes it different from legal objectivity) is that it is objectified. Technological objectivity is measured, controlled, plugged into a network, interchangeable with anyone else's. It is a resource, like any other resource. On this account, notice, the close relationship between the words "objectivity" and "objectification" does not indicate any special relationship between the ideas. Technological objectification is a characteristic of a form of experience; making an objective judgment is one of many experiences that can take this form.[13] Technological subjectivity is just as objectified, for instance, as technological objectivity. A radiologist's judgment can be an objective one or a hunch, but in either case, it is thought of as a resource.

The Objectification of Technical Writing

I began this chapter by saying that it is a mistake to think of technical writing as being particularly objective. We can now see how people make that mistake. They confuse the distinction between the form of experience and the experience itself, led on by the similarity of "objectification" and "objectivity." Taking technical writing to be objective (which it frequently is) and recognizing that technology objectifies, people think that the objectivity of the writing is what makes it objectified. Put this way, of course, you can see that they're making an elementary error in logic.

What are the consequences of rectifying this error for the teaching of technical writing, in particular, and writing, generally? Perhaps very few. Objectivity itself ceases to be a crucial concern of technical communication. The particular objectivity required in a particular technical document is determined by the situation and by the practices which constitute that situation. We, as teachers, no longer even have a particular responsibility toward that objectivity. Usually we are not members of the group; we are not engaged in making the technical judgments; and we are not in any special position when it comes to teaching the practices, though sometimes we may be able to do our part. Our responsibilities as teachers are only those dictated by common sense, which is encouraging, given the murky waters we've been through.

The only possible consequences have to do with technological objectification. How do we, as teachers, respond to that? There seem to be two separate issues. First, if Heidegger is right, and technology is imperialistic, how is technology taking over writing? How is it flattening writing, quantifying it, treating it as a resource, and making it useful? We have been looking at this question already; it is now time to go into it more deeply. Second, if on this account we don't like technological objectification—and if you read Heidegger, it's hard to like it—then should we be teaching technical writing and thereby helping to "technologize" (objectify) writing? Aren't we morally implicated? The first kind of question is essentially empirical; the second, moral.

We have seen some answers to the first question already. In part, technological practices make writing into an instrument by fiat, at a stroke legitimating certain other management and production practices. The fiat does require setting up systems that evaluate the instrument's utility and diagnose its failures; those systems have been the focus so far. They, in turn, depend on the idea that technical writing presents facts; the amount and quality of fact transmission has been what was measured. So far, I have been arguing that such measures give us meaningless results.

I need, however, to carry this argument a little farther. The fact that a measure of utility has no theoretical foundation and gives no meaningful results does not mean that people will abandon it because it may have other functions within the group. (I have been describing some of those functions.) Neither does it mean that no more satisfactory measure of utility can be found.

The question is, in fact, purely empirical: "Can a community be gotten together that can develop a consistent measure of the utility of any particular technical document?" Obviously, the answer is "yes." A bunch of us writing teachers could sit down and evaluate a manual on the basis of the number of grammatical errors in it. The measure would be consistent and objective. The trouble is that the actual use of the manual is probably not affected by the number of grammatical errors.

Please do not laugh. In fact, a measure of usability, called "readability," has been used for years by many technical writing teachers. As we will see in chapter 9, the test has been automated. It has even been treated as evidence that a State of New York plain language requirement has been satisfied. Yet this measure has no more demonstrable a relation to the usability (or even the readability) of documents than a test of grammaticality has. A test of grammaticality I describe is, moreover, much more accurate.

Use of such tests does, however, have precisely the effects I describe. It flattens language and treats it as a quantifiable resource. As we will see again in chapter 9, not only the language suffers, but also the thinking processes as well. In some hands, the distortions can be extraordinary. I once interviewed "the most promising young engineer" in a technological group, the manager of which had heard somewhere that no sentence should be longer than fifteen words. I asked the engineer whether he ever revised his reports, reports which he spent one-quarter of his time writing. "Oh, yes," he said, "I always go through and count the words in each sentence, and if I ever go over fifteen, I throw out the extra words." And as Madame de Sévigné says, "Je sais encore mille petits contes agréables comme celui-là." ("I know thousands of other good little stories like that one.")

Let us refine the question. Can one get a community of users, then, to give an accurate judgment of usability? On occasion, we certainly can. There are many things in our culture that we pretty much agree on: that *War and Peace* is a good book, that democracy has certain advantages, and that word processing is handy. The question here, however, is not whether on occasion a community of users can be gotten to agree about the usability of a document, but whether the community can render such objective judgments consistently and reliably, the way the community of radiologists does. This is, let me say once more, an empirical question, but the weight of the empirical evidence is, so far as I know, against it. Judgments of the usability of technical documents seem closer to judgments about the latest novel (for example, widely varying) than they do to judgments about X rays.

Let me remind you of the reason for this. Judgments about the usability of a document are based primarily on how useful something is to the reader, and that usefulness will depend heavily on what the reader already knows, what the reader's purposes are, and so forth. Even slight variations in the reader's Background may make a huge difference to a document's utility. So, in order to get an objective judgment about the general utility of a document, one would have to be able to make all that background knowledge explicit, which is impossible. (Notice that a similar argument about the quality of freshman papers or CEEB achievement tests can be made.)

But even if we could, would we want to? Or would we want to implement the many other strategies for treating technical writing as a resource? One such strategy, for instance, is to denigrate individual judgments, even though they are precisely the best that we can do. My objection to this strategy is not that it treats foolish individual judgments as unworthy of attention; it is that even idiosyncratic, unusual, or unsupported judgments can give the author insight into how the Background and network are being deployed, which could lead to material improvement. Again, the same argument can be made about the judgment of freshman papers or CEEB achievement tests.

Resisting Technological Objectification

So far, I have been talking about strategies for global objectification of technical documents. There are numerous other strategies for taking over the language of technical documents. A second question, which may be of some concern to teachers of technical writing, is whether objectifications of this kind can or should be resisted.

The major part of the answer to the second question is already clear. We, as teachers of language, are not particularly implicated by technology. We wouldn't be unless there were some special, technological way of converting thought into language. As we have seen, there isn't. But we may well be able to make a special response to this moral problem, a response appropriate to our situation. Such a response is not demanded because we are especially implicated; it's demanded because we are in a special position. (The difference is the difference between the moral demands made of a person who causes a traffic accident and the moral demands made of a bystander.)

The position may, in fact, be particularly advantageous. If technical writing is difficult to understand as being useful, it may be particularly resistant to technological objectification. If we can diagnose the forms the resistance takes, we may be particularly effective in resisting it.

Indeed, the word "objectivity" gives us a clue about how this resistance works. Remember, even though it shouldn't be, it is still an issue for many teachers of technical writing. Indeed, it can be taken to ridiculous extremes. Simple common sense, for instance, even without the benefit of the foregoing chapter, ought to make us agree with Tom Pearsall that linguistic objectivity ought not to be an issue in technical writing (see chapter 2). Yet many people still tell students that there are certain linguistic devices that they must use in technical writing because technical writing is particularly objective. These are the devices that conventionally indicate that the judgment expressed is an objective one. They include such things as using the passive voice, using nominalizations, and (the one I will concentrate on) avoiding the use of "I" in papers except when one is expressing an opinion.

I should add that this chapter should change our view of these devices. If one has the normal intuition about objectivity, then there is some reason to believe that these devices are necessary—if an objective judgment were made by following a particular method, it would be important to signal the fact that one is using that method. That's probably why these devices have historically loomed large on the technical writing scene. But once one becomes a holist, there is no reason to cling to any of these devices.

Let me be clear about what the convention is. Teachers tell students to reserve the words "I" or "we" for statements of opinion. Where matters of fact are concerned, students should use the passive voice. Instead of saying, "I started the machine" or "I observed that precipitation began," one says, "The machine was started," or "Precipitation began." Logically, this stipulation is absurd. The choice between the two sentences depends not on a formal rule about fact versus opinion, but on how much the agent of implementation should be emphasized. In the first case, for some reason, it's important to say who started the machine; in the second, it isn't. Under this analysis, the word "I" is functionally equivalent to "Randall" or "the gorilla"—keep it if needed; throw it out if not. In this situation, the use of the word "I" says nothing about the mental state of the author, and the reader recognizes that.

What, then, is the stake in this silly rule? I think the rule is one of those strategies for making technical writing "efficient," that is, objectified. As always with such strategies, there is a superficially plausible reason for imposing it, and underneath there are other, more powerful functionalities. The superficial reason is that, in much technical writing, the agent is presumed to be specified by the context. If the data show that the number of bald males named Reginald over the age of thirty in New York City correlates with the prevailing mortgage rate, I need not say, "I observed this" or "I concluded this from the data." If I give a chi-square, I show that I am being objective, as far as my community is concerned. Saying "I concluded" doesn't just add unnecessary words—it clouds the issue, since it implies that I had some special way of doing it. (As with "Read all instructions," the non-obviousness condition operates. Since agency is too obvious to be worth mentioning under the normal interpretation, there must be something special about the agency.)

A more powerful reason is that suppressing the "I" can rid the document of some inconvenient individuality. In the passive voice, the organization we are speaking for might speak more loudly: naming the agent that might assert, for instance, a proprietary claim for the agent's actions. If I say "I" in this book, the reasoning goes, I remind people that it is the economic entity "David N. Dobrin" whose ideas these are. That's fine if I work for MIT, but not if I work for Bolt, Beranek, and Newman. In private companies, it is not the performer, but the owner whose work it is, and the reader should not have this fact confused.

The overtones of this are not just legal; they are practical. Suppressing the agent gains another kind of efficiency: linguistic fungibility. Not using "I" at Bolt, Beranek, and Newman makes the product more like other of their products. Words from one document can easily be moved to another; we have instant boilerplate. This may be an attempt, moreover, to make writing more susceptible to technical analysis. It looks as if the more sameness one imposes on documents, the easier they are to evaluate. Of course, this efficiency does risk an inefficient backlash because people—all of them, interchangeably—don't like to have their work appropriated. And in any case, other things in the situation may require that agency be specified. But at least, the reasoning runs, it's a first step.

As Marcuse suggests they might be, these reasons are remarkably incoherent. Requiring the use of "I" might be equally efficient, and it might make bringing the document under the control of the organization equally easy. If we are going to be objectified anyway, why doesn't the use of "I" become the norm? At least it would be a nice, graceful norm to have.

An easy answer is that the use of "I" resists alienation because it reminds people that there is a real, human speaker. Unfortunately, if Heidegger is right, this answer is wrong. According to Heidegger, no particular linguistic usage would, in itself, permanently resist objectification; anything *could* be taken over. The "I" that you are reminded of might be a perfectly technologized, entirely fungible "I." Is there a more complicated answer? Frankly, I don't see it. Nevertheless, the fact remains that, at this historical moment, certain uses of language are proscribed because they are taken as resisting objectification. It is perhaps our responsibility as teachers of language to sniff out those uses and encourage them.

But which uses? Let us imagine for a moment what a perfectly technologized language would be like. Surely it would have some of the fungibility that purveyors of advice about impersonal constructions would like it to have. Surely, too, the favored constructions would be inefficient because they are imprecise and confusing. (This inefficiency would, however, be ignored, its price paid with aplomb.) A technologized (as opposed to a technical) language would surely be a deracinated language. It would, like any technology, disappear as it was used, pushing the user "past" it to the end for which it is a means. Like the snow, which disappears qua (beautiful, shiny) snow as it becomes an obstacle, or like the people in a public works department, who become snow-removers, a technological language would disappear as it turns us into users. Uses of language, then, that prevent language from disappearing would be uses that help us resist "technologization."

What could those uses be? We can't, as I say, simply point to some. But we can remember that a technologized language is a language that doesn't matter very much. It is invisible and it is blunt because all that people want from it is to "get the idea," to "get the message across." When language doesn't matter, given our technological need to make things fungible, it's all right to give up: for example, the clarity about agency that a correct use of the personal pronoun gives us. Uses of language that help us resist technology would then be uses that matter, for some odd reason. These uses cannot be constant; what they are depends on the situation at the time. No usage always matters, since all uses can be taken over.

At the same time, we also need to sniff out usages that somehow make language matter less, usages that blur distinctions or obscure relationships. Sometimes, as I have said, they themselves won't surface; rather, like the use of the word "I," they'll appear as alternatives to arbitrary prohibitions. Obeying this prohibition obscures relationships, purposes, and agency. But obeying it also simplifies

dealing with the documents, making the documents more susceptible to technological analysis. Used as if language mattered, there
would be nothing wrong with these usages. Used as they are used
now, they deracinate language.

When you develop a nose for these usages, it's amazing what you
can find. Consider a sentence such as the following:

> The fluid passes through a filter to remove impurities from it.

This usage obscures both agency and causality in one fell swoop;
yet it is very common, particularly these days, when teachers are
encouraging students to use verb forms like infinitive phrases rather
than the dread "nominalizations."[14] How does it do that? There are
two conventions governing the use of adverbial infinitive phrases.
The first is that the agent of the phrase is the agent of the main verb;
the second is that the phrase contains a distinct link in a causal
chain. A sentence like "George went to the store in order to get
some bread" satisfies both conventions; George does both acts, and
the causal relationship between the two acts is clear. But in the other
sentence, "fluid" is not the agent of "filter," and the causal relationship is not distinct. Since filters usually remove impurities, the
sentence resembles a sentence like "I went to the store in order to
get to the store," a pleonasm writ large. In order to correct the first,
the sentence needs to read, "The fluid is passed . . . (and so on)
. . . " and in order to correct the second, "to" needs to be changed
to "that."

People are not led to making this mistake because they have a
false idea about objectivity. Rather, they make it because they don't
have the time or the energy to be clear about the causalities with
which they are supposedly concerned. The effects, however, are remarkably similar to the effects of avoiding "I." Meaning is blurred;
so is emphasis. As far as administrative purposes are concerned,
this is probably an advantage—in this case, because people concerned with the usability of the document don't really care about
precision, in other cases because the relationships of purposes or
causes need to be hazy. There may be an administrative cost: the
user can't use the document as effectively. But when documents are
understood in terms of their overall place in the network, that cost
has to be balanced against the savings in time for the writer.

Please remember that the objection to such sentences has nothing
to do with their efficiency or lack thereof. That would be a technological objection. My objection to these sentences is that writing
them makes language matter less; it encourages the flattening of lan-

guage, which is one of the effects of technologization. My grounds for this objection are purely moral. If you accept my argument, you are against these usages because you don't think language should be taken over by technology. Because you teach writing (presumably), you are in a position to do something about this. Thus, if you accept my argument, there is one moral responsibility for you as a teacher—to make sure that language matters.

6 Know Your Audience

In chapter 3, I made a distinction between the Background and the network: between a complex of non-Intentional skills and a web of Intentional states, like beliefs and desires. The existence of a Background is what distinguishes the Searle-Dreyfus account of mental functioning from a holistic cognitive account. In the areas we've covered so far, like the possibility of measuring human information transfer or the one-to-one relationship of words and things, the Background has not been that important because the two accounts would arrive at the same place. Why, then, am I insisting on its existence?

The one place where the notion of the Background has been crucial is in the discussion of the coffee mill. I suggest there that the safety instructions are misdirected. The instructions are trying to teach Background skills in the use of small electric appliances; unfortunately, written instructions, which express Intentional states, don't, by themselves, teach Background skills. Knowledge can't just teach know-how. You may know that cords hanging over the edge are dangerous, but that doesn't stop you from leaving them there.

This kind of misdirection is common. In this chapter, I want to look at an example of similar misdirection, one that is far removed from coffee mills and computers. In the coffee mill example, the instructions writer apparently forgot that skills were necessary. In this new example, the people dispensing misdirected instructions have a theoretical commitment to the idea that only knowledge, not know-how, is needed to perform the task. This commitment, unfortunately, vitiates their efforts.

The task is one part of that endlessly mysterious phenomenon, the writing process. The misdirected instructions are those that teachers give in order to get writers to write for their audience. This chapter marks a transition in subject matter: from technical writing to the technique of writing. As we shall see, people in technical writing have often been concerned with writing to an audience, but the problem of how to do it is universal.

Very quickly, this chapter will present an intricate discussion of the advice teachers give about audience, their characterizations of writing to an audience, and my alternative ones. You should bear in mind that this chapter also has two other themes. First, I want to demonstrate why the Background is needed in accounts of writing. Second, I want to show that giving instructions requires that one take into account the skills (not only the knowledge) required to execute a task successfully. In this case, I will show that having knowledge of an audience by itself does little or no good. Indeed, where knowledge is helpful, its usefulness arises from a skilled interpretation on the writer's part of the audience's relationship to the material, which I call the "sense" of an audience.

What Does "Know Your Audience" Mean?

We are all agreed about one thing: writers should "pay attention to their audience," "keep their audience in mind," "respect their audience," or, as a chapter title in one textbook has it, "know your audience." The problem is to figure out exactly what it is to know your audience. As with the Rathbone example in chapter 4, I am going to pick somewhat arbitrarily on that last formulation and try to clarify it.

In ordinary English, the word "know" has many senses. Exactly which sense is meant depends first on the grammatical form of the object and second on the kind of object. In other languages, like French, it's easier to distinguish among the senses because the French use two different words where we use one. Where the object of "know" is a proposition (usually a clause or a pronoun or noun that is defined by a clause), the French use the verb "savoir." Thus, the French know (savoir) that Paris is the capital of France (a proposition), the fact that Ader is the father of aviation (a noun defined by a proposition), or where the best champagne is made (near Reims). As I have said before, what you know in this sense is an Intentional state, a representation of a state of affairs in the mode of belief.[15]

When the object of the word is a name, the French generally use the word "connaître." The French know (connaître) Paris or my friend Paula or particle physics or President Reagan. In all these senses, the knowledge denoted is familiarity or acquaintance with the thing named. To know Paris may be to have visited there; to know Paula may be to have some kind of social contact with her; to know particle physics may imply an in-depth knowledge; and to know Mr. Reagan may be, by analogy, to have studied his actions and to be able to anticipate accurately how he will behave.

Consider, now, the difference between knowing that Paris is in France and knowing Paris. From the first, you can infer that I also know that Paris is a city and that France is a country. Knowing a proposition involves knowing a certain web of other propositions as well; knowledge exists within a network. From the second, you cannot necessarily infer that I know anything in particular, but, if you believe the claim, you can assume that I have available to me a cloud of interrelated facts. You cannot know which ones, but you can assume I have an ability to work with them, so that if, for instance, you want to know where the American Embassy is, it is reasonable to suppose I could tell you it is in the Place de la Concorde.

Similarly, if "I know particle physics," I know a huge cloud of things and can work with that knowledge. Indeed, this use suggests the possession of Background skills (know-how) as well as knowledge. When, for instance, we say that we know auto mechanics, what that amounts to is that we can fix cars (or that we know Al and Mike down at the service station). Or, when we say that we "know" Ronald Reagan, we are not usually referring to any personal acquaintance.[16] We are saying, rather, that we have know-how when it comes to understanding his behavior.

These senses are listed below:

Sense	Object	Meaning
savoir (1)	Paula is in Paris	Know a fact
savoir (2)	Where Paris is	Know a related fact
connaître (1)	Paula, Paris	Familiar or acquainted with
connaître (2)	Particle physics	Work with a body of knowledge
connaître (3)	Printing	Have skills in an area
connaître (4)	President Reagan	Understand thoroughly

Which sense of "know" is being used in the sentence, "Know your audience"? The imperative mood complicates things. Strictly speaking, one can't order somebody to know (savoir) a proposition because knowledge of a proposition depends on its truth, and the person being ordered can't control the truth. One can order somebody to know (savoir), for example, the names of the major arteries in the body, but really the order is to acquire the knowledge. I can, in other words, get up a subject like astrology, knowing it in the connaître (2) sense, but whether what I've learned is knowledge depends on how well astrology works.

Audiences, of course, are neither a body of knowledge nor an area of skill. So neither the connaître (2) sense nor the connaître (3) sense can be the one meant (unless you are a rhetorical determinist and think of rhetoric as being like auto mechanics). The connaître (1) sense is implausible; it suggests social contact in the case of people. Connaître (4) is, perhaps, the most plausible, since it suggests an ability to understand how the audience would behave in certain situations. Again, the imperative mood makes things difficult, and the depth of knowledge implied seems greater than most writers have. Besides, as we shall see, it is phenomenologically implausible.

Perhaps, then, "know your audience" is a solecism. Like "to hear a color," the phrase couples a verb and an object that just don't go together. Nevertheless, something is meant by it—and by the other characterizations I gave. So let me go one step further and try to cash out the term by paraphrasing. There seem to be two possibilities. One is a slight perversion of the connaitre (1) sense, which can be explained as follows: in anything one writes, one takes it that a relationship exists between reader and writer. In this chapter, for instance, I take it that I am talking to my professional colleagues. This relationship does not just exist only in my mind (as Walter Ong would seem to have it); it isn't the relationship between the "author" and his "idea of an audience." It involves real commitments that I, the author, make to you, the actual reader.[17] "Know your audience," then, can be construed as reminding people of that fact. "Remember that your audience exists," it might be saying. A more accurate way of putting it might be as follows: "When you're writing, say things that are appropriate both to the relationships you're trying to set up and to the actual relationships you have with your actual audience." This is good advice, but it's limited.

The other is a mild twist of the connaître (2) sense. It is evidently what is meant when, for instance, Linda Flower says that writing is a "problem-solving process" and that part of the problem is meeting "constraints exerted by the nature of the audience" (Flower and Hayes, "A Cognitive Process Theory," 1981). Since Flower uses a cognitive approach, the "nature of the audience" must consist of a body of facts. This knowledge, then, would be at the disposal of the writer, who would be able to apply it (detect and satisfy the constraints) at the appropriate times. The difference between this sense and the ordinary connaître sense is that the knowledge about the audience is not organized and shared, the way particle physics is. The only disciplinary knowledge one might have relating to audiences would be a knowledge of the techniques for garnering and applying knowledge about particular audiences; that is, you would know audience analysis.

If this were the process people used—and I admit, it sounds plausible—then teachers of writing would have to give two kinds of instructions: instructions in how to get the knowledge and instructions in how to apply it. In fact, to my knowledge, teachers of writing have concentrated entirely on the first kind. They have tried to describe the kinds of knowledge writers should have and have tried to show writers how to get that knowledge.

What might such knowledge look like? Following is a list of facts about an audience that various technical writing textbooks say should be determined before an author begins to write, say, a manual.

Age.	Educational level.
Educational specialization.	Knowledge of English.
Technical knowledge.	Familiarity with similar machines, mode of operation, interface.
Attitude toward machine.	Reason for reading the manual.
Reason for using the machine.	Situation in which the manual is read.
Ways they might abuse the machine.	Knowledge of safety.
Social position.	General knowledge.

The list is not complete, of course, but right now all we need to worry about is how the information in these categories is used. Sometimes, of course, it is obvious. If the audience is uneducated, for instance, they might not understand certain words, appreciate a certain manner of talking, or be familiar with the principles underlying the operation of the machine. I remind you, though, that the claim is stronger than that: the information in every category exercises constraints on the writing process. Without it, the claim goes, the writer will not be able to write successfully. "Know your audience" is in the imperative mood.

Let us take this claim seriously, for a moment, and see how filling it out would be useful if we were writing the instructions for the coffee mill. Early on, we confront the categories "educational level" and "knowledge of English." The constraint being exerted is obviously on the language (simple, complex, Latinate, and so on) that the writer should use. For the coffee mill, we can assume that the users in the United States are largely upper-middle-class and that their knowledge of English and educational level is roughly the same as the knowledge of English among all members of that class. Thus, lists like the following might be correct. (I doubt it, though; I made them up.)

Knowledge of English		Educational Level	
Fluent	85%	College	70%
Some	7%	High School	20%
Little	7%	Less	10%

It would be nice if the figures correlated, but they don't. Many people who have little knowledge of English have been well-educated in their own tongues, and many people with little education are fluent. So if these facts do make sense of the audience, then there are actually nine target audiences, one for each combination of the three categories. And for each target audience, a different level of English is required. Addition of more facts would create even more target audiences: auto mechanics with little college, no English, excellent technical skills, and a feeling of distrust and superiority over the machine, or Ph.D.'s with good English, no technical skills, and a slavish attitude toward instructions, to name just two.

This is, of course, yet another version of the infinite regress argument. If facts about the audience exert constraints, then rules about how to sort out the constraints exerted by different facts need to be established. The same statistical jumble would not be sorted out even if the audience were only a single person. The information amassed might be contradictory (Ph.D., propensity to break things, brilliant technical skills).

Yet another objection to the strong claim that Flower makes (which applies in a slightly different way to any weaker versions) is that even a single, uncomplicated fact about a single audience doesn't seem to exert enough of a constraint. Let us consider another, more realistic example. Imagine I am a technical writer, and I am supposed to explain a computer's operating system to you. I know every fact about you in every category. Crucial to the notion of operating system is the notion of file. (An operating system, for those of you who don't know, handles the mechanics of dealing with the computer. From the user's point of view, it's job is pretty much to organize access to batches of data called "files.") My question is whether and how I should explain the notion of file? Should I use the filing cabinet analogy?[18] Should I distinguish among kinds of files (batch, ASCII)? Where in the text should I do either? According to the strong claim, the answer ought to be determined by facts about the audience. But no list of facts could provide that determination. (Notice that even the one obviously crucial fact, whether you have dealt with operating systems before, doesn't necessarily answer my question.) Let us then turn to the weak claim, that certain facts help at certain times. I've already admitted this claim; I will also admit that in certain cases, certain facts may make a huge difference. Say we discover that the audience for the coffee mill instructions consists entirely of people who have previously owned a coffee mill made by a competitor. Suddenly, we have an obvious way of approaching the problem. Or say we know that the audience consists entirely of English professors. We might introduce an especially literary tone.

The trouble with this, however, is that it leaves out any account of when a particular fact might be required. Under what circumstances does the need for such a fact emerge in consciousness, or under what circumstances does a particular fact become relevant to the writing experience? Most of the time, of course, most facts don't apparently bear on what you write. Is that an illusion? Do they always affect your writing, albeit unconsciously? Then this weak claim seems very implausible. If it is not an illusion, though, then the weak claim needs some account of when the needed facts emerge and why.

We are, of course, in the territory of Background. It is the Background that permits needed facts to emerge into consciousness at the appropriate time. It is a Background skill that "takes into account" the audience. How can the Background do this without specifically taking into account facts and having those facts exert constraints? Only a descriptive answer is possible, since, by definition, the full process cannot be made explicit. To make the description a little easier, let me introduce a new term. Rather than having knowledge about an audience, let me say that a writer has a "sense of an audience": skill at organizing and combining facts, intuitions, and hypotheses about an audience, imagination of an audience, and so on. I could describe it equally well as a continuing interpretation or appraisal of the audience. As one writes, this skill, sense of an audience, is deployed, along with many, many others. In particular, this skill enables us to see the need for particular facts about an audience or to see the bearing that a particular fact has.

What Is a "Sense of the Audience"?

The basic argument for adumbrating such a Background skill is phenomenological; not that I or anyone else is directly conscious of deploying the skill. Rather, from a description of what happens as one writes, the fact that the skill must be operating and some of the ways it operates become apparent.

Let me start by considering the nearest example. In writing this book, I made no attempt to amass knowledge about you. I didn't make lists of people who might read the book; I didn't ascertain much about the situations in which you might be reading it. Somehow, though, I am writing. Certainly, if I were asked, I might be able to say a few things about you—your approximate age, the kind of job you hold, your memberships in professional societies, your command of language—all within certain very broad limits and with lots of uncertainty. As I'm writing, though, I'm not thinking about any of these things. Perhaps I ought to think more. When, earlier in this book, I used the word "fungible," I didn't think about whether you knew it. (Later, I did, but I decided to keep it because it was the right word and if you didn't know it, maybe you would like to learn it.) But frankly, I don't know what it would be like for me to sit here and worry about you and then respond to my worry by changing what I say. If I did sit here and worry, I wouldn't be able to write.

Instead, as I write, I'm primarily engaged with the material, not with you. I am in the position of a pianist or a dancer in performance. I have my music or my choreography before me, and I'm working through it. I'm working through it for you, certainly, but my attention is being paid to the material, not to the audience. My efforts as a writer go into making this material available, into realizing it. The process is exactly analogous to what you do when you read this. You do not think (usually) about the efforts I am making; you, too, confront the material. My confrontation has succeeded if yours has.

This sounds weird, but really we do this whenever we engage in any cooperative activity. If I'm helping you push a car, I am not thinking about you. I am pushing. Yes, I'm doing it for you, and as I'm doing it, I'm taking your activity into account. But if you, not the car, were my primary concern, I wouldn't be able to push. In writing, both the writer and audience are grappling with certain representations of the world, trying to understand them in a certain way. The writer is in front doing most of the work; the audience is just behind, finding the way through that the writer has worked out cooperating.

If, of course, there's a problem, then as I push, I might turn to you. The car reaches a slope, and perhaps I try to coordinate my acceleration with yours. Or perhaps we need to stop and discuss it. At such moments, the need to consider directly some aspect of our partnership emerges. Or perhaps we are not in synch, and I suddenly notice the pace of your footsteps. If something goes wrong, I know that my appraisal of our relationship in this activity has been working because that appraisal is what has found the thing that went wrong. And, if there's a problem in my relationship with the audience, then either a fact or a need for a fact relevant to that problem emerges.

Rhetorical or cognitive treatments of writing mask this fact: that writing is a cooperative confrontation of material. Instead, they treat it as an interactive activity. In their story, I'm writing this word because I expect it to have a certain effect. Nothing could be further from the truth. I do not choose a word so much as come to it. What rhetoric forgets is that writing is always about something, and what it's about matters profoundly. A skilled rhetorician affects people but does so by taking a view of certain material, a view that can be grasped by and shared with people. Taking a view of certain material is not at all the same thing as trying to achieve a certain effect.

As I write, the instrument I play is myself, not you. As I write, I am organizing the horizon of my mind so as to have true, intelligent thoughts in an orderly fashion and to express them for others. I know from experience that, if the horizon has been organized properly, you, my audience, will be able to follow in my footsteps, to understand me. But as I am writing, this knowledge does not significantly affect me. It's as if I were playing piano for you. I know you might be affected, but if my main concern were the effect, my playing would suffer.

Modern cognitive theorists of composition obscure this point, too, when they talk about "reader-oriented" and "writer-oriented" prose (Flower and Hayes 1977; Flower and Hayes, "Cognition of Discovery," 1980). They imply that different locutions can be directed more or less toward a reader. But, in fact, any writing is a confrontation of material for a reader. If some prose loses people and other prose doesn't, that's just an effect of the way the material has been confronted. If the writer doesn't like the effect, the writer may want to confront the material again, in a different way, for a different reader.

How can I be focused on the material itself, yet at the same time be confronting the material *for* a reader? How, after all, can we be doing something for somebody when we're not thinking (Intentionally) about them? The answer is that we do it all the time. A vivid example is what happens when you talk to somebody for the first time. Such a conversation inevitably has a subject. You talk about something, however painfully. But the selection and handling of that subject is attuned to facilitate the process of discovery in which the two of you are engaged. The two of you are busy *finding a relationship* with each other; you're discovering what the other person thinks, what that person knows, what concerns you share, and so on. As you talk, you gradually adapt your conversation to the emerging relationship. But it is a rare person who does this consciously. If necessary—if something goes wrong, for instance—you can direct your attention to the relationship, but most of the time you don't. Most of the time, what you're paying attention to is what you're talking about.

Much the same thing goes on as one writes. In the process of writing about something in a certain way, one finds a relationship with the person being written for. True, the person is more remote physically, but that only means that the relationship is often more fragile, if not more amorphous. True, too, you have no way of confirming the relationship with the reader. But that still doesn't mean that you are not finding one.

"But," you might object, "you don't even know that the relationship will actually be established. You're just pretending that it will be; your audience is merely a convenient fiction" (Ede 1979; Ede and Lunsford 1984). This kind of argument makes a simple logical mistake. As you write, you're not pretending that the audience you're writing to is real; you are taking it that it is. Pretending is Intentional and nonessential. Taking it (a Background skill) that an audience exists (some audience, maybe just yourself) is something you must do every moment you write. A different audience may materialize, but if that happens, you have not written to a fiction; you've merely made a mistake about who you were writing to. If you thought the audience was fictitious, you'd go about things quite differently.

How Good Writers Exercise
Their Sense of an Audience

All right. I have some new terminology. Writers, in the process of confronting the material *for* an audience, find a relationship with that audience. In that confrontation, they use (and develop) a sense of that audience. Does this terminology answer any questions? How, for instance, does the sense of an audience affect the confrontation for, and how can one improve this sense? How does one develop this (or any other) Background skill?

We can begin to get answers by looking at how people who are very good at writing do it. One group I know of is clearly confronting material for an audience, yet also clearly not thinking about an audience as they write. I refer, of course, to novelists and poets.

Such a writer often describes this period of apprenticeship as the period when "I found my voice." Having found that voice, each has a unique, identifiable style. ("Style" ordinarily refers to the arrangement and choice of words; here, however, I want to include such things as choice of subject, way of approaching material, or method of structuring a piece.) Their individual styles, they say, allow them to get through the material they're trying to write.

That style, I think, is the way each novelist and poet has of establishing a relationship with an audience. This relationship may or may not be an easy one for the audience to enter into. With the later Joyce, it's not; with Dickens, it is. Either way, though, it sets up a relationship. You'll notice that creative writers do not change their style to accommodate the audience. Instead, the audience finds its way through that style.

I am not a novelist or poet, and I am not a stylist, but I think the same is true for me. My style carries me through the material in a way that establishes my relationship with you. In a way, my style of writing is much like my style of dress—my own, for better or for worse, with plenty of faults and coarse areas. When I establish my style of dress, I don't think of any particular people who will see it; I just pick clothes I like and wear them as I happen to wear them. Yet that style very definitely presents me to others and establishes a certain kind of relationship with them.

The "material" in this analogy is our normal, everyday activity, as it involves others. The style carries us through bus rides, the checkout line at the supermarket, or classes. The style structures our encounters with others in a way that we scarcely pay attention to, but which is, nevertheless, very powerful. A different style, that of a street person or Oscar Wilde, would make of these activities quite a different thing.

When a successful writer establishes a successful style, one might say that the writer has an accurate sense of (or understanding of) the material, a deep sense of self, and a formidable sense of the language. In this chapter, I am arguing that it is also proper to say that such a writer has a good *sense of the audience*. Strictly speaking, it is this last sense which allows the successful writer to confront the material *for* that audience.

One common experience argues for the correctness of this characterization: when a writer with a particular style is asked to write

something for a completely different sort of audience, the style col-
lapses. Consider what happens when our experienced author is
asked to write, say, advertising jingles. The style isn't enough to
carry this writer through the task: a new voice, one appropriate to
the task and the audience, must be learned. Until that voice is
learned, the writing won't be any good. It is as if the writer were
suddenly asked to wear a top hat, use a cane, and hold a lily in the
other hand. For a long while, the task would be impossible to carry
off.

How Does One Get
a Sense of One's Audience?

The argument of the previous section can be summed up as follows.
Good writers do not need to amass a lot of knowledge about an
audience because they don't need or use this information. These
writers find their relationships with a particular audience by developing a style of confronting material. As they are doing this, they
are developing a sense of the audience. The crucial word as far as
this section is concerned is "good." Good writers may do this, but
we are not at all sure how. We are sure, however, that they are
often self-taught and that it takes them years. What about bad writers? Can they learn to have a voice? And can they be taught?

We can see that the way people teach audience analysis has nothing to do with what is crucial about writing for an audience. Amassing facts is, as I've said, misguided. So there is not much empirical
evidence about how to teach style. The common wisdom ("Le style
c'est l'homme") is that the development of a style is ineffable, something that just happens. And this is probably right. Perhaps,
though, we can do a few things to help people develop one. In all
probability, much of one's ability to do this lies in one's personality;
the way we establish new kinds of relationships depends on the
way we have established other kinds.

Before we go into this any further, however, let's go at it from the
other end and ask what it is that's necessary to learn. The following
paragraph was written by a student who had actually done some
audience analysis.

> (1) Opiate drugs are thought to produce analgesia by inhibiting
> certain neurons from firing. (2) How and where do these drugs
> act on the nerve cells? (3) This question became a particularly
> hot issue after the discovery of enkephalins and endorphins, the
> body's endogenous opiates. (4) These compounds occur natu-

rally in mammalian organisms in brain and enteric (gut) tissue. (5) Enkephalins are polypeptides. (6) Certain amino acids in these polypeptides show significant amounts of homology with morphine, indicating that the two compounds act in a similar manner on the molecular level. (7) One type of opiate found in the body, met-enkephalin, has tyrosine in its polypeptide chain. (8) Tyrosine contains a benzene ring with a phenolic hydroxyl group. (9) This residue seems also to be responsible on the molecular level for the analgesic action of morphine.

This is a fairly dense paragraph, but in itself, that's not the problem with it. The problem is that the author is switching audiences in mid-paragraph. In sentences 1 and 2, the audience is a sophisticated one but is unfamiliar with neurology or mammalian biochemistry. (Otherwise, the sentences would be obvious.) In sentences 3, 4, and 5, however, the audience knows the meaning of "endogenous" and the significance of "polypeptides" and has heard of the recent discovery of enkephalins. The audience is apparently a group of biochemists who don't, however, know the meaning of "enteric." By sentences 6 and 7, the audience apparently knows not only what a ring with a phenolic hydroxyl group is, but also how it might be important. Perhaps there is an audience that would know exactly what the writer expects them to know, but I doubt it.

In all probability, the paragraph should look like one of the two following paragraphs.

(1.) The recent discovery of enkephalins and endorphins, the body's endogenous opiates, has suggested that a benzene ring with a phenolic hydroxyl group (located on tyrosine in the endorphins) is responsible for the analgesic action of all opiates.

(2.) By 1960, empirical evidence had strongly suggested that some group on the morphine molecule reacts with unknown molecules in the neuron membrane and prevents the neuron from firing. There was no way to confirm this, however, because the process could not be studied directly, and no other molecules that worked in an analogous way had been discovered. Ideally, these analogous molecules would occur naturally, since it's unlikely that the morphine molecule would have such a subtle effect on the membrane if there had been no evolutionary preparation for it, . . . [etc., etc.] . . . .

Notice that both the diagnosis and the remedies depend entirely on the specific facts of the situation. The conjunction of those words, that audience, and that writer is creating the problem. We can't abstract missing formal features; this is not a failure of technique.

Notice, too, that actually coming up with either of these paragraphs is probably well within the writer's capabilities. But before being able to write either of them, the author would have to do two things: realize that a mistake had been made in the first one and then figure out what the mistake was. Both are terribly difficult. Why, after all, should the interesting fact about the audience be whether they are familiar with the kinds of biochemical questions about the action of molecules which were being asked by the investigators? And after discovering the problem, how can the author discover that the first two sentences are weak, that certain types of explanations are in order and that they must precede the actual account?

If we want to teach the development of a sense of an audience, we ought to lead the writer carefully through situations where one discovers the need for diagnosis of the preceding kind, makes it, and then repairs the writing. Unfortunately, there are two difficulties with this. First, when writers make adjustments in their own material for an audience different from the teacher, the teacher has no authoritative idea about the diagnosis to be made. Second, when writers are doing this with somebody else's material, diagnosis is relatively easy, because in each case the writer is the audience. Still, these activities need not necessarily be conducted rigorously to produce an effect. A teacher unfamiliar with the audience may still have a certain sympathy with the writer.

Another approach would be to make the writer confront the material with an actual audience. The writer writes; the reader reads; and the writer discusses the experience with the reader. Readers, of course, are not very trustworthy with their reactions; what they say they are reacting to and what they are actually reacting to might be very different things. But they are reasonably good about judging alternative versions. Test audiences, of course, must be close to the real audience. One of the problems that those of us who have conducted Elbow-style groups run into is that the other members of the group are not the audience of educated readers that we want the writer to be writing to.

Experienced writers have noticed that they can often develop a sense of an audience even without trying out specific material on actual readers. The writer who sets out to construct jingles might well spend time talking to ordinary people, seeing how they think and feel, discovering their concerns and their language. This jingle writer might also read what the audience reads, listen to what they listen to, and so on. Know-how is being developed; later on, an "Aha, this means I should alter my style this way" would be a verbalization of something that has gone on in the Background. Of course, this way works better for experienced writers because they have more resources available to them when it comes to diagnosis.

Along the same lines, many people, inexperienced or experienced, try to visualize their audience in an organized way. The following is a rough transcription of an account given to me by a middle manager of how she gets to know her audience.

> Sometimes I have to write something which I know an audience won't like to hear, and yet I don't know these people. I often spend some time figuring out who they are. Are they managers? What kind of experience do they have with the issues? What are their interests in this? Answering these questions helps me to figure out the organization of the piece and to make sure I haven't left anything out.

From this account, you might well think she is amassing facts— just what the technical writing books recommend. But look more closely. Logically speaking, would the facts she's amassing actually tell her how to overcome hostility? In themselves, no. However, in the process of getting those facts, she is discovering how her piece will be for them. As she is saying "George is a manager and he is responsible for safety," she will realize that George will resist this idea because he won't want to be responsible for implementing it. Indeed, the whole reason she picked out those facts about George was that they would lead her to the genuinely relevant consideration.

This, then, is why amassing facts works, when it does work. In the process of concentrating on the facts, the writer develops a Background sense of how those facts fit together. Remember, my objection is not to amassing facts, per se; it is to wasting effort on it. Much the same effect (visualization of the audience) could well be achieved by writing a two-paragraph piece on how the audience views the situation being discussed. I myself often find that, as I write, I think of one particular member of the audience—not imagining the audience member reading this, just thinking of that person—and I find that in certain places I have put in things that I learned from or discussed with this person. Other writers whom I know tell me that, in this sense, they, too, write for a single person, often their editor. Any member of a strange audience whom one talks to is likely to become the person one writes to. Again, these are processes of visualization.

I think, also, of transforming "writer-based" prose to "reader-based" prose as a form of visualization. I have no objection to the technique itself; my earlier objection was to the characterization of what it does. The trouble with the technique is the trouble with all visualization. It may or may not have much effect when it finally comes down to diagnosing specific problems or coming up with specific remedies.

This is not an authoritative discussion of ways to learn or teach audience analysis. There may be numerous other, wonderful ways that I've never thought of or heard about. The important thing that these ways of teaching share is that they treat the writer's activity as a skill, not a technique. The writer learns by trying, failing, succeeding, trying again. This kind of learning is nerve-wracking for the teacher. It proceeds in fits and starts, and it is very hard to evaluate. But it is the way one learns.

Last Thoughts on Developing a Sense of an Audience

Experienced writers who tell novices to "Know your audience" want the novices to write things that are suited to their audience. This is a laudable goal. Such people can, themselves, generally reach the goal. If they ask why they can and the novice writer can't, in some situation, they usually can point to some fact or other about the audience that turned out to be crucial. If only the novice writer had just known that fact, a blunder might have been avoided. No wonder the experienced writer wants the novice to collect relevant facts in advance and pay attention to them. What experienced writers don't realize is that the facts do not matter. The difference between the good writer and the novice is not that one has a fact, while the other doesn't. The difference is that the good writer can find the needed fact, and once that fact is found, the writer can do the right thing with it. Finding the fact (or "zeroing in," as Dreyfus calls it [Dreyfus 1979]) and using it are Background skills, however, so they're relatively invisible even to the giver of advice; therefore it's much harder to advise people on how to use them. Think how silly, "Develop a sense of your audience" sounds. It's easier to offer simple advice that doesn't work.

Still, I think, if "Develop a sense of your audience" is right, then that's what has to be said. True, we're essentially admitting that it's very difficult to confront material in ways that make an audience happy. True, we're admitting that even the people who can do it well don't know how they do it. True, we're admitting that, often, it isn't done. In writing, much gets lost, ignored, or misunderstood; many times we hurt or offend people; but at least we're telling people that the Background skills we need in order to take account of our audience as we write just take a long time to develop. They are developed by writing for people, seeing how they react, reading what they write you, and learning from the inevitable mistakes. And at least we're admitting that these skills can't be developed by following facile advice.

The deeper problem raised by this chapter, however, is still with us. Once we admit that what we're doing—whether writing coffee mill instructions or telling people how to take account of an audience—is getting people to develop skills, how do we go about doing it? The general answer, obviously, is to apply these skills in situations where people have to practice them. With coffee mills, this is not easy; with teaching audience analysis, it isn't impossible. The moral of this chapter is that we should be directing more of our efforts toward inventing more effective ways of imparting or fostering skills. These ways will not, unfortunately, be systematic and reliable. As we will see in the next chapter, a skill cannot be taught by reducing it to a methodical process and then having people learn that process. How can a skill be taught? I keep on evading that question because I'm not sure what the answer is.

7 What Outlines Do to You and for You

In the last chapter, I argued that the standard way of teaching one part of the curriculum was a misdirection of effort because it teaches the writer to get knowledge, when, in fact, the writer needs to learn a Background skill. I tried to demonstrate the existence of the Background skill by giving a phenomenological description of what happens when I write and by showing where the Background skill operates.

Phenomenological descriptions are not even arguments, much less hard empirical evidence. One gains conviction about such processes as similar ones are described and as one discovers how the processes mesh. In this chapter, therefore, I am going to offer another description. I will reject another standard way of teaching another important part of the writing process, present a phenomenological description of the process, and describe the consequences for teaching. My purpose is not so much to convince people not to teach in this particular way, as it is to demonstrate the weaknesses of any teaching of this type. At the same time, I wish to advance my own description of the writing process, to convince you of the accuracy of the psychology I describe, and to show you how adopting that psychology pays off.

In the last chapter, we established that, when we say we are writing *to* someone, we are, in fact, confronting material *for* someone. When a writer decides to confront material for someone, how does that writer go about organizing the confrontation? The answer advanced by the profession has been "methodically." (I am referring, of course, to the process, not to the final result. I can write a methodical chapter without being methodical about writing it.) The more Grundian textbooks confidently describe a step-by-step procedure: the writer confronts the material by collecting information, deciding on a unifying theme, preparing an outline for the paper, and then writing the paper.[19]

This procedure sounds wonderful—it sounded wonderful to me

when I first learned about it. However, it never worked for me, and I doubt that it works for most people. In this chapter, I want to tell *why*. I am going to concentrate on the outline step alone because, in outlines, the various ideas about planning a paper are condensed.

Some Observations about Outlining

I assume that we all know what I'm talking about. The idea is that before we start writing we set down in order the important points to be made. With labels and indentations, we indicate the relative importance of each item and its relationship to the items surrounding it. Thus, for this chapter, an outline of these first few pages might look like this:

  I. Transition from previous chapter
 II. Some observations about outlining
    A. People feel they're supposed to, but don't
    B. Many situations when they don't need to
      1. When they know what they'll say
      2. . . . [and so on] . . . .

I must confess now that I took an instant dislike to outlining when I was taught it in junior high school. My teachers often required that I turn in an outline along with the paper. I did, but I wrote the paper first, then made the outline. I was not ashamed. Today I often encounter writers who do what I did in junior high school but have never gotten over it. They think they ought to outline, don't, and feel guilty about it. Outlining is, for them, like losing those five pounds or giving up cigarettes. Consultants like me are often asked to give courses in outlining, but like diet programs, they have little enough effect (Paradis and Dobrin 1984).

Conflicts with authority figures in early life have always interested me. So over the past few years, I have kept a weather eye out for outlining. In the process, I have made the following observations:

- Documents we're used to writing don't usually need to be outlined or planned for in any way. We just write them. This has little to do with their length or complexity.

- When we do prepare an outline for a document, by the time we've gotten halfway through the writing, we've gotten pretty far away from the outline. The outline of the new document can't be gotten just by juggling the old outline.

- Experienced professional writers rarely outline. At most, they keep a pad of paper next to the typewriter or terminal on which they write ideas or notes. This is not to say that they don't organize in advance—far from it—it's just that they don't use an outline.

- The standard outline form is most appropriate for organizing a certain kind of material: research papers or essays with standard arguments. This material lends itself to outlining for three reasons. First, it consists of a vast body of facts (often from note cards) that must be put in arrays. Second, the arguments and facts are public property: papers are written for the general, educated audience—the audience of newsmagazines or "60 Minutes." Thus, there is usually a natural way of organizing the material. Third, the internal relationships of the ideas in any such paper are relatively simple. If, for instance, I'm doing a paper on the geography of Egypt, I can divide it very naturally into two sections, Nile delta and desert, and I can be confident that the two sections won't have that much to do with each other. As soon as the relationships get more complicated, as when the geography of Egypt is part of a discussion of Egypt's political economy, then what happens in the rest of the paper severely constrains the structure of the current section, a constraint that will not be easy to represent in outline format. This observation underlies much of the argument in this chapter.

- A corollary to this observation is that, after one gets out of school, outlines are most often used in the preparation of talks or lectures intended for people who are not in command of the material, who need to have it organized for them, and who need a guide to what's happening during the lecture.[20]

- Our outlines in school were made as much for the teacher's convenience as for our own. If a teacher wished to criticize the plan of a proposed paper or get a quick idea of what the novice writer thought the structure of the paper was, then outlines were more serviceable than prose. The teacher read the outline and altered freely, and then the student had to follow the instructions.

I take it that all these observations are not problematic. I am not trying to criticize outlines yet; I'm just trying to see how they work as a method of planning. If, however, you feel dissatisfied with them, they can be verified empirically.

The Outline as Architectural Metaphor

Now I want to offer a criticism, one that can't be derived empirically. The metaphor upon which the idea of outlining implicitly relies is, at best, limited and, at worst, suspect. Let me explain. When we use the word "outline" in a sentence—for example, "I see a figure outlined against the sky"—the outline is an aspect of an existing spatial entity. Pieces of writing, however, are not spatial entities and, when we outline, not yet existing entities. They have no visual aspect. So there is little actual resemblance between an outline of a building and an outline of a paper. Where does the metaphor come from? Perhaps—I'm really guessing—an outline of a building looks like an architectural plan or sketch. (Certainly, the abstractions are somewhat similar.) An architectural plan would resemble an outline of a paper in that buildings are built from the plan, and a piece of writing is built from the outline.

The comparison gains some plausibility, if not cogency, because architectural or spatial metaphors are standard in discussions of writing. We often say that a paper has a structure, that its argument is solid or well founded, or that ideas support other ideas. Usually, though, we use such metaphors when the paper already exists, just as when the building already exists. Even then, such metaphors are not particularly compelling. When we read a paper, we don't take in the whole paper at once, as we do the structure of spatial entities.[21] When the paper doesn't exist (the situation I'm discussing), the architectural metaphor is not very illuminating.

"But," you might say, "whether a paper exists or not, the metaphor is a good one. The point of the metaphor is that both blueprints and outlines are plans; each precedes the construction of the building itself and forms the plan for the finished product." There's a difference, however, between the two kinds of plans. With a blueprint, the relationship between the plan and its realization is clear. Each line corresponds to something important in the finished product, and there are standard ways of converting the line into the realization. A plan of a building is what one might call a strong representation of the actual building. Outlines of papers are not strong representations of the actual paper because (1) many features of the final product are not represented in the outline, and (2) there's no clear way of getting from the outline to the final product.

A better metaphor for how we get from plan to paper would be an organic one: a paper grows from its seed. This, too, is a standard way of talking; we say that "ideas have developed." But with this metaphor, the status of the outline is sadly diminished. For one thing, it is unclear how the "I . . . A" format is like a seed. And, for another, the growth pattern is not well determined; in development, that is, nurture affects the way the final product will turn out.

What Outlines Represent

Obviously, your choice of metaphor depends very much on how you think the plan determines the development of the paper. So let us inquire into how this works for outlines. How do the materials that outlines use guide the later work? How do outlines represent information (in the common-speech sense, not the mathematical sense)? And how much information can be transmitted with that form of representation?

In the standard outline format, information is conveyed by the numbering system, by the relative positions of the numbers, and by the content of the statements that come after the numbers. The relative positions are redundant, however; the outline would be equivalent if the numbers and letters were set flush left. So in fact, the outline contains information along four different axes. The content line indicates the ideas to be stated; the numbering system indicates the order in which the ideas come and their relative importance. (Ideas in an "A" line are as important as those in a "B" line but are less important than and are contained by the ideas in a "I" or "II" line.) And, by agreement, an idea in an inferior line is taken to be contained by the idea in the superior line immediately preceding it.

Does this representation system attain any of the power of architectural blueprints? Obviously not. But if not, how much power does it have? Clearly, that depends on the extent to which the content, relative importance, order, and containment of ideas are important in the construction of the paper. If they are very important, outlining is crucial. If not, then, as we shall see, it may even be confusing.

We can see now why outlines might well prove beneficial for lectures or for straightforward student papers. In both cases, it is important to be clear about what the ideas are and what order they belong in. Notice that the importance is conventional. Lecture audiences and teachers of student writing expect to have ideas presented to them in order, with the major and minor ideas clearly marked. In these cases, the audience is often trying to get from the writing back to the outline; teachers make sure the ideas are there, so students can retell them in a test. Of course, where the flow of ideas, the argument, and the prose are important in themselves to the audience, then extracting the ideas becomes proportionally less important.

In a sense, then, teaching someone to outline is teaching that person to work on a certain level of communication; it is to say that a paper is like fossil-bearing ground, where ideas are embedded, waiting to be found again, the detritus chipped off. As we shall see in chapter 9, computer outlining aids, both the kind that help you create an outline and the kind that analyze a completed paper and construct an outline of it, implicitly treat a paper this way. When that's right—when the audience is sitting there with a yellow highlighter or a red pencil—they work well.

How We Get from Plan to Paper

Outside those situations, the metaphor on which outlines are founded is impoverished. To understand how we plan in other situations, we need new metaphors. Metaphors are, of course, all we ever can have; any account of how we get from a plan to a realization is metaphorical.[22]

So let me propose the following: Getting from plan to paper is something like traveling to a location by following directions. The directions are the plan; the actual travel is the paper. Particular kinds of plans, like an outline, resemble particular kinds of directions. An outline is like the directions that were given at the beginning of the book. These, you will remember, consisted of a list of intersections and a set of instructions to follow upon reaching each intersection. The assumption was that the general structure of the technologies at your service would constrain you between the intersections. "Go north along this road" would be all that was necessary. The trick was to identify each intersection, so that you would know when to stop doing the obvious thing. To that end, the instructions gave you identifiable signposts. When a signpost emerged from the landscape, you could take appropriate action. Outlines are like "signpost instructions" to the writer because they, too, presume that, once you've gotten to a listed idea, the technology available to you will carry you to the next one. You merely "develop" the idea and then provide a "transition" to the new idea.

Let's consider another set of directions called "landmark instructions." These contain landmarks, features of the landscape that you can refer to and use during the entire traverse. The archetypal "landmark" instruction is, "Head towards that radio tower on the mountain." During your entire journey, you can look up whenever you have a problem and decide which path to take by seeing which one will bring you closer. Landmarks, in other words, constantly help you make sense of the landscape, while signposts presume upon technology to make sense of it for you.

Both landmark instructions and signpost instructions can get you where you want to go. If you were in Manhattan and wanted to go to Bellevue, a landmark instruction might say, "Head toward the Empire State Building, and when you get near it, head east toward the East River until you hit Bellevue." A signpost instruction might say, "Head up 5th Avenue until you reach 34th Street, turn right, and go straight to the river." When following either set of instructions from, say, NYU, you are likely to get there.[23] With one, though, you always know how well you're doing, and you know you haven't made a mistake. With the other, if you miss a signpost, you are lost.

Signpost instructions work best when the signposts emerge from the landscape properly and the technology constraining the route in between is working. Landmark instructions work best when there are many ways to get from A to B, if specifying one way would get very complicated, or, most important, when you are exploring out in the wild and the way from A to B isn't known. Landmark instructions allow you to pick your own way, making sure that you're on the right track by consulting the landmark.

Sometimes, of course, a particular feature can be both a signpost and a landmark. The Empire State Building can be used as a landmark when you are walking toward it, but it can also be the signpost at the corner of 34th and 5th. Apparently, 34th Street is a signpost, but since the streets are numbered, it is also a landmark since you can orient yourself by the numbering system. Usually, though, the appropriate signpost (the one that emerges most readily) is quite different from the appropriate landmark. And even when they are the same object, the representation that makes them most functional is almost always different. The Empire State Building is a good landmark, but at the corner of 34th and 5th, it is hard to look up; if you were using it as a signpost, it would be better to identify the sign on the side of the building.

You can see why entries representing the content, order, relative importance, and containment of ideas are like signposts. Each new content line represents a turn. This idea is reached through development of the previous idea; reaching it indicates that the previous line of development is finished. A "transition" from the previous idea must be found; at the end, a similar transition must be provided. In the analogy, the area around a turn is the most difficult to navigate. In between, though, all is straightforward. Development consists of explanation or justification of the idea represented in the content line. Under this model, therefore, the most effective kind of representation in the content line is a sentence, which can be most easily incorporated and then justified.

Unfortunately, signposts aren't usually that useful. When we're writing, we only rarely know how precisely to get from one signpost to the next. "Develop" and "provide transitions" might be good ex post facto descriptions of how we proceeded but not of how we should proceed. To put it another way, the landscape between ideas is usually rugged and without trails. We have to constantly be making sense of it ourselves ("lighting it up," I will say, following Heidegger) because no preexisting technology guides us. Most of the time, therefore, when we're planning a paper, we should be using landmarks, not signposts. True, in certain cases, where we've been through the territory already, as in the preceding lectures, signposts might be more useful. But these cases are surely rare.

If we give signpost instructions, even to ourselves, we must be sure that the areas between the signposts are made sense of by the skills of the user. These skills always involve appraisal and discovery of the factors involved in an activity—the metaphorical landscape. The activity can be structured so that the appraisal involves little more than following existing guides, or it can be structured so that much of the landscape is lit up. In general, the latter kind of structure is better and more useful; it is better to understand Bostonian place names than those in Los Angeles. (The more the landscape can be lit up for you and for the reader, the more is said, the more accurately, the more clearly.)

Extending the Analogy

But how can an entry in an outline (or in any plan) be a landmark? The difference between a landmark and a signpost, as I have said, is that the former facilitates our journey between ideas and the other leaves us open to our own devices. This would be true even if they both represented the same idea; the difference would then lie in the form of representation. To show how this might be true, let me return to the difference between the topic outline and the sentence outline. A topic outline contains a telegraphic entry; a sentence outline contains complete sentences. The outline at the beginning of this chapter is a topic outline.

In theory, a sentence outline is the more useful one. But for me, and I think for most people, the topic outline is actually better. This observation is routinely denied by most commentators on writing (Hays 1982; Plung 1982). And, I admit, it doesn't seem commonsensical. The better worked out a paper is, the easier it seems to write, and sentences are better worked out than telegraphic entries. Nevertheless, my analysis shows why it has to be right. When we read the few words in a topic outline, many different ideas occur to us; a great wealth of disparate ideas comes readily to hand. But when those few words are locked into one relationship—bound, so to speak, by a verb—their relationships to other ideas are occluded. The explicit idea is good to have if we're working with a few ideas in a small space, but it is not so good when we're trying to find our way in a larger landscape.

All right, so a landmark allows you to have ideas. It also makes approaching it easier. You have surely noticed, for instance, that it's much easier to write a paragraph when you know only approximately what's coming in the next one. Writing a new paragraph to fit between two existing paragraphs is the very devil because the flow between paragraphs has already been established—the connections between ideas have been made, and even an aside interrupts the flow. Thus, a topic, rather than a sentence, allows you to set up an array of notions (ideas, impressions, tones, themes, examples) that can be drawn on when the topic is taken up, without being forced to cleave to a particular pattern.

This phenomenon, that too much explicitness impedes the flow of ideas during the early parts of creation, is a curious one. To be convinced of its truth, you should look for evidence in as many areas as possible. Here is just one. You surely have noticed that, as we write a single sentence, many ideas occur to us. Those ideas can be continued or referred to in the next sentence. But as we write the next sentence, still more new ideas occur to us, and these new ideas squeeze out the old ones. On the other hand, when we are trying to write up to an existing sentence, those good new ideas don't come because we're trying to set up the sentence so as to reach the next one. A landmark, then, encourages a wealth of ideas, many of which are not used.

We are far enough along now for me to locate this in the psychology I have been talking about all along. An Intentional state, a representation in a mode, only exists against one's Background and network, which are deployed in order to make sense of that state. The form of the representation affects the deployment greatly. In thinking Empire State Building, a certain Background and knowledge are deployed; in thinking 34th and 5th, a very different Background and knowledge are deployed. Certain representations of ideas help us organize the Background and network in ways that make sense of many related ideas, that make sense of the landscape. Other representations do not. When we're being creative, we have to be very careful not to settle too soon into a rigid organization of our horizon; habit, as William James says, is sedimented very quickly.[24]

I find giving directions to be a powerful metaphor, in part, because it emphasizes the fact that Intentional states are always in flux. A representation never exists by itself. In thinking, we are always going from somewhere to somewhere else, and we're making sense of what's in between in terms of both. When we have landmarks, what is around us is lit up and the route is clear; when we don't, we just muddle along. When what is around us is clear, we can write well. When it's not, when we've planned badly, we write badly.

If you buy this metaphor, you can now allow me to clarify somewhat the differences between a plan for a paper and an architectural sketch. A plan for a paper is more temporal than spatial. In a plan, we are working out a succession of horizons, which can only be thought of in terms of movement, not just the working through of a sequence of ideas, which can be thought of as static and spatial. Our aim is not merely to reach an idea, but to reach that idea *as* related to other ideas, *as* having come from previous ideas, and *as* leading to yet other ideas. The idea at the turning point, the idea noted in an outline, may be paramount, but it is paramount because it focuses the other ideas, not only because it seems important in the abstract. This, incidentally, is why, when we get to a crucial turn—a new theme, say—we often don't set it down the way it was in an outline, not even the way it was in a topic outline. When we get to the turn, we are in a horizon, and, to get everything in that horizon organized correctly, we have to do a lot of fiddling around. The landmark has to be made into a signpost.

We can also see more clearly why outlines are useful when the territory is familiar. When the ideas are known, the representations in the content line are phenomenologically richer, and "developing" may really be what we do as we write.

But we have also come to something quite new. This argument suggests that entries in a plan do not need to be ideas (or even representations) at all. If, for instance, what is phenomenologically rich (what serves as a landmark) is not ideas, but a way of presenting them, a particular rhetorical tone, then the landmark may be something that establishes that tone even though the ideas expressed are completely different. Or, if the crucial issue is the "shape" of a paper, the plan may be entirely pictorial. What we do with such an entry no longer has anything to do with "development," as it is commonly understood in descriptions of the writing process; but it still may guide us through the writing.

In any way (not method) of planning, however, the particular form an entry takes is still crucial. Just as slight changes in wording can turn a landmark into a signpost, slight changes of tone or even (in an entirely pictorial representation) slight changes in shading can extinguish the light shed by a plan.

Using Better Kinds of Plans

We can now see why planning is not methodical and why using a formal (content-free) method is restricting. The efficacy of outlining (or any other method) depends in large but delicate measure on the nature of the thing being planned. If that thing requires a different kind of planning, then the paper will get written only in spite of, rather than because of, the outline. This is the experience described at the beginning of this chapter. Perhaps, though, there are classifications of planning methods, each suited to specific kinds of writing? No. A planning approach is appropriate to the content but not the form of the thing being planned. A small change in content could change the whole approach that is required.

We can see that many kinds of plans exist; in fact, there seems to be no limitation on their number. Consider how much is possible even in the small area of pictorial representations. Grouping ideas on a page, abandoning a linear format, could prove very suggestive; so might drawing arrows between related ideas by using blue ink for some ideas, red or green for others. Many people in fact do have some such system. I, for one, often put ideas down at random and then add lines, question marks, notations, and doodles. I'm not sure what the doodles do, but the rest of the representational system provides relationships that the three-dimensioned list cannot. It is functional for me.

I use the word "system" advisedly. The greatest single advantage of outlining is that the conventions governing the representation are well established and instantly familiar. To come up with better ways of making plans (I will call these planning techniques, but adjure you to remember that they are not formal) is not to make up a new way each time you plan a paper. If planning is a skill, and I say it is, then the techniques used must be relatively constant and coherent, or the skill will never be developed. Rather, coming up with new ways is coming up with techniques that will be fruitful over and over again.

The use of circles or blue ink is not wonderfully promising as a general technique for several reasons. First, the crucial thing about finding landmarks is getting the representation right, and circles and blue ink don't represent very well. There is, of course, no reason why they couldn't be made to represent; if someone wants to develop such techniques, it might prove very interesting. But right now, our culture has few notions about the relationships of ideas (in this context) that correspond to colored arrows. Second, the biggest single leap in writing is still between the plan and the prose, between the horizons suggested by a landmark, and the relationships established by the prose. What we want in creating most papers is to work out the flow of those ideas, prepare the ground for new ones, and move into them. A pictorial planning environment doesn't do that for us.[25] Again, this is not an objection to working out richer planning environments; it's just a suggestion that the effect will not be powerful.

"But," you might object, "you are saying (1) that standard outlines are rarely useful because they usually don't represent what needs to be planned; (2) that planning techniques must be adapted to the content of the thing being planned; (3) that planning techniques must be systemic, reusable; and (4) that in our culture we simply haven't worked out many useful systemic planning techniques. This is puzzling for three reasons. First, points two and three seem to be contradictory. Second, it looks as if we're stuck with outlines because nothing else is developed. Third, it seems empirically false since people do use outlines (and other planning methods) and somehow or other get things done."

This objection evaporates once you realize that more than one skill or technique is used as one plans or realizes a plan. The people who do use outlines are not, I would think, using them according to the standard strategy. Rather, they are embedding many different techniques in the entries. Experience, moreover, has given them practice with these techniques, and they can use them effectively. My arrows and doodles have become a system for me. For other people, outlines in blue and red ink have become a system. Richer planning environments are being developed all the time and used appropriately, but each time by individuals.

Last night, I stopped writing this paragraph at the end of the last sentence, and I wrote out some notes for what to say today:

Just as a mnemonic device.
Sometimes lose it, sometimes change.
Loses effectiveness, revising.

These notes tell me what I wanted to take up today in the rest of this paragraph. This morning, the notes look a little peculiar, but, gradually, I am recovering what I meant. Now, as I look at the notes, I recover a whole array of ideas that were part of the horizon I had when I wrote them down originally. This horizon is for me the important thing. Without it, I couldn't write this sentence and the next. Sometimes I forget; sometimes those mnemonic devices are wrong. Sometimes, too, a new idea intervenes, and I change my mind. The point is, though, that the planning environment I use makes little difference to the recovery of the horizon, especially since I'm used to this system.

People who habitually use outlines are doing the same thing. They don't use them the way they say they do. Instead, the entries are mnemonic devices; essentially, they are used as landmarks. The entries are not crucial points, but reminders. This distinction is very subtle and largely invisible. But you can tell whether people are using signposts or landmarks by looking at the way they treat entries that come near the end of the outline. People who use signposts will incorporate these wholesale or virtually so. People who use landmarks, on the other hand, will often find that the plan has gotten away from them. In such cases, the later entries won't make much sense, and they won't be used. Far from indicating that a plan has failed, I think this can often mean that the plan is being formulated more thoroughly in the writing, which is just as it should be.[26]

In my experience, then, useful outlines don't so much represent ideas as recall or invoke them. This distinction has two practical consequences. First, it means that the outline, when it is used, should be regarded as a highly mutable document, one that should be revised whenever new ideas come up. The last part should be less useful than the first. Second, it suggests why other kinds of plans work. If one is planning by setting up the format of the page—the generic content of the paper (for example, Introduction, Literature Review), or even the audience response (building excitement, lull)—the content will be carried along by the plan. In using it, the writer will be reminded of the content; just as with outlines, the content reminds the writer of the generic structure or generic response. In certain kinds of work, like script-writing or brochure-planning, this is actually done. Where it's not done, it's due to people already having the format or generic structure under control but not the content.

But wait a minute. What does it mean to have the content under control?

Working Through a Paper

Planning a paper requires a group of skills for appraising the content that are very much analogous to the group of skills I have been calling the "sense" of the audience. When a paper is planned properly, the entries in the plan serve as landmarks, which focus these skills. The skills can then locate the content properly within the horizon, setting up the proper relationships among ideas, a proper order. This group of skills is not operating in isolation; it works along with one's sense of an audience and the numerous other skills one uses as one writes. Changes in one's sense of an audience may change the structure of a paper (we all know that), or they may just change the luminosity of some landmark.

A cognitivist picture of the writing process suggests that these things are not skills but systems of rules and also suggests that they can be disentangled. Such a picture offers the hope that systematic, formal planning techniques can be developed. I believe that this picture is wrong, that all these skills are interrelated, and that their use depends on the content.

The content is only under control when the relationships in each horizon and their succession have been established. And these can only be established by a process that has gone largely unnoticed in the literature, a process I call "working through" the material. Since we can't guess what a horizon will be like in advance, we actually have to sit down and visit each horizon. We need to resolve how everything bears on what we want to say at any moment. And this is the real work in planning a document, the *working through*.

What do I mean by "working through"? Let me describe a few ways of doing it. The order is from worst to best.

- *Writing the first paragraph of a paper.* Many writers, particularly fiction writers and reporters, tell me that they work for hours on the first paragraph of a paper, and once they've gotten that, the rest flows easily. I think what they're doing is working out the paper by finding a tone and an audience, even finding a plausible order for treating the material and finding the most important interrelationships among the parts of that material.

- *Writing an abstract of a paper*. Scientists, engineers, and "lazy humanists" frequently have to do this because they submit abstracts to program committees at professional conferences. An abstract contains the essential arguments or contributions in a paper and presents them in a tone which approximates that of the final paper. Some people find it relatively easy to write a paper from its abstract.

The fact that these methods work suggests that finding the actual wording one will use in a paper is important. In some mysterious way, making the horizons succeed each other properly is done best by actually writing down the sentences which will make that flow work, not by taking snapshots of various points in the flow and putting those snapshots in a row. Notice that, in these cases, the sentences are acting as landmarks; ordinarily, of course, they don't.

- *Talking to somebody*. In conversing, the writer can work out the flow in some detail. Having a real audience also helps objectify what will be said. If the audience of the disquisition is part of the audience of the actual paper, so much the better, but anyone will do. (It's better to tell warm bodies than chairs; even though you're just trying to work through the material, having to work it through for somebody is better.)

- *Giving the paper as a speech*. Often the notes for the speech become landmarks after the speech is given because they now make sense of the material that has been worked through. The writer, of course, must actually work through the material as the speech is given, not as it is being read from a previously prepared text.

- *Preparing the charts and figures for the paper*. This, again, is extremely effective for scientists and engineers. An effective graphic illustration is probably the best possible landmark for the interior of a scientific paper. In an essay, the analog of a good graphic illustration is a good example. I often find an example even before I write the paper, and the example focuses my approach throughout.

- *Last and clearly best—writing a first draft.* Writing the paper does help people work out what they want to say in the paper. Even if little verbiage is kept from the first draft, the route (and often the landmarks) is usually kept. It's much easier to write an outline after the first draft, and the resulting outline now contains landmarks.

All these ways of working through a paper accomplish the same sort of thing. They establish the relationships among ideas, the writer's intentions, the sense of the audience, the conventions that govern organization, the habits of thought, the rhythms of speech and language, and so on and so forth, in each horizon and in successions of horizons. They are not, notice, the actual writing of the paper; that is what can now be managed, once the material has been worked through. "But," you might say, "why is there such a range in the amount of detail worked through; why is it that sometimes a paragraph is enough and at other times a rough draft is barely sufficient?" This is a good question because it sharpens the distinction between planning and working through. For some kinds of documents, remember, it is actually possible to have worked through most of the material before it is written. These are the documents one just sits down and writes, having already developed one's experience with one's audience, with the formats, with the material, and a sense of how the presentation should go—all Background skills. With those skills in place, one can just start writing, and out it comes. So working through a paper is as much developing Background skills for handling the material as it is clarifying and developing the thoughts expressed. In some situations, then, a paragraph may be all that's needed; in others, nothing; and in still others, the first draft itself barely suffices.

In terms of the metaphor I've been using, writing a paper that doesn't need to be explicitly worked through is like finding your way in a neighborhood you already know fairly well. Even though you may not know the exact route, the territory is familiar, and once you are on your way, clues to the right way keep showing up. Writing a paper that does need to be worked through can be more like wandering blindfolded on the surface of Mars, searching for a well.

Plans for Other People

With this description in place, we can now evaluate the usefulness of outlines when authorship is shared or when writing is monitored.

To begin with, it should be obvious that reading and understanding an outline or getting from outline to finished product is no easier for a teacher, supervisor, or coauthor than it is for a writer. A topic outline may give some idea of the topics and the order of coverage, but it won't thereby give the reader of the outline an idea of the tone, the subsidiary relationships between the topics, the way the paper serves the audience, or its usefulness. A canny reviewer who knows the situation may be able to infer a lot from an outline, but the outline by itself isn't "telling" that person. Thus, it's not surprising that, even when a writer and supervisor agree on an outline, the finished product may turn out to be quite different from what the supervisor expected. This haziness, as I've said, isn't necessarily bad. In the outline stage, ideas should be flexible, and a certain amount of talking around a subject is usually in order as a way of beginning the working through.

When such a discussion does occur, or when the outline is for some reason luminous for the reader, then looking at the document does have at least one advantage. Often in technical writing, external constraints on the structure of a paper may have escaped the writer's notice; showing the outline to someone else may bring those things into relief. People who are close to a project may not realize that certain audiences need to be addressed or may have an exaggerated idea of how much treatment a subject deserves. An outline that contains an explicit discussion of such things as page length or audience served may be helpful to both writer and monitor. As I've noted before, sometimes planning a format, and so on, helps the writer. And the explicit discussion can often help a supervisor tell when somebody has gone way off.

Of course, if both writer and reader are exceptionally skilled in the area under discussion, the outline itself may be the working through. The writer will have put down the proper landmarks; the supervisor will recognize them as such. Then, any discussion of the outline will really be a refining of the paper, a refining comparable to what usually goes on in the review of a first draft. Most people apparently think that this is usually what goes on in a reading and discussion of an outline, but I doubt it.

There is one last advantage of monitoring with outlines. If a writer never works through a paper, due to inexperience or lack of discipline, writing an outline might start that writer on the way. As we've seen, however, it's not much of a start, and there ought to be better administrative devices for seeing to it that papers are worked through.

Beyond these obvious points, however, not much more can be said. In working situations, the outline's very shortcomings are advantages; they make the outlines readable. More complex outlining systems are harder for monitors to decode. More thorough working through takes much longer to read, and it's harder to take cognizance of external constraints on the document. So, in working situations or in many teaching situations, outlines will remain, limited as they are.

Conclusion

People are taught that planning is the crucial step in the preparation of a document, when working the document through is really the crucial step. Outlining in the standard form is, at best, only a small first step; at worst, and this happens fairly frequently, the outline is an impediment. In planning a document, one needs to work it through, finding landmarks that will serve as mnemonic devices. It is unlikely that simple topic entries will work as landmarks, especially when the territory has not already been crossed.

Despite all this, I am not against outlines per se. Remember, people can produce wonderful things with them despite their inutility, just as the Egyptians managed to build the pyramids through dogged application of the lever and the lash. But I do think that we should take a much freer attitude towards these preliminary planning documents. We should recognize the variety of the representational resources available to us—in mentioning colored ink and arrows I have just skimmed the surface—while at the same time recognizing the difficulty of interpreting these representations. We should recognize that such documents are most useful when the paper has already been worked through. We should recognize that if we do have a preliminary document, we need to revise it as we're working through. We should recognize that using outlines is a difficult skill to learn and that we accomplish very little when we do teach people this skill. We should also recognize that the primary user of the standard outline is not the writer but the monitor, teacher, or supervisor. And we should further recognize that we help a person more by talking a paper through than we do by reviewing an outline. We can do all of this if we realize that planning a paper involves not so much sketching a spatial structure as planning a succession of horizons; if, in other words, we replace our old, confusing metaphors for how a paper comes into being with some new, more accurate ones; if we think of a paper as developing organically rather than mechanically; and if we think of writing a paper as taking a route through an unknown land.

8 What Makes a Paragraph Coherent?

In the last two chapters, I have been criticizing attempts to reduce descriptions of the writing process to descriptions of technique. I have been arguing (1) that the writing process does not have a formal structure, so that describing the rules, constraints, or (formal) techniques governing it is impossible and (2) that using formal techniques in writing is limiting and misdirected. Instead, I have been saying that the various elements of writing are interrelated skills. They should be analyzed as skills, and when people are learning how to write, they should be taught to develop skills, not to employ techniques.

Unfortunately, the subject of these chapters has been mental processes, and these are not exactly tangible; and the technical analyses I have been criticizing do not stand on very firm ground and have not advanced very far. If they are examples of how writing is being converted to technique, then they are scarcely worth getting exercised over.

In this chapter, I want to examine the possibilities for technical analysis of something apparently more tangible: the paragraph. Because the subject matter is something we can look at together, my approach will be quite different. I will take the attempts at technical analysis of the paragraph very seriously and push them as far as they can go. A major criticism will be, then, that they don't go far enough. The effort, after all, is there. Analysis of paragraphs has received much attention in the literature and promises to receive more.

Indeed, it deserves this kind of attention. If any idea is central to the possibility of taking cognitivist approaches to the study of writing, it is that paragraphs have a formal structure. For this idea provides the most direct analogy between the modern composition paradigm and modern work in cognitivism. In modern linguistics and cognitive psychology, an article of faith is that sentences have a formal structure. For modern composition, then, the analogous article of faith is that paragraphs have a formal structure.

The "Intelligibility" of Sentences

How can a sentence have a formal structure? The standard argument (which comes from Chomsky) begins with the following two sentences:

1. Colorless green ideas sleep furiously.
2. Sleep colorless furiously ideas green.

Both sentences are nonsense, but the first sentence is *intelligible*, because the parts of speech are correctly located relative to each other. The adjectives precede the noun and the trio occupy the subject; the verb and adverb follow, occupying the predicate. The subject and predicate are called "formal characteristics" because any sentence, no matter what its meaning, needs them in order to be intelligible. More specifically, the claim is that the appropriate formal characteristics are necessary and sufficient conditions for the intelligibility of the sentence; any sentence is intelligible by virtue of having these characteristics.

I do not wish to pass on the truth of this assertion, but I do want to describe the consequences it is meant to have. First of all, the claim is supposed to have some critical content. We can tell whether a sentence fails to be intelligible and why by determining whether it has these formal characteristics. If, moreover, we know and understand the formal structures of sentences, we can correct the sentences by giving them the correct characteristics. If, for instance, we were given sentence 2, most of us would be able to convert it into sentence 1.

Second, the observation is meant to have some heuristic value. Knowing the relevant formal characteristics, we can construct text that has them. Two sentences, for instance, like "The wheelbarrow was in the barn" and "The barn was red" can be combined into one: "The wheelbarrow was in the barn, which was red."

Assertions about the formal structure of paragraphs would have similar critical and heuristic value. In the investigation of both sentences and paragraphs, these critical and heuristic uses partially validate the formal analysis. The formal structures are taken to be not just surface features that happen to be there, but the very structures we use in constructing, as well as comprehending, paragraphs (or sentences). In the study of sentences, however, this validation is nowhere near as important as it is in the study of paragraphs.

The investigation into sentences relies more on quite a different sort of validation: the fact that (educated) native speakers of a language can tell instantly whether a sentence (even a nonsense sentence) is "grammatical" or "intelligible." Thus an investigator can test whether the presence or absence of a feature makes a difference to its grammaticality merely by asking native speakers. With paragraphs, however, there is no analogous test.

The "Coherence" of Paragraphs

If a paragraph has the appropriate formal characteristics, researchers do not say that it is intelligible; they say that it is "coherent" (Faigley and Witte 1981; Halliday and Hasan 1976; Markels 1984). Claims about coherence are not easily testable empirically (Halliday and Hasan 1976; Markels 1984). Native speakers do not agree about whether paragraphs are coherent; their judgment, moreover, frequently depends on the content of the paragraph and its relationship to what goes before and after. Thus investigators must rely far more on validations provided by critical and heuristic applications of their concepts.

The basic concepts are obtainable from analysis of actual paragraphs. Let us, then, look at some paragraphs and see what the formal features of paragraphs are and how they operate. I must add, however, that, in my analysis, I also rely on quite old-fashioned notions of paragraph structure. I do this merely because the current research effort implicitly builds on these notions.

The following paragraph was the beginning of a student paper. (The numbers are added for easy reference.)

> (1) Water polo combines many aspects of a variety of sports, including soccer, hockey, and basketball. (2) The "field" of competition is a swimming pool, thirty meters long and twenty wide, over seven feet deep. (3) Obviously no one can stand on the bottom, and for those unfamiliar with meters, this is about twice the size of an average family pool (larger by far than most community pools.) (4) There is a goal at each end, eight feet wide and stretching four feet from the surface of the water. (5) Some markings on the pool define areas of play—the two yard line, like soccer's penalty zone for offsides or hockey's blue line; the four-yard line, like soccer's penalty shot mark; and the mid-pool mark, akin to basketball's center circle where the jump is played.

We are not yet sure what a coherent paragraph is, but we can be pretty sure this isn't one. What's wrong with it? To begin with, the *topic sentence* is unrelated to most of the rest of the paragraph. The paragraph is about water polo, but the topic sentence suggests that water polo will be introduced by way of a comparison with other sports, and that comparison isn't forthcoming until the last sentence. Even then, the comparison is inadequate.

We can remark on a few other faults. The information given about water polo in sentences 2, 3, and 4 doesn't seem to follow a logical progression; it has no visible *pattern of development*. Sentences 2 and 3 are connected to some extent because depth, the concluding idea of the second sentence, is the subject of the third. "Depth" provides a *connection* between sentences. Unfortunately, no similar connection between the third and fourth is provided. The fifth, similarly, is connected very weakly to the fourth but is strongly connected to the first. This last connection, however, is not so strong that the writer could just reorder the sentences; the paragraph has to be rewritten.

I offered the student the following rewrite, which kept the idea of the first sentence, but little else:

> (1) Water polo is similar in many respects to soccer, hockey, and basketball, and dissimilar in one crucial respect: the players are swimming. (2) The playing field is slightly larger than a basketball court, 94' × 64' as opposed to 90' × 50', and considerably deeper, 7 feet. (3) The object of the game, like soccer, is to put the ball (which is the same size as a soccer ball) in a net. (4) The net itself is somewhat smaller than a soccer net, 8' wide and 4' off the water, but much harder to defend, since the goalie is treading water. (5) The rules governing the flow of the game have some features of all three sports. (6) The game begins at a center line with a face-off, like hockey; like soccer, much of the play involves positional maneuvering between the offside line (2 yards in front of the goal) and the penalty-shot line (4 yards in front); and like basketball, the play moves wildly and rapidly from one side of the court to the other.

I do not defend this as an example of elegant style. (Don't even trust it as an account of water polo.) It is meant to illustrate a point. Like the first paragraph, the topic sentence introduces a comparison, but here, it is carried through. To carry it through, I have to introduce new information, information which may have been the basis of the comparison for the author, but which was not originally provided. The connections, now, are slightly more subtle; "basketball" provides one connection between the first two sentences and "considerably deeper" a secondary, somewhat flip connection. "Like soccer" connects the third to the first and puts it in parallel with the second. "Net" provides the primary connection in the fourth, soccer a secondary, and "treading water" a tertiary. Number 5 breaks with number 4; the connection to the rest is implicit. The last sentence is connected to the first and fifth by way of the three sports and to the fifth by an implicit connection between "rules governing the flow" and the description of the game itself.

The pattern of development is subtle but nevertheless there. The paragraph moves from a description of the playing field to the object of the game to the course of the game.

The Standard Wisdom
on Constructing Paragraphs

So far, this is a commonsense account of the problems with the first paragraph and the virtues of the second. Three terms have been emphasized: topic sentence, pattern of development, and connection. Each term indicates a feature of paragraphs that can be thought of as formal: something a paragraph must possess no matter what its content. Thus, to convert this commonsense account into an account of formal structures, it is only necessary to cash out these particular terms.

Before I begin, though, let me make a distinction. A coherent paragraph is one that "makes sense," one that is "about one thing." In common speech, this notion of coherence, therefore, contains a semantic evaluation. The idea of formal analysis, though, is to get rid of such semantic evaluations. To that end, researchers in the field have taken to calling paragraphs that have all the correct formal features correctly aligned "cohesive." The assumption is that "cohesion" produces (or is at least a necessary condition of) coherence.[27] A persuasive indication of the truth of that assumption would be a cohesive paragraph analogous to "Colorless green ideas sleep furiously." Short of that, we must examine how each formal device works. If, qua formal device, they turn out to be essential to the operation of the paragraph, then the assumption will look good. If, on the other hand, something else produces the coherence, it will not.

Topic Sentences

When a paragraph is "coherent," that is, "about one thing," it is often said to contain a central idea or "topic." All the other ideas in the paragraph are "subordinate" to the topic; the topic brings each of them into relation. Very often, in a paragraph, one sentence actually states the topic; this is called a "topic sentence." Usually, the topic sentence is the first one in the paragraph; sometimes it is the second, or the last; occasionally it occupies some other position.

The notion of topic sentence is deeply tied to the notion of exposition; nonexpository paragraphs need not have topic sentences. A narrative paragraph, for instance, may well begin with an event and continue with the sequence; no central idea need ever be stated. A descriptive paragraph of the pointilist school might avoid explicit connections between descriptions. By analogy, a few expository paragraphs also elide the central idea, leaving the reader to infer the coherence without explicit aid. But these expository paragraphs are the exceptions. Most of the time, the exposition proceeds by asserting an idea and then elaborating, extending, or proving it, the specific position of the assertion being determined by the manner of elaboration.

In an expository paragraph, when some "idea" is being expressed, and the other ideas are "subordinate" to that, the function of the topic sentence is to facilitate both the expression and the subordination. One has a topic sentence so that one can place the ideas in relation more easily. Thus, analysis of a topic sentence cannot be independent; it must be part of the analysis of the exposition: of the ideas and their relationship. And analysis of a topic sentence must somehow explain how the expression of the idea allows the ideas to be put into relation.

The analysis so far does not make topic sentences formal. The description is merely a commonsense one. "Topic sentences" are not defined in terms of "idea," "expression of idea," and "subordination," which are themselves semantically defined. For a description of paragraphs as formal to suceed, formal counterparts for those terms must be found. In the literature, these counterparts are usually called a "pattern of development" and "connections." Having a pattern of development gives a paragraph "structure" and having connections gives it—the usage is confusing—"cohesiveness."

Patterns of Development

Historically, grammar has only been ascribed to completed sentences. The grammatical structure assigned to the sentence, moreover, has been static and architectural; it can be laid out in a diagram, for instance. To do this is, of course, to ignore, and perhaps to falsify, the way sentences function in time. When we read a sentence, its grammar allows us to understand the sentence as we read. We don't suspend understanding until the pattern is worked out (unless we're reading James or Heidegger).

The pattern of development of a paragraph is similarly static, and this notion therefore falsifies the experience in the same way. Still, the architectural pattern often stands out. Consider, for instance, a paragraph that begins with the following topic sentence:

The wide-rimmed soup bowl has three uses.

The paragraph will develop by making those three functions explicit, namely:

1. The bowl holds soup, the rim offering a convenient place on which to wipe the soup spoon.
2. The bowl acts as a cup, the rim serving as a convenient handle for those who wish to dispense with spoons.
3. The bowl acts as a missile, the rim providing a convenient grip to those who wish to fling the bowl at unruly waiters.

The three sentences describe the uses mentioned in the first sentence: thus they can be said to "support," or "extend," or "give examples of" that idea. The examples are both independent and parallel, so that in theory they can be given in any order. Any order chosen, however, constitutes a development; it indicates a certain relationship among the ideas.

Very often the development lends itself to abstract (formal) description. If, for instance, I present the sentences in the preceding order, I may be presenting the most important or most useful idea first, the least important or useful last. Presenting them in the reverse order, I would then be going from least important to most important.

In the pedagogy of paragraphs, descriptions of paragraph development on this abstract level are common. When writing paragraphs that make independent points, students are told, order them in terms of importance. When presenting a spatial description, order the elements in terms of spatial position. When presenting comparisons and contrasts, use an AB–AB–AB pattern or else an AAA–BBB pattern. Figure 8-1, for example, is a list of the ways paragraphs may be ordered or developed when all the parts are parallel. I drew the list from a technical writing textbook.

1. Expanded Definition	5. Enumeration
A. Features-Term	A. Occurrence
B. Term-Features	B. Importance
2. Time	C. Familiarity
A. Past-Present	6. Comparison-Contrast
B. Present-Past	A. Aa-Bb
C. Present-Past-Present	B. AB-ab
3. Space	7. Cause and Effect
A. Right-Left	A. Cause to Effect
B. Left-Right	B. Effect to Cause
C. Etc.	8. Partition
4. Logic	A. By structure
A. Input-Output	B. By cost
B. Output-Input	C. By principle of
C. Most Important-	operation
Least Important	D. By weight, etc.

Fig. 8-1. Patterns of development for expository paragraphs.
(Based on: Rathbone 1966, 79–80. Reprinted with permission.)

Let us take a minute to see how these work. The earlier paragraph was describing the functions of the bowl. Another paragraph might partition the bowl by structure. Say, for instance, our topic sentence were, "The bowl has three parts." The three following sentences might be:

1. On the outside is the rim, by which one grasps the bowl.
2. Towards the middle are the sides, which hold the soup in.
3. At the middle is the bottom, which keeps the soup from going all over the table.

If the development of every paragraph could be explained on this level, the explanations would be very powerful. Unfortunately, however, the method of ordering or developing the ideas in the paragraph often depends on the nature of the thing being described.

Say, for instance, the topic sentence continued with, "one which is common and others less often called upon." Here the development is in terms of "frequency of use." (Sentence number 1 might begin with, "Most frequently, it is used as a . . . ," and the other two would be changed to match.) If the topic sentence ended with, "only one of which, however, is employed in polite society," the order would again be based on a particular concrete fact about soup bowls. (Last, for instance, would be, "Least polite, but most satisfying is the use of the soup bowl as a missile, . . . [and so forth]

. . . .") Or again, the sentences could be developed according to a sequence of events entirely particular to soup bowls. "While the bowl is full, it is used as a bowl, the wide rim being . . . . When it is nearly empty, it is used as a cup . . . . After the soup has been fully consumed . . . ."

Admittedly, we can create an abstract description of the relationships between these sentences, but such descriptions are ex post facto accounts, not descriptions of structures that many paragraphs share.

Cohesion Devices

People who believe in topic sentences and patterns of development acknowledge that a paragraph can have both a topic sentence and a pattern of development but still be incoherent. Consider, for instance, this version of the soup bowl example:

> The soup bowl has three uses. A spoon can scoop soup out of it. Raising it to the lips, it becomes a cup. Or, one can fling it at unruly waiters.

The paragraph has a topic sentence and a pattern of development, but the relationships between the sentences are not clear. For the paragraph to be coherent, the sentences must be tied together or *connected*.

The simplest kind of connection is the direct connection between sentences. Let me show how they work by taking a sample sentence and connecting it to subsequent sentences, each of which is connected by a different technique. The sample sentence comes from Dewey's *Democracy and Education* (1924):

> The pupil has a body, and brings it to school along with his mind. (p. 165)

In such a sentence, certain words occupy important positions: in descending order, they are, roughly, the subject, the verb(s), the end of the sentence, the object of the verb(s), and everything else. The simplest technique for connecting two sentences is to take a word in an important position from the first sentence and use it in an important position in the second. (Note that this is a formal description.) A good example is Dewey's next sentence:

> And the *body* is, of necessity, a well-spring of energy (p. 165)

But many others of the same kind are possible:

Yet the *mind* is the teacher's only concern.

The teacher, too, has a *body*.

Yet the *pupil* must pretend he has brought only the former.

Notice, by the way, how difficult it is to make an unimportant word in the previous sentence be the source of the connection. Plausible sentences connecting with "school" are rare:

The *school* imprisons the body while it frees the mind.

Generally, the more important the word and the closer it comes to the end of the previous sentence, the better able one is to delay the connection until the end of the current sentence. Thus, the first example can probably be improved to:

Yet the teacher is often only concerned with the mind.

Pronouns, synonyms, or demonstrative pronouns can also provide the connection:

Would that *this* were not the case.

The teacher who forgets *either* creates for himself no small annoyance.

Yet the *mental* is the only concern of education.

Phenomenologically speaking, the connection seems harder to see when a pronoun or synonym is used.

The connections so far we may call *explicit* connections; others are possible. In the following two sentences from the previous page, Dewey relies on a *logical* connection:

The very word pupil has almost come to mean one who is engaged not in having fruitful experiences but in absorbing knowledge directly. (p. 164)

Something which is called mind or consciousness is severed from the physical organs of activity. (p. 164)

The relationships between the two can be inferred by the reader. This method is quite common; see, for instance, the following examples:

1. Ruth hit the ball sharply.
2. Tinker broke to his right.

1. The unemployment rate dropped last month.
2. For the first time, the military was included in the calculations.

1. Few men paid any attention.
2. For women, it was a beacon of hope.

In each pair, you will notice, the reader must have some prior knowledge of the situation. If you know nothing about baseball or about how unemployment rates are calculated, those examples will seem mysterious. And the third must seem mysterious to us all, until we know what "it" is.

As we have seen, correct placement often helps the connecting devices to work properly. This suggests that connections can also be made syntactically. Consider, for instance, the following sequence of sentences:

> The bear has its claws.
> The dog has its teeth.
> The scorpion has its sting.

If you remove the parallelism, you have a mess:

> The bear has claws.
> Dogs are endowed with teeth.
> A scorpion is provided with a stinger at the end of its tail.

Sometimes even a combination of explicit, logical, or syntactic connections is insufficient. In those cases, English allows you to signal the connection with what are called "proleptic devices." If, for instance, the connection between first and second sentence is that between generalization and example, we can indicate that with the words "for example" or "for instance," as in the following, rather silly continuation of Dewey's sentence:

> Johnny's, for instance, weighs 80 pounds and is moving constantly.

If the sentences are in contrast, one can indicate this with devices like "but," "however," and "conversely":

> Once the pupil is there, however, the body is ignored.

If the sentence merely adds extra information, devices like "also" and "as well" are appropriate:

> The pupil brings his lunch pail as well.

Obviously proleptic devices can also signal a sentence's place in the pattern of development. In the soup bowl example, for instance, where, properly speaking, only a weak syntactic connection links the sentences, the place in the overall pattern could well be marked by "First," "Second," and "Third," at the beginning of the appropriate sentences.

We can now see that the paragraph given at the beginning of this subsection can be repaired simply by adding explicit connections and proleptic devices.

> A soup bowl has three uses. As a bowl, it remains stationary while a spoon scoops soup out of it. As a cup, it is brought to the lips and soup is slurped out of it. As a missile, it is flung at unruly waiters, the soup, in this case, removing itself.

Connections would be very simple if at any point only one kind of connection were possible or appropriate. Unfortunately, different kinds of connections can easily substitute for each other. A logical and syntactic connection can easily replace an explicit one; an explicit connection can easily replace a proleptic device, as in the previous example. Links between sentences, moreover, are very often multiple. A logical connection is supplemented by a secondary explicit connection; a proleptic device simultaneously connects to the foregoing sentence and reminds one of the place in the pattern of development.

But, no matter how tight the sentence connections and no matter how many of them there are, the paragraph will not cohere if the ideas in the sentence are not connected. Consider, for instance, the following paragraph:

> MIT is on the Charles. The Charles flows into the sea. The sea contains small amounts of iridium. Iridium is used in the manufacture of jewelry. Jewelry is worn infrequently at MIT.

Perhaps something could be made out of the paragraph by connecting MIT's attitude toward jewelry and iridium, but it would be uphill work.

Criticizing and Building Paragraphs with These Ideas

We have now ascertained that, according to the standard wisdom, a coherent paragraph usually has the following features:

1. A topic sentence.
2. A pattern of development.
3. Devices that connect sentences.

The modern researcher would like to say that together these devices give a paragraph its coherence. It ought to be clear, however, that, as described, these features do nothing of the sort. Paragraphs can lack any of the three features and still be coherent; they can have all three and not be coherent.

Worse, each of the concepts looks as if it were produced ex post facto. Paragraphs don't have topic sentences because of some inner necessity; they have them because analysts can't fail to find one. (Try an experiment; go back and find the "topic sentences" of five consecutive paragraphs in this paper. Do they really express a main idea that is developed by the rest of the paragraph?) Patterns of development aren't a scaffolding upon which ideas find themselves, but a weakly abstract description of relationships among ideas that proceed out of the ideas themselves. A connection is a similarly abstract description of relationships between sentences.

Still, the analysis would be persuasive if we could show that the concepts are vital critical or heuristic tools. The latter possibility does look promising. Rhetoric has a long tradition of generating things to say from formal models, and one ignores such long traditions at one's peril.

Besides, it sounds plausible. I can imagine looking at something, wondering what to say about it, and saying, "Well, what caused it?" Or in technical writing, I can imagine someone looking at a piece of machinery in order to describe it and thinking, "Shall I go left-to-right or spiral out from the center?" Well, I sort of imagine this.

A lot of the plausibility, though, depends on the level of abstraction. Phenomenologically, it's implausible to say that people begin writing a paragraph by saying, "Well, I had better write the topic sentence that states my main idea first," if only because the constraints from the required connections to previous paragraphs are usually great. But they might think, "What am I going to say in this paragraph" and try to state it in the first sentence. Similarly, people don't begin a new sentence by thinking of which proleptic device to use, but they might look back at the "powerful" words in the previous sentence as a way of finding a new sentence.

Unfortunately, as a justification for analysis, the idea that we use formal characteristics as heuristic tools is scarcely compelling. Surely they are more useful as critical tools. Both bad paragraphs, for instance, could be and were criticized with them. (The soccer paragraph was criticized because it promised a pattern of development but didn't deliver. The individual sentences, moreover, had very few connections between them. The simpler bad soup bowl example also lacked those connections; inserting them repaired the paragraph.) But even that value must be limited, unless we can explain the basis for it (referring to value). Why, for instance, is the fact that a paragraph lacks a topic sentence a criticism?

The cognitivist would have it, let me remind you, that these formal features are necessary features of a cohesive paragraph and that cohesion is necessary for coherence. But remember, the basic argument for this position is the heuristic and critical value of the analysis. So if the heuristic value is limited, and the critical value is sporadic, then unless some explanation of the underlying process is forthcoming, the cognitivist account is not going to be convincing.

The questions are, "Why do these features of the paragraph exist?" and "Why does noting their absence help us to repair paragraphs?" To answer them, with either a cognitivist or a noncognitivist account, we must look more deeply into how and why these features of paragraphs actually function. And, since criticism of paragraphs has revealed them most clearly, let us begin the investigation with the following question. Under what circumstances do we think a paragraph has failed? The simple answer is that a paragraph fails when it fails to make each successive idea relevant to what has gone before.

Another Failed Paragraph

The following paragraph is the beginning of a letter that a former student of mine showed me. (I've numbered the sentences for easy reference.)

> Dear XX:
>
> (A1) I would like to publish the findings of my master's thesis, "Successful MRP System Implementation: Managing the Organizational Transition." (A2) The thesis shows how a general management framework can help analyze and plan for the introduction of information systems technology into a corporation. (A3) It is a case study of the ABC Corporation's gradual implementation of an MRP (Management Resources Planning) system, a computerized management tool which helps managers plan the allocation of internal resources. (A4) The thesis uses the QRS

> Framework (a system for analyzing corporate culture developed at Harvard) to follow the attempt from its beginning and show how the various parts of the corporation responded to it.

This paragraph has all the requisite formal features. It has a topic sentence, a clear pattern of development (more about the thesis), and clear connections between sentences. (Each new sentence has "thesis" or a reference to "thesis" as the subject.) But still, it's not a good paragraph.

In intuitive terms, one might say that the paragraph goes off in several different directions, that it doesn't pull things together. Look at sentences A3 and A4, for instance. I don't immediately see what the MRP and the QRS have to do with each other. If I look at sentence A2, I get a clue: apparently the general management framework, evidently the QRS Framework, is being used to analyze the introduction of an information systems technology, evidently the MRP system. So in A3 and A4, the writer is explaining A2, although in reverse order. Maybe something could be done to bring this paragraph in line with an ordinary formal pattern of development. Could the writer just switch sentences A3 and A4, so that the pattern of development forecast in A2 is used? No, since sentence A4 requires information explained in sentence A3. Maybe the writer can use more careful links between sentences A2 and A4. The notion of using a "framework" to "analyze" something is peculiar; if the writer had said the framework was used to "analyze the attempt," maybe that would have helped. But no, it wouldn't, since the attempt is being followed in this case study, not analyzed.

If you want, you can spend quite a lot of time introducing formal fixes (for example, proleptic devices) and still do nothing about the problem. What is that problem? Well, for one thing, I don't understand the problems companies have with introducing an information systems technology and thus why or how one needs to analyze the introduction. In looking back at the first sentence for help, I get none; instead, I get more mysterious terms. The MRP system is not merely a technology and a tool (sentences A2 and A3) but something that is implemented. And somehow implementation makes a difference to the organization, creating an organizational transition. To put it bluntly, the first sentence doesn't tell me the "why's" and "how's" of the situation, and even after the next few sentences, the situation is still murky.

I talked to the student for a while and came up with the following new version:

Dear XX:

(B1) I would like to publish the findings of my master's thesis, "Successful MRP System Implementation: Managing the Organizational Transition." (B2) The thesis is a case study of how the ABC Corporation gradually implemented a Management Resources Planning (MRP) system, an information system which helps top management plan the allocation of resources. (B3) The thesis follows the implementation from the beginning, using the QRS Framework (a system for analyzing corporate culture developed at Harvard) to show how the various parts of the corporation responded to the attempt. (B4) The attempt was not successful because the lower-level organization resisted the imposition. (B5) Since similar resistance can usually be expected, the thesis shows how a QRS Framework can be used for planning the introduction of similar information management systems.

In the corrected version, the problems don't come up because I haven't let them. The connecting words in the sentences and what is developed in the paragraph are familiar terms—thesis, case study, implementation of a (now-defined) system. When an unfamiliar term comes up, I define it. The pattern of development is now more available, as well. Since the paper is based on a thesis, and since the letter is written to an editor, I've organized it around the contribution of the thesis, not its subject. The thesis is a case study (contribution 1), and the case study uses a particular method (contribution 2). The case study is not merely worth reviewing in itself; it also shows people explicitly how to avoid these problems in the future (contribution 3). There are, of course, other threads. With case studies, people are always interested in what happened, so I also throw in a tidbit.

This student asked me how I came up with the new version. I told him that I followed a standard rule of thumb, "Begin with the familiar and move to the unfamiliar."[28] He objected, and after some argument, I agreed; this description covers too many different activities to be illuminating. Let's look at some of them.

For one thing, I wasn't happy with the fact that an MRP was both a tool (A3) and a technology (A2). I called it a "system." True, I was no longer mentioning the fact that this thesis was making a contribution in the study of technology transfer, but the idea remained implicit, and I felt the loss was not that great. For another, I let the central fact be the attempt at implementing the system, and I gave a chronological order to the descriptions of the attempt, justifying this partly by giving the words "case study" new prominence.

I could go on, of course. But I want you to notice two things about this kind of explanation. First of all, it is not a description of what I actually thought as I was rewriting the paragraph. Then, the best I can remember, I had a whirl of thoughts out of which sentences emerged. Second of all, this explanation can't be brought to bear on any other paragraph. What I did and the reasons I did them are sui generis. Attempts at generalization, like saying that I put the familiar before the unfamiliar, are simply too imprecise to be useful.

I would like to suggest that what is true of "Put the familiar before the unfamiliar" is equally true of "lacks a topic sentence" or "unclear pattern of development." Explanations at that level cover up more accurate explanations at a deeper level, each of which is applicable only to the paragraph at hand.

If this suggestion is correct, then the picture of paragraph coherence given by the modern researcher is radically incorrect. What is at issue when a paragraph fails to make sense is just that: it fails to make sense. And whether it makes sense depends on a welter of factors, among which the formal factors can claim no special status.

We are left with two questions. The first, more important one is, "How can we tell which picture is right?" The second is, "If this suggestion is right, what is the status of formal features in a paragraph?" To answer the first question, we're going to have to tackle another question I've simply avoided up until now, the question of, "How do we actually understand paragraphs?" This question must necessarily treat a paragraph as something experienced sequentially, not as an architectural object. As such, it is extremely difficult to answer; an adequate answer presupposes an adequate account of how we experience things in time, something I certainly don't know much about. Therefore, all I can do here is present two very limited, inadequate stories of how we might understand paragraphs; the first is the picture of the cognitivist, and the second is the picture I have had throughout this book. With both pictures in front of you, you will be better able to choose between them, and you will understand slightly better how I think the formal features work.

How We Understand Paragraphs:
A Cognitivist Account

The modern researcher's account of how we understand paragraphs relies on cognitivist accounts of understanding in general. One well-known account is Marvin Minsky's (1981). For Minsky, the basic question is, "How do human beings manage (1) to organize their knowledge and (2) to utilize that organization in making inferences about what they are told." He suggests the following answer.

Each human being puts knowledge in "frames," collections of data about something that are related in a particular way. When a human being is, say, discussing a subject, this frame is activated in the mind, and that person's ideas about the subject are, at least initially, given the same structure as the frame. Minsky gives the example of a child's birthday party (1981, 105–6). Tell a child that he or she is going to a party, and the child will know already that the party takes place at a certain time, lasts a certain amount of time, includes activities like playing games, involves eating ice cream, and so on and so forth. This particular party may not have some of these features, in which case the child will remove the appropriate "default" values and substitute, for instance, "no ice cream," for "ice cream." These substitutions leave the structure of the frame alone; the implication is that knowledge of a birthday party just has a certain structure.

Within the frame are items that deserve their own frames: ice cream, for instance. In the ice-cream "slot" (place where information may be filled in) is a "pointer" to the ice-cream frame. When required (What kind of ice cream will they have?), the ice-cream frame can be "activated" by way of the pointer.

You can see why this is an attractive account. It acknowledges the fact that when one idea is invoked, relationships to other ideas are also invoked, even though they're not made explicit. If I begin a discussion of a "birthday party," it's natural for certain details about the party to be made an issue by my auditor, even if not doing so consciously. In acknowledging this, the account also admits that what is invoked and how are content-dependent; it doesn't admit any general, formal descriptions of logical relations of the comparison or qualification kind. Most important, it says that this knowledge does have some structure.

There are not, you see, an infinite number of frames, according to Minsky. Some concepts are primary; others are subsidiary. The primary concepts are the labels for the frame; the subsidiary are inside the frame. When one invokes a frame, it's usually easier to invoke it by its label than by some element of it. When one is filling in slots in the frame, it's usually easier to fill them in according to the pattern dictated by the natural structure of the frame. Thus, for instance, when one invokes the birthday party frame, certain slots (time, for instance) have to be filled in first, and others can wait.[29] Thus, if one accepts Minsky's account, one has a way of figuring out the proper structure of the paragraph; just figure out the structure(s) of the frame(s) one is invoking and act accordingly. The coherence devices, and so forth, then, may or may not be invoked, depending on whether they're needed to help move around in the frame.

This is very sketchy, but for my purposes it doesn't matter. Right now, it's important that you see how the idea (and others like it) works. For Minsky, any concept has a group of ideas naturally associated with it. (Everybody agrees with this.) For Minsky, though, the group is relatively small, and it has a certain natural structure. (All cognitivists would agree.) Minsky creates this account because he wants to solve the problem of what might be called "static interaction." Given that we are talking about birthday parties, how is it that people know so much about them even when not much has been said? The account solves this problem well. Frame (or "script") descriptions founder, however, when they are asked to solve the problem of dynamic interaction.

The problem is that sometimes what happens in the world just doesn't fit the frame. Imagine, for instance, that we are dutifully filling out a child's birthday party frame when we discover that it takes place at 11:00 p.m. Suddenly we have to alter either the "birthday party" part of the frame or the "child's" part of the frame. Unfortunately, in the Minsky account of frames, this just isn't possible. If it were, we would have to have another frame that "evaluates" the frame as it's being filled out, so that it can tell whether this frame has the right information. That frame would itself require a frame for checking it—the old infinite regress. This problem, which is known in the literature as the "frame problem," has not been solved (Dennett 1984).

The frame problem has led Minsky and others to feel very hesitant about frames. There is yet another problem, which creates even more difficulties for an account of paragraphs. To put this problem in the terms we care about right now, the problem is that even the pairing of two simple sentences "activates" too many frames for the notion to have any use in, for example, the study of paragraphs. To put it in more general terms, the problem is that there is no natural limitation on the size of frames.

Consider, for instance, the following two sentences. Imagine that I am describing a man named John, who is in a wheelchair.

A1. John drives a large car.
A2. John flies a small plane.

Now, after reading the two sentences, what would you feel able to say about John, and, in particular, the extent of John's motor skills? Quite a lot, I would imagine. If so, then what sorts of knowledge did you use when making those conclusions? What, in other words, were the contents of the frames you used? You knew, among other things:

1. That for each machine, one person (or more) controls its motion, which is speedy and covers large distances.
2. That the physical situations of the driver and pilot (seated in a central position) are relatively similar.
3. That the motor operations (controller responds to outside environment by making small adjustment in the controls) are relatively similar.
4. That differences in the actual method of movement of the plane and the car don't matter in this context.

You have, moreover, a number of facts that are waiting in the wings, so to speak. Among them are the following:

1. In one case, the controls are a stick; in the other, they're a wheel.
2. Planes tip; cars don't.
3. The speeds and media of travel are quite different.
4. The laws governing both activities, and the costs.
5. Pilot's licenses are far more difficult to obtain and keep than driver's licenses.

And so on and so forth. Notice, by the way, that for one to know about all these things, one must also know a good deal about things ranging from the operation of mechanical devices to ownership and responsibility.

Now, try to imagine preexisting frames for "handicaps," "drive," "large car," "fly," and "small plane" that would contain this information structured in such a way that (1) the frames weren't impossibly large and (2) the specific comparisons we need would emerge. Don't spend too much time on it; I don't think you can. For these and only these things to be salient, you have to bring into the frames too many facts that, properly speaking, belong in other domains.

You can see this point more clearly if you change the sentence pair slightly. Consider, for instance, the following, which has the same context:

B1. John drives a large car.
B2. John flies a small hang glider.

The answer to the question about John's disabilities changes greatly. Balance and physical dexterity, perhaps, are being compared, where before coordination was. You make this conclusion, notice, on the basis of entirely different comparisons between the two activities. For some reason quite different information in the "handicaps," "large cars," and "flying" frames has become salient. Yet the frames are the same. Within a frame explanation of understanding, explaining this phenomenon requires invoking enormously complicated metaframes, meta-metaframes, and so on—the infinite regress once again. (If you're still not convinced, imagine how those metaframes would have to be changed if we had sentences A1 and A2 but used them instead to make a point about John's wealth, not his motor skills.)

Frame explanations are intuitively sensible when they suggest that we group certain information together. But they provide no explanation of how we are able to "zero in" on salient information. A simple frame story like Minsky's tries to account for our ability to do this by saying that it's built into the structure of the frames. One might keep some of this simple account by imagining that many, many frames are activated in the course of the comparison. But then we have to imagine a mechanism for seeing which frames are activated, a mechanism that does all the interesting work, but which is not at all part of the account. Introducing such a new mechanism is always fatal to a scientific account because it smacks of deus ex machina.

How Formal Features of Paragraphs Operate:
A Noncognitivist Account

The basic strategy in any cognitive account is to compartmentalize ideas, describe a structure for those compartments, and describe mental processes in terms of these compartments. The basic strategy for arguing against such accounts is to show that the compartments are too large to be useful or that the dynamic interaction of these compartments or their elements requires introduction of a new mechanism. What does this mean for paragraphs?

It means simply that when a paragraph makes sense, it makes sense because myriad ideas (all the ideas mobilized by the succession of sentences, like the A1-A2 pair) are made to have sensible relationships. Success in making a paragraph make sense depends on all the ideas involved. Yes, it also depends on the formal devices used, but those devices don't have any special status. Sometimes an idea tells us how to put everything in relation; sometimes the word "however" does. But they both do this in the same way.

I would like to offer a justification for this claim, but unfortunately, I can't. All I can really offer is another sketch, also drawn from outside sources, of how understanding works. The source is Heidegger, the same source I've been using throughout the book.

Early in *Being and Time*, Heidegger examines the simple activity of hammering. The act of hammering, he says, involves our making sense of our entire current situation. Hammering is not just swinging a hammer, for the way one swings a hammer depends on a number of things: ranging from one's previous skill and experience with hammering, to the pattern of light and shadow in the room, to one's knowledge of and experience with the object being hammered, to one's purposes in hammering. Constantly, as we are hammering, we are adjusting the hammer so as to satisfy the constraints exerted by all of these things.

If, for instance, we are hammering a nail into a board that will be used in a cabinet, as the nail gets closer, we hammer more lightly, in order to preserve the surface. The activity, for Heidegger, is not "hammering more lightly"; it is purposive—it is, rather, "hammering more lightly in order to preserve the surface." But the purposes (the "in order to's") don't just stop there. It's also "in order to make finishing easier in order to have a beautiful cabinet in order to be pleased when I enter the kitchen," which can easily be added. Indeed, the "in order to's" extend infinitely. According to Heidegger, any activity of ours is at the center of a vast web of "in order to's"; that web is the horizon (Heidegger 1962). At any moment in that activity, to put it another way, we are organizing a set of involvements or commitments within the world that allows us to understand the activity in the way we do.

Reading requires a similar organization of involvements. The structure of the involvements, however, is quite different. In hammering, we are engaged in altering the physical world in order to accomplish certain goals of our own. In reading, as we have seen, we are ordering our own experience of the material in a way that's guided by the writer's experience. Part of being led, certainly, is understanding the formal rules of the language itself and also, of course, understanding conventional signals provided by the language. But there is something more important about that language that we have, as yet, left out. That is the other self.

The person writing—me, right now—has his own horizon and his own involvements. The person reading must be open to that horizon, those involvements. Indeed, this openness is at the foundation of the reading experience. We always subordinate our interpretation of the language to our estimate of what the author wants to say.

To see how this works and also just to show you how delicate the array of involvements is and how easy to shift, I want to bring up two final examples. Consider this version of a sentence pair used earlier in this chapter:

1. Ruth hit the ball sharply.
2. Tinker broke to his right.

Given our knowledge of baseball, we naturally assume that Tinker was going after the ball. (If we don't assume something like this, the sentences have no connection at all, since no formal connecting technique is used.) A frame account provides a perfectly satisfactory explanation of how we make that assumption. What a frame account doesn't explain is the fact that any of the following continuations are also acceptable:

3A. With luck, the lead runner, Gehrig, could be erased and the rather slow batter, Ruth, could be doubled off at first.
3B. The end of the bat came whizzing by his left ear; he had barely gotten out of the way.
3C. But before the ball could get to him, Evers had speared the line drive, and the inning was over.

Each requires a radically different picture of the situation. We had none of those pictures before we read the continuation. But we were perfectly ready to allow these continuations. We read so as to leave these possibilities entirely open. Indeed, it may be wrong to say that we "assumed" that he was going after the ball. That assumption may only have emerged after we were given time to reflect on the sentences. Perhaps we simply mobilized involvements that left us appropriately open to the author's ideas.

How can we be sure that this leaving ourselves open genuinely dominates our understanding of a sequence? One way is to look at what happens when the various kinds of signals conflict. Say, for instance, we have a sentence pair such as the following:

1. John F. Kennedy was elected in 1960.
2. The twenty-third president was not noted for his legislative achievements.

Kennedy, of course, was not the twenty-third president. Nevertheless, we are sure that he is the subject of the second sentence. The reason: people don't talk about one president and then suddenly switch to another. It is overwhelmingly more likely that "twenty-third" is a typo.

We can explain our leaping to this conclusion in another way: "It is conventional, as we've seen, to refer to approximately the same thing in successive sentences. Thus 'the twenty-third president,' which violates the convention, is a likely candidate for a mistake." But such an explanation puts the cart before the horse. Formally speaking, as we've seen, it is entirely possible to switch foci of successive sentences. The reason we can zero in on this as a violation of convention is that we know that this author has little reason to jump around like that.

Learning to Write Paragraphs

I have offered a competing account of how we understand paragraphs, if "account" is the right word for a metaphorical explanation that reduces itself to "Well, you just understand them." I do not claim this is incisive, only that it is true. It remains for me to evaluate it in the same way that we tried to evaluate a formal analysis. Evaluation was in three areas: analysis, heuristics, and criticism.

As far as analysis is concerned, this account is not superior to that of the formalists. It merely suggests that formal analysis is incomplete and not likely to get any better. The formal devices identified are, at most, conventions. No rule-governed system of conventions, such as those governing sentences, is likely to be discovered; perhaps because, as a unit of meaning, "paragraph" is not as well defined as "sentence" or "word."

This account does not deny the heuristic value of the devices just described, but it suggests that their heuristic use is limited. People ought not to think, "OK, now I've got to write a topic sentence"; they should, most of the time, be thinking, "What should I say next?" When you're stuck, sometimes it's good to think of things in new ways, and, in those cases, perhaps thinking "Should I spiral outward?" may do precisely that. But equally good, according to this account, might be to write one sentence about one idea and then link it appropriately to another about a second.

This account does suggest that criticism of purely formal features in paragraphs is likely to be superficial. The criticism may allow one to find and correct faults, particularly when the faults are rather prominent. But most such mistakes in form come out of mistakes in content. Thus, the most thorough way of diagnosing a paragraph is to discover the places where things aren't clear. This is, I admit, at best, difficult, and at worst, ineffable. But it is the right way of going about things.

Thus far, there don't seem to be many advantages to knowing that paragraphs don't really have formal features. In fact, since this account requires you to pay more attention to the content, which may, in the case of some freshman papers, be a positively noisome mélange of old hat and stale ideas, you may be worse off knowing all this. It would be easier just to write "No topic sentence" in the margin.

But there may be one advantage. These ideas suggest a better way of teaching people how paragraphs work and how to write more coherent paragraphs: simply, to have them read, write, and revise lots of paragraphs—good paragraphs, bad paragraphs, other people's, their own. As they do, they'll begin to see that a coherent paragraph is one that makes sense. And they'll see that one makes a paragraph coherent by revising it until it makes sense.

9 Computers and the Techniques of Writing

Introduction

The last three chapters have been about theoretical attempts to reduce writing to a technique. So far I have argued that such theories are superficial and that teaching the use of techniques is limiting. The discussion has been on an abstract, highly theoretical level, and it has dealt with subjects (for example, a sense of an audience) that are annoyingly abstruse. In this chapter, I want to take up more concrete attempts to reduce writing to a technique. I want to look at what happens when certain writing tasks are performed not by a writer, but by a computer.

What is the relationship between the two? In theory, the relationship is close. Cognitivist analyses are by definition formal: the processes described occur independently of the meaning of whatever they operate upon. Computer programs are formal by definition. And since formal processes are replicated (not just simulated) on a computer, an analysis of computer writing tools is precisely an analysis of certain formal theories of writing. Conversely, then, if a formal theory proves impossible to replicate on a computer, then the formal theory is inadequate.

In fact, though, the realms of theory and of practice are far apart. No one has ever tried to take a theory of audience analysis and write a computer program that exerts the constraints imposed by the theory. No one has even tried to write a program that analyzes the formal features of paragraphs. Some work has been done in outlining; we will look at it. But the theories of planning embedded in those programs are so reactionary that few modern composition theorists would feel comfortable in the same bed with them. Indeed, the theories of language and language production embedded in most computer writing aids—aids that were largely developed by computer programmers with no professional training—are equally reactionary.

Even so, I regard the existence of the computer and computer

writing aids as the conclusive test for the arguments in this book.
And I regard the recent history of attempts to create computer writing aids as the most concrete evidence for them. The formal theories
we have seen so far depend on a lot of hand waving because the
processes described are of incredible complexity. (Admittedly, it is
also fair to say that my theories depend on a lot of hand waving and
Heidegger.) But a computer program can, at least in theory, work at
that level of complexity. Even a very plausible theory on the macro
level depends on many tiny interactions, which may behave unpre-
dictably. Computer modeling can let one look at those tiny interactions.

What we will see, however, is that computer implementations of
formal theories run into apparently insuperable problems long before they can even begin to test the formal theories we have been
looking at. The structure of these problems, moreover, is exactly
what my theories predict. In order to show this, I am going to look
very carefully at the way in which several different kinds of computer programs fail. To follow this, you don't need any expertise in
computer programming. But you will have to look at the problems
and try to think through the ways that might be found to overcome
them.

Much is at issue here. Computer writing tools have mostly been
developed by people who think of writing as a technology. The
thrust of their efforts, therefore, has been to make tools that substitute for specific tasks that writers are known to perform or tools
that permit closer monitoring and control of the writing. The prevailing conception has been that computers would take over some of
the boring and mechanical writing and editing jobs, such as checking grammar or identifying mistakes of style or diction. Unfortunately, most of these jobs are even harder for a computer than they are
for a person. Better (and easier) would be to make tools that can be
turned to a writer's purposes. Rather than substituting for known
writing tasks, the computer would open up new possibilities for
writers. But little has been done along those lines. The developers
have had the wrong theory.

Even the choices of what programs to develop have not really
been motivated by a consideration of what writers need. Instead,
they have been driven by the capacities of the computer. People
have seen that such and such a program would be possible to build,
and they have built it.

But how are formal theories involved, here, if the programs are not explicitly testing them? In two ways. First, formal theories drive the developer's ideas of what the user ought to want. Second, formal theories, by definition, describe the capacities of computers. The test of the theories, then, is in the utility of the programs. Do they do any good? Could the same thing be accomplished more simply? Is their use potentially harmful?

In the following pages, therefore, I will say that (a) certain tools are not useful and that (b) they are impossible to improve. Such claims always run into two responses that I would like to anticipate here. The response to (a) is, "Well, I use it, so it must be useful." In chapter 7, I made a similar argument—that outlines are not useful—and mentioned that believers in outlines make this response. My reply was that the believer is ingenious about putting a bad tool to a good use, and I want to make the same type of reply here. Arguments about the merits of a tool are always about the *intended* use of a tool, not the actual use. They treat whether the tool itself helps people in meeting the intended ends, whether other tools are more effective, whether use of the tool is unreasonably expensive or involves unreasonable effort, and so forth. One can use a sledgehammer as a tool for hitting golf balls, but that does not mean a sledgehammer is an effective golf-ball hitter.

The response to (b) is "How can you say that computers will never overcome this limitation? Look at all the surprising things technology has done. They laughed at the Wright Brothers, you know." The answer to this objection has to do with whether the problems confronting a potential technological advance seem to have any in-principle solution. The Wright Brothers knew perfectly well that such a solution existed; birds had found it long before they had. We shall see that no similar solution seems possible for these problems; by contrast, it seems that the limitations are principled.

This very long chapter is organized as follows. In the next section, I describe how computers work. The description will show the close relationship between theoretical analyses and computer analyses. It will also show what the limitations are and how they occur. In the section after that, the way current computer programs work is described in some detail. The detail is necessary because each type of application performs its own kind of formal analysis, and thus each type fails in a different way. The last section asks whether the limitations now encountered are ever likely to be overcome. The short answer is no; in an appendix, I describe some likely near-term developments in computer writing aids.

How Computers Work, Hacks,
and the Limitations Hacks Impose

To understand any of this, you need to understand the distinction between a letter, for example, "a," and a symbol, for example, 'a'. The letter is a *meaningful object*, part of the alphabet, with a certain pronunciation. The symbol is a *formal object*, distinguishable from other such objects by its shape.[30] You can easily see that the two are different if you realize that either one can change while the other stays the same. The symbol 'a' and the symbol '**a**' are different, but they both represent the same letter "a." The symbol 'a' remains the symbol 'a' in a letter-substitution code like that used in Poe's "The Gold Bug," but in such a code, the letter "a" might be represented by the symbol 'w'.

When we use the computer for word processing, we normally don't notice any difference between letters and symbols. When I type the letter "a" at the keyboard, as far as I am concerned, the computer is storing and displaying the letter "a." But as far as the computer is concerned, it is storing and displaying the symbol 'a'. We don't notice anything because storage and display of the symbol effectively simulate storage and display of the letter. The distinction between meaningful object and formal object becomes slightly more salient, however, for other kinds of objects, such as words or sentences. A word like "word" is, to us, a meaningful object, something with a meaning in some language. To a computer, however, 'word' is just a collection of 'letters' surrounded by 'spaces' or 'hyphens'.[31] The computer defines the formal symbol syntactically, that is, in terms of other symbols. Its syntactic and our semantic definitions don't necessarily tally. To us "bbbcsgeds" and "PresidentReagan" are not "words," but to the computer, 'bbbcsgeds' and 'PresidentReagan' are 'words'. To us, "clear-cut" is two words; to the computer it is one.

Similar inaccuracies occur in the handling of other meaningful textual objects. The computer only understands the object as a formal or syntactic object, defined purely in formal terms. When the definitions break down, the simulation is imperfect. The syntactic definition of 'sentence', for instance, is a collection of 'words' terminated by a 'period' or 'colon' and two 'spaces'. So if we ask the program to count the number of "words" in a sentence containing "clear-cut," we will get the wrong answer: if the sentence containing "clear-cut" were this one, the colon would throw off the answer completely.

Notice that the inaccuracy of simulation introduces a certain, shall we say, suspicion into our dealings with a computer. We must always be ready to make up for the computer's failings. I have a command on my word processor: *Delete Sentence*. If I had applied that command to the previous sentence, it would only have deleted two words because my word processor defines 'colon' as something that ends 'sentences'. Thus, whenever I use that command, I have to be ready for the possibility that it will not be applied as I wish.

Or, let us move away from word processing for a minute. Imagine I am programming a computer to score an arithmetic test. The answer to a question like "2 + 2 =" is a meaningful object, one which has many formal counterparts—"4" is a correct answer, but so is "four," and, to some smart-alecks, "teatime." But the computer only accepts '4'. If I have the computer score the test, I must always wonder whether or not the computer has actually gotten it right.

To make up for these inaccuracies, somebody has to do some work. For the command *Delete Sentence*, I must check each time I use the command—not too difficult, really. With computer scoring, either the students must be taught to give answers with the correct formal shape (the usual strategy), or the teacher must check all the answers, or the simulation must be improved. Taking the usual strategy, though, does have a cost. Remember that, for pedagogical purposes, not all answers are equally wrong. The answer, "22," for instance, betrays a certain idea about the arithmetic process that should be discussed with the student. Disallowing those kinds of answers and responses loses certain opportunities for teaching.

Could we allow any answer, but then get the computer to find and evaluate the interesting incorrect responses? The short answer is "yes"; the long answer is "no." The computer defines a 'correct answer' as any symbol string that exactly matches a symbol string in the list of 'correct answers' given to it by the programmer. If we can anticipate every possible 'correct answer', and, by the same token, every possible 'interesting incorrect answer', then the computer can accurately simulate our response. The problem, then, is to construct the right lists.

Think what motley lists those for "2 + 2 =" would be. There would be 'four' and '4', of course, but also, perhaps, 'School's out', 'school's out', and 'schools out'. Such a list couldn't be constructed in a systematic manner. Instead, each item would be obtained by outguessing the students and added ad hoc according to the judgment of the teacher. A similar list for "11 + 11 =" could not be generated from the list for "2 + 2 =." The teacher would pretty much have to start the list fresh, again outguessing all those creative little minds.

In the computer trade, this kind of ad hoc fix has a name: *hack*. Hacks, as the name implies, take care of a problem by chopping at it until it goes away. The trouble with computer hacks is that, occasionally, they chop out the heart of the program. That's why, generally, hacking is not a good idea. It is the resort of a bad programmer who doesn't know why the problem occurs and doesn't have the time or patience to find it. Far, far preferable is an in-principle solution: a change in the structure of the program that genuinely adapts it to the problem at hand. An in-principle solution to evaluating the answers would be to generate the list of 'correct solutions' and 'interesting incorrect answers' in a systematic way.

One way of putting the thesis of this book is to say that any formal description of our way of treating meaning is simply a concatenation of hacks. Rule-governed manipulation of symbols (what computers do) has no natural relation to our meaning-governed manipulation of meaningful objects. An apparently successful hack (like the definition of 'word') breaks down in certain cases because meaning, and not any rule or collection of rules, defines what counts as a word. Where the hack breaks down, no in-principle fix is available. Either the repair must be left to the user, or an enormous number of complicated, weird, unrelated hacks must be applied, the application producing a scarcely perceptible improvement in quality at an enormous cost in computer time and memory.

Now, there are good hacks and bad hacks. Defining a sentence, for instance, as a string of words ended by a period or colon is not a particularly good hack. You can imagine a better one. You could, for instance, take each 'word' in a putative 'sentence' and determine its 'part of speech', using the computer's 'dictionary'. (This, too, wouldn't be entirely accurate, but if you added still more rules, for instance, that only adverbs, adjectives, and nouns can follow prepositions, you could improve the identification somewhat.) Then, you could test each potential sentence group for the presence of at least one free noun and verb. The tests would produce more accurate results but would still not be perfect. The situations where they failed would still have to be dealt with ad hoc. In fact, something very much like this hack is used in electronic typewriters that check 'grammar'. It's relatively inaccurate, but for its purposes the hack works. To improve the hack, however, is so costly in terms of computer time that, with one exception, to be described later, the improvement, though technically feasible for the last ten years, has not been implemented.

But are these hacks? This question gets us to the heart of the matter. "A sentence," one might say, "really is a collection of words with at least one free noun and verb. When a computer identifies a sentence with syntactic tests, it is doing exactly what we do. The tests, therefore, are not hacks." If this objection is right, I am wrong, and I have been wrong throughout this book. I have been arguing throughout that formal features simply don't define paragraphs or methods of writing papers or whatever. If they don't, then computer simulations must be hacks. If they do, then an accurate computer simulation —a nonhack—is possible.

This is, of course, exactly the subject of chapter 8. If a paragraph really is a collection of sentences that are about one subject, that include a topic sentence, and that have a pattern of development, then we understand them (we detect their coherence) on the basis of those formal features, and a computer program that detects or evaluates paragraphs on that basis can be built. If not, then computer analysis of paragraphs will always be a collection of hacks, as will formal theories.

Let me remind you once more of why the analysis would have to be a hack. Take the example of the sentence. When we parse a sentence, we do not do so by looking up the part of speech of each word in our internal dictionary. Rather, our understanding of the syntactic structure of the sentence comes out of our understanding of the meaning of the sentence. That meaning, as we have seen in chapters 2 and 3, is a matter of who is talking, the conversational situation, and the background and network of both parties. For a simulation to be a nonhack, it must find and utilize formal reductions of all these matters.

When a computer program cannot find formal reductions of all these matters, its responses, whether accurate or inaccurate, are fundamentally different from those of a human being. When we are responding to a piece of text, we are embedded in a human situation. In this piece of text, I am talking to you. You are reading my words. Your understanding and your response arise out of that situation. If you say, "Good job," you mean it (or you are lying). By contrast, a computer is only simulating, so when it says, "Good job," it is not responding to my text and is not bringing its understanding of the situation to the response. For the computer's simulated response to have a meaning, some human being must be responsible for it. Someone must check the computer or else structure the situation (as with the evaluations of the test) so that the computer's response is necessarily meaningful. This point is a subtle one, but it becomes clearer in other contexts. When, for instance, the computer tells you your account is overdrawn, you believe it because you know that human beings set up the program that looks at your account, but if you think there has been a mistake, you don't believe it until human beings have verified it.

One way of describing the suspicion mentioned earlier, then, is that the user isn't sure how the simulations of responses to meaning are being backed up. With the command, *Delete Sentence*, the backup must be performed by the user—it is up to the user to check whether the simulation worked. In other contexts, like the hack for checking sentences, the designer creating it is saying implicitly to the user, "For your purposes, this is good enough." And in other cases, as in the analysis of responses to the test, no one is backing it up, and as a result, there is a small degradation in the relationship between the two human beings actually involved.

Let me put these ideas in a series of steps.

1. Human beings manipulate meaningful objects; computers manipulate symbols.

2. Computers can simulate the manipulation of meaningful objects by manipulating symbols, but the more meaningful the object, the more onerous the simulation.

3. The simulation cannot be made perfect with ad hoc fixes called "hacks."

4. With a simulation, a human being must back up the computer's responses, which include making up for the inadequacies of the simulation. In analyzing the success or failure of a particular application, one must find the places where the inaccuracies are remedied.

5. As we shall see, some of the remedy may consist of denying the appropriateness or the importance of a human response to text. The formal simulation is taken to be "good enough," and the fundamental fact about human communication—that humans do it—is denied.

Invention Aids, Idea Processors, and the Writer's Workbench

One traditional account of the writing process describes four stages: invention, arrangement, production, and correction. Writing programs for each of the nonwriting stages have been developed. Invention aids are meant to help writers find something to say. Idea processors are meant to help writers outline (organize) what they have found. And the Writer's Workbench programs are meant to help them analyze and correct what they have said.

Invention Aids

In chapter 7, I was concerned with the way people plan and work through a paper. Invention aids were originally developed to get people (specifically students) to the point where they could begin planning. These aids are meant to be substitutive. They substitute for dialogues between teacher and student, where the teacher helps the student to find an idea and focus it. As a teacher, I have always felt that these conversations were remarkable for their banality. In each, the teacher apparently asks the identical questions: what are you interested in, what do you know about, tell me more. The dialogue thus seems a natural for computerization; put the questions on the machine, have the student respond there, and give the teacher more time for research.

Once developed, the programs seemed to have other applications. Finding an idea, focusing it, planning the paper, and working it through are not distinct, sequential steps; nor are students the only ones stymied by having nothing to say. So invention aids have been used even after a subject and treatment are found for purposes closer to those of rhetorical invention in order to develop an idea or to find a good way of presenting it. They have also been marketed commercially. In commercial applications, the aids have not usually been used to develop and focus ideas; rather, the assumption has been that there is a standard format for expressing the ideas, and the programs have been guiding them through the format.

Invention aids have always consisted of a series of questions. These questions are asked no matter what the answers, so they effectively embody a primitive formal theory of how people find and develop ideas for papers. A session with the aid might look like this (Burns 1979):

> * What is your name?
> S: Karl.
> * In one word, what is the subject of the paper you're planning?
> S: Dolphins.
> * Good, Karl, what do you want to say about Dolphins?
> S: Dolphins are beautiful.

> * OK, Karl, can you think of other things that are beautiful like
> Dolphins?
> S: My mother is beautiful.
> * How many different kinds of Dolphins are there?

There is nothing conceptually new about this. The questions themselves are drawn from the rhetorical topics, which were described by Aristotle. They could be presented equally well on a piece of paper. Having the computer present them offers only two, slight advantages. First, the questions can be posed sequentially, so the student can't read ahead. Second, the answers are put onto the computer, so they are available for word-processing or mail.[32]

There is, however, a fundamental difference between having the teacher present the questions and having a computer or a piece of paper do it. The teacher is, in fact, responding to the student's answers, evaluating their meaning and presenting the next question on the basis of that evaluation. Even if the teacher asks the identical questions, the student knows that the questions are meaningful and that the teacher has judged to ask this question rather than another. In fact, of course, the questions are rarely identical. The teacher helps the student control the material generated by wording the questions in the correct way and zeroing in on the interesting answers.

For the computerized questions to be meaningful in the same way, they would have to embody a formal theory of how people find and develop ideas that has been tested and found adequate by the people who made the question sequence. The primitive questions shown previously are obviously not adequate. Such a sequence would have to pose questions that were responsive to the student—that would help the student zero in—no matter what the answers were. Here is one attempt at such a sequence. This time, a failure is shown:

> * What is your name?
> S: Karl.
> * In one word, what is the subject of your paper?
> S: Dolphins.
> * Now, use that word in a sentence, which expresses the main
> idea of your paper.
> S: Dolphins are large mammals, which live in the sea.
> * Good, Karl, now give me a reason for believing what you just
> said.[33]

The theory is based partly on the format that the idea will be plugged into, the standard thesis-and-three-supporting-reasons structure. Unfortunately, these answers don't work. Karl doesn't know what a decent theme or, presumably, decent support is, so he'll have a banal or uncontroversial thesis and arguments that are beside the point. If he already knew how to write papers in this format, the answers would work out reasonably well. But in that case it isn't the questions doing the work—it is the student.

This problem illustrates a dynamic we will encounter again and again. The ignorant user of the program can't really be helped by it. The knowledgeable user doesn't need it.

Perhaps, though, a better set of open-ended questions can be found. One kind of structure, which I am drawing loosely from Stephen Marcus might be the following. (The questions are asked after the one-word statement of topic.)

* In what ways are Dolphins and bread boxes the same?
S: They're both sleek and shiny.
* In what ways are Dolphins and forest fires alike?
S: They both go very fast through their natural element.

The theory here is that the writer needs to be jogged into thinking of interesting relationships among the ideas and that the focusing will be done automatically in the answers or else at a later step. Marcus developed these questions to help students write poems, and for this purpose, the technique seems vaguely plausible. But as we saw in chapters 6 and 7, what is really crucial in the development of a paper is finding the internal relationships among ideas, and something like this might well be a distraction.

Obviously, before these programs could satisfy the purposes for which they were developed, they would somehow have to be responsive to the meaning of the answers. Is this impossible, given that computers are formal systems? I have asserted that it is, but let us now put the assertion to the test by seeing what would happen if we tried some hacks.

Perhaps we could perform a formal analysis of the subject chosen and select questions according to the results of the analysis. We might, for instance, take each 'concrete noun' and match it to an appropriate 'abstract noun'. Dolphins, for instance, are species of animals. So when we see 'dolphins' in a subject line, we see that it lies in the category, 'animal species', and we structure the question accordingly:

* What an interesting subject! Where do Dolphins live?
S: In the ocean.

> * And how big are they?
> S: A lot bigger than I am.

Or, we could put it in the class of unusual or specialized subjects and create a sequence like the following:

> * What do you know about Dolphins that your five-year-old sister doesn't know?
> S: Dolphins are large mammals that live in the sea.
> * Good, S, why don't you use that as a topic sentence.
> * Now, tell me, does your five-year-old sister know what a mammal is?
> S: No.
> * Then you should explain that.
>
> (And so forth . . . .)

Unfortunately, these don't solve the meaning problem because they don't solve the problem in general terms. I've set up the first question sequence so that it works for the subject 'dolphins'. But for other 'animal species', it doesn't. What if "cells" were on the subject line? Questions about where they live or how big they are get quite complex. If "whippets" were the subject line, the answers wouldn't be complex, but they wouldn't be interesting either. And if "unicorns" were the subject, the sequence might be plausible, but something important would be left out. The second sequence depends yet more on a response to meaning. It must know, for instance, that the first response is largely correct and that "mammal" might not be recognized by the five-year-old sister.

Classifying the responses and then matching question structures to the classifications works in some situations but doesn't in others. The amount of work, however, that creates an even semi-plausible aid that works along these lines is staggering. Can you imagine categorizing every word in the English language? The preceding dialogue, unsatisfactory as it is, is mere science fiction.

If invention aids are used, who compensates for the deficiencies? The students do. They compensate by wasting their time. The more skillful students waste time generating answers to foolish questions, and they waste more time sorting through the answers and throwing them out again. The less knowledgeable or less accomplished students also compensate by suffering from the delusion that the idea of writing a paper is to generate material rather than saying something that needs to be said. The teacher does end up compensating some, either by helping the student sort through the material or dealing with undigested compilations. There is one further cost.

Using such programs requires that students constantly evade, misunderstand, or ignore the meanings of the questions the computer asks. Later on, the teacher will have to unteach what was unwittingly taught.

Idea Processors

"Idea processors" are computer programs that make the mechanics of outlining easier. Outlining with pencil and paper, we only have room to make the branches in the tree go three or four levels deep, and when we wish to emend or move items, the marks that are already there get in the way. Outlining with a word processor, we can keep our copy clean, but we still can't go very deep. Indentation on word processors, moreover, is often a little tricky, and changing indentation levels or moving blocks is usually clumsy, particularly since, in the latter case, all the labels must be updated. "Idea processors" get around all these problems. A user can move, reorder, zoom in on, renumber, expand upon, or delete entries with a push of a button.

For writing down an outline, an idea processor has some marginal advantage over pencil and paper though, as you will see, even that is limited. But the use pictured by its creators is not actually for outlining, but for working through a paper. Their picture is that a preliminary outline will be written down, and then the paper will be created as the entries are reordered, relabeled, shuffled, hidden, or expanded upon. Notice, of course, that the computer does no manipulation on the basis of the meaning of the entries; that is left up to the user. But most imaginable, nonmeaningful manipulations are possible.

The theory of this use (again, a formal one) is that the writing process works by setting out and developing ideas in hierarchies. It is one version of what I was once told by a seventh-grade teacher— that the way to write papers is to write the outline and then to gradually fill in the outline with entries and subentries. Neil Larson, the developer of an idea processor named MaxThink, recognizes that this simple procedure doesn't usually work, but he thinks that a more complicated version does.

Larson and the many other commercial manufacturers of such programs are not bashful about this theory.[34] Indeed, the extent of their claims is implicit in the name *idea* processors. Taking their inspiration from a branch of artificial intelligence that is committed to the idea that thinking is symbol-processing, they believe that manipulating symbols according to their form (for example, their position in the hierarchy) is manipulating ideas.[35]

Larson, for instance, claims that his idea or "thought processor" is a "radical departure" from other computer writing aids because it can "interact directly with higher-level thinking skills" and thus "improve the productivity of your thoughts" (P: 1–3). The thought-processing commands "expand your writing and thinking abilities," and "improve your insight, perception, imagination, and creative thinking" (P: 2). The programs are, in short, "mind-expanding software" (M: 3).[36]

This is quite a different claim from the one about outlines examined in chapter 7. The idea is not that the entries in an outline help you plan; it is that moving the entries around "improves the productivity of your thoughts." Still, a few parts of our discussion from chapter 7 are relevant here. An outline, remember, is an attempt at establishing a route through material. Entries are signposts at important turns. The writer follows the route by writing the paper; the signposts emerge at the proper time. The value (meaning) of these signposts is determined by the meaning of the entry itself, its relative position along the route ("before this . . . after that"), and its importance in the hierarchy.

An idea processor makes it easier to change the latter two, and it also permits, as I have said, greater articulation of the path. In theory, one can set out a signpost, and then set out mini-, mini-mini-, and mini-mini-minisignposts, which define the exact route between the posts at a higher level. One cannot, unfortunately, see all the signposts at once. Usually an idea processor shows only two adjacent levels; to see other levels, one must "zoom" in or out. (This limitation is where the program might be inferior to paper.) But according to the theory, this is not important. The lower-level chunks are implicitly part of the higher-level ones, so working out a paper can consist only of articulating chunks and then moving the chunks around.

We have seen, however, that the really important thing about an outline entry is not the detail it provides but its luminosity. We have seen, too, that the representational techniques used in outlines (creation of a hierarchy) only contribute to the luminosity in certain special circumstances, when the relationships among items are well known and when, therefore, significant amounts of manipulation are not going to be necessary. Thus, it seems unlikely that shuffling entries around is going to help, and it may hurt.

To put it another way, the basic assumption of all idea processors is that the meaning (luminosity) of an outline entry does not shift when its position is shifted. But clearly the meaning of an item in a list is not stable. It depends on the other items in the list, the reason the item appeared, facts about the item that are known to be relevant, the purposes of the author, and so on and so forth. It depends on the context, on the background and network that were in the horizon when the item was placed there. Shift the context, and one shifts the background and network, and thus the meaning.

This simple fact has a simple consequence: to use the programs effectively, you have to be constantly updating the lists. Since the meaning of items changes whenever you move them around, whenever you change your purposes, and so on, you can't change the lists with any precision by using the program's commands alone. Whenever you use a program command, you also have to adjust three things: (1) your idea of what the item means, (2) your idea of what other items mean, and (3) the representation.

Some examples will help. I am in the habit of making lists of things to do. When I first got MaxThink, I thought I could make my life much simpler by putting all these lists together. Say I had a list of things to do such as the following:

Things To Do This Week
A. Work on Idea Processing Paper
B. Buy groceries
C. Do laundry
D. Write letter to A.
E. Grade papers for Technical Writing Class

I now want to move elements of this list to a new list, "Things to Do Today." If I use only the program commands, the best I can get easily is the following:

Things To Do Today
A. Work on Idea Processing Paper
B. Buy groceries
C. Grade papers for Technical Writing Class

But what I want is something like the following:

Things To Do Today
Develop Second Section more fully
Buy cucumbers
Grade 3 (?) papers

This is, I admit, a simpleminded point, and in this form, it doesn't seem to be too serious an objection. I can, after all, change the new list or else remember that, in the new list, the meaning of, for example, "buy groceries" is now different.

The trouble is that, if I'm doing any complicated list processing, it's not easy to do either of these things. For a big list, updating is a tremendous chore. Yet failing to update requires that I remember the new (or old, depending) meanings, and I, at least, have a very hard time doing that.

Not that updating is required only when I move an item. Even changing the surrounding context changes the meaning. Consider the following three-item list. Consider what happens to the meaning of the first two items when I change the third:

> Lions
> Tigers
> Wolves

This looks like a list of Asian carnivores. Now, subtract the last item and add a different one:

> Lions
> Tigers
> Pistons

This is a list of Detroit's professional sports teams. Now, make another switch:

> Lions
> Tigers
> Bears

Oh, my! Even changing the title can make a huge difference. If I were to take the first list and call it "Large North American Carnivores," "lion" would now mean "mountain lion," and there would suddenly be the distinct but implicit suggestion that all the animals were in the same ecosystem.

Now, in a sense, this is a feature, not a bug. When entries change meaning, you may get new ideas, new associations, new relationships. This is, in fact, one reason why Larson claims it helps generate ideas. But in the overall scheme of things these idea-generating abilities are relatively unimportant, just as Stephen Marcus's comparison-eliciting questions were. When these abilities are used, moreover, then the organizations of the Background and network that had been established are frequently lost, and this loss, necessarily, is invisible.

We've seen that the best planning environments are those that permit us to be creative, that allow us to roam as much as possible through the territory we're exploring. MaxThink, with only two levels visible at any one time and with virtually no visual capabilities, is scarcely a rich planning environment. (The newest version of ThinkTank on the Mac is better, but not much.) Paper and pencil outlines, by contrast, are much richer. True, it's hard to move things and change the labels. But updating is much more purposive and much clearer because, while you're doing it, all the relevant information is visible. And with paper and pencil, moreover, you can move to less rigid kinds of environments more easily. You can underline, draw arrows, circle, shade, highlight, cross-out, and the like. The delicate adjustments that these create can't be made with an idea processor.

As an environment for working through, the idea processor is even worse. What is kept through the manipulations are, as I've said, the hierarchical entries and the literal text. For working through, these are not usually luminous. To put it another way, the idea that you write by filling out elements in a hierarchy is just wrong phenomenologically. At a certain level, the entries would actually interfere with thinking, for the same reason that sentence outlines do.

I used MaxThink. When I did, I constantly wanted to reach into the computer and drag out some idea that I couldn't even find. I wanted to have all the ideas around me, the way I lay out note cards on a desk. I managed, despite the urges, but it was like walking uphill backwards. Other people do not have such big problems. Indeed, I know people who swear by the program, not at it. But again, let me say the fact that someone uses a program doesn't mean that the program is useful. All it means is that they've found ways around the program's inconveniences.

Notice how different these programs would be if people like Larson were not committed to the idea that list processing is thinking. These people might, then, have freer ideas about what goes on when you write and be able to build environments that provide tools for writers, not substitutes for writers' tasks. The technical capacities of computers could enable us to build good planning tools. I have seen systems with very large screens and multiple windows, with the ability to create numerous icons (screens to be saved for later use), with the ability to draw on the screen, with the ability to find text anywhere in the system and grab it immediately.[37] Combinations of these abilities might really extend one's ability to plan because the tools would be genuinely richer than paper and pencil. Interestingly, these systems were designed for LISP programmers who feel they need to program flexibly. In developing these tools, the programmers didn't think abstractly about the tasks they thought a computer could substitute for; they built what they needed. If only writers could do the same thing for themselves. But as long as programmers are building them for writers and are thinking of writing as list processing, idea processors will be the result.

Text Analyzers

Invention programs and idea processors take the user from no text to some (disordered) text. Text analyzers take the finally completed text and pull it apart. All of us are familiar with one such analyzer, the 'spell checker'. (The invidious marks around the term are meant to remind you that it doesn't actually check spelling. On the assumption that one reminder is enough, I'll drop them from now on.) Other text analyzers evaluate the style of a text, point out errors in word usage, find doubled words, and so on. Of these, the most notorious are STYLE and DICTION, two of the so-called Writer's Workbench programs distributed by AT&T.

These are all substitutive tools; they check spelling, diction, and so forth for you. The problem with them is that meaning determines, for example, whether words are spelled correctly, and since these programs cannot respond to meaning, they are inaccurate. The inaccuracies mean either that the user must accept imperfect analysis, or that the user must check it, effectively redoing the work. So the programs don't actually substitute; they either replace a superior analysis with an inferior one or they require that the work be done over again. All of these tools could be significantly better if they didn't attempt to substitute but did try to extend the writer's abilities.

For the sake of simplicity, I will spend most of my time on spelling checkers. These programs go through a text and compare each 'word' to a list of 'words' in their 'dictionary'. If a word in the text doesn't match any of the words in the 'dictionary', it is put in a list of 'misspelled words'. Note the marks around the words; 'misspelled' is syntactically defined. In this case, though, that doesn't seem so serious. Correct spelling is, after all, apparently defined syntactically; a correct spelling is one that has the correct symbols in the correct order.

In fact, however, correct spelling is defined semantically. The syntactic definition of a spelling checker breaks down in at least five areas.

1. 'Misspelled' words witch (for example) happen to look like other words in the 'dictionary' will not be 'misspelled'.

2. When the standards for correct spelling vary, 'misspellings' can in fact be correct. Aeronautical engineers prefer 'gage' to 'gauge'. My spelling checker prefers 'gauge'.

3. Nonstandard notations, like "d-o-l-p-h-i-n-s" will be 'misspelled', but not misspelled.

4. Unusual words not in the 'dictionary' will be 'misspelled'. So will made-up words, technical words, proper nouns, and foreign words.

5. Permissible suffixes, prefixes, and combinations of words are defined conventionally, so legitimate constructs will be 'misspelled' and illegitimate ones will be missed.

I ran a well-known spelling checker on an earlier version of this chapter up to this point, and the following is part of the output. (Formatting commands and index codes, which increase the length of the output, while decreasing utility, have been quietly removed.)

Aha	backhoe	bbbcsgeds	Carnivores
commerical	e.g	emend	Fodor
Gerrard	MaxThink	PresidentReagan	rote
Solip	teatime	ThinkTank	WANDAH

Now this isn't bad. There were 4,000 words, and only 16-odd errors. The error ratio, the chance that a correct word will be identified correctly, is about 99.6 percent. Still, the garbage ratio, the percentage of mistaken entries in the output, is very high.

Even if it were low, the fact that it is nonzero does mean that the user has to make up for the errors, this time by picking through the garbage. The user has to look at each 'misspelled word' and decide whether it's a misspelling. This is easy enough, but a few problem words emerge: Is "teatime" one word or two? Why does "e.g" lack a period after it? Is "backhoe" a word?

All these questions are decidable, in principle. I can look them up in the dictionary, but usually I don't; it takes too much time. Instead, I look at the word, decide whether it falls into one of the classes of errors listed above, and if it does, I ignore it (or add it to the dictionary). With this procedure, of course, all I can ever catch are inadvertent errors. With a genuine misspelling, I will persist in my belief about the spelling of the word, and I will assume that the error is the computer's, not mine. I will find "commerical," that is, but I won't be helped to the right spelling of "teatime" (which is spelled "teatime," "tea time," or "tea-time," depending on the dictionary you consult).

I am, mind you, a good speller. This means first that the list is relatively short, second that my checking of the checker is reasonably likely to be good, and third that the program won't be very useful to me. The garbage ratio is so high that I don't want to waste time running through the program and poking through the output, especially when I will catch most of the typos in proofreading. But what about the bad speller? Where the garbage ratio is lower, is the program more useful?

The voice of the people has spoken on this subject: "Yes, it is useful." But just how useful remains an empirical question. Bad spellers, too, have to make up for the program's deficiencies by picking through the garbage. Bad spellers, moreover, take more time to pick through it, partly because there's much more and partly because they are far less able to make correct decisions on the fly than I am. Bad spellers also have many more problem words. My problem words are "backhoe," "e.g," and "teatime"; the bad spellers might also include "emend," "Aha," and "Gerrard." This is not to mention the problem words they fail to notice.

The usefulness of such programs to bad spellers largely depends on how they deal with the problem words. If they look them up, well and good. If they don't, they have a number of choices, all of which are bad: they can do what I do, in which case they are wasting time; or they can make a guess, which is scarcely productive; or they can figure that, if the word appears on the list, it must be a mistake, and they can change the word. This last choice is genuinely pernicious. If they make it frequently, actually using the speller will reduce the size of their vocabulary.

If the discarded problem words were always misspelled, at least the bad spellers would only be losing words they were unsure of anyway. But many problem words are correctly spelled; they appear only because the computer doesn't recognize them. So bad spellers run the risk of losing words they already know. They can obviate that risk only if they display great strength of will, stubbornly knowing what they know, ignoring the appearance of "rote," for instance, on the list of 'mispelled words'.

How willing are people to use these programs correctly? In my (limited) experience, people are not willing. In two years of working with students in the MIT computer rooms, I have never even seen any dictionary besides mine in the room; I have often seen students use spelling checkers; and I have often seen them change words rather than go through the effort of finding the correct spelling.

I have noticed one other problem with spelling checkers, a problem for me and a problem for the students. In a peculiar way, they are a distraction. Waiting for the occasionally very slow checker to finish, poking through the garbage, and figuring out which errors are the computer's can be forms of procrastination. Worse, when I'm feeling particularly lazy, I use the spelling checker as an excuse for not proofreading. I figure that I've reduced the number of errors, and thus there is less reason to have to go back. As far as I can tell, the students feel that way, too.

Still, I am in the minority. For most people, the benefits outweigh the costs. Notice, though, that this balance would shift markedly if either of two things happened. If there were no inadvertent errors, like "commerical," then a significant benefit would be lost. And if the problem words were more difficult to deal with, that is, if what counted as an error were less clear-cut or if there were no final authority, like a dictionary, then the difficulty of dealing with the problem words would be much, much greater.

Unfortunately, with other text analysis programs, the balance does shift. Take, for example, DICTION, the Writer's Workbench program. The errors caught by DICTION are due to ignorance, not oversight. To make up for those errors, users must have a knowledge that they have demonstrated they do not have. The users have, moreover, no readily available authority that can help them make up for this ignorance.

DICTION works in just the same way a spelling checker does. Instead of a dictionary, however, the program has a list of 'words frequently misused'. If a 'word' or group of 'words' in the text matches one on the list, the word and its context are outputted to the screen. I ran DICTION on an earlier draft of the text. Here is the first part of the output. The repetitive catches are eliminated.

> If the list of formal features were complete, the job would be boring and mechanical, *[rather]* like checking for missing commas.

> Any computer program *[which]* tests paragraphs for formal features , *[in fact,]* any program *[which]* tests any text for any formal features, is testing a formal theory.

> This limitation, not surprisingly, is the same limitation as that on theoretical analysis of writing: formal analysis of *[meaningful]* text produces inaccurate results.

This *[very]* long chapter is organized as follows.

The detail is required because each type of application performs its own *[kind of]* formal analysis, and thus each type fails in a different way.

One can use a sledgehammer as a tool for hitting golf balls, *[but that]* does not mean a sledgehammer is an effective golf-ball hitter.

What exactly is meant by the term is a *[very]* difficult philosophical problem, as Fodor *[indicate]*s.

If I have the computer score the test, I must always wonder whether the computer has *[actual]*ly gotten it right.

If we can *[anticipate]* every possible 'correct answer', and, by the same token, every possible 'interesting incorrect answer', then the computer can accurately simulate our response.

number of sentences 498 number of phrases found 99

Hmm, I'm not doing very well. One-fifth of my sentences contain 'diction errors'. Why so many? A companion program called EXPLAIN makes recommendations. According to EXPLAIN, I should use "suggest" for "indicate," "that" for "but that," "rather" for "kind of," "?" for "rather," "expect" for "anticipate," and nothing at all for "very." Hmmm. Garbage—*[rather]* like telling me that "Fodor" is misspelled. But wait a minute. I see an error. I'm being too arcane when I say it's a golf-ball hitter. It should be golf club. All right, I'll change that. (Or *[rather]*, I won't, so as to preserve the example, as I did with "teatime.") What about the rest? All garbage.

If I know what I'm doing, I don't need the program. The garbage ratio is even higher than that of the speller, and there are virtually no inadvertent errors to catch. What if I don't know what I'm doing? If all the garbage were clear-cut garbage (peculiar metaphor!), the program might alert users to their errors. Unfortunately, for people whose strength of will about language is weaker than mine, many of the catches pose problems. Some people do not know the difference between "expect" and "anticipate."

The problem catches are like the problem words in the list of 'misspelled words'. The user can try to resolve the problem, can ignore it, or can take the computer's word for it. The first is good, the second is a waste of time, and the third is pernicious. Unfortunately, the first is much, much harder to do than it is for spelling checkers. Remember that we, at least, know why some of these words appear on the list. Less *[sophisticated]* users do not. They, for instance, look at the word "sophisticated," do not know it is an overused intensive, and immediately doubt themselves.[38]

How are users likely to *[deal with]* the *[situation]*? There are a *[number of]* possibilities. *[They]* can turn to the dictionary but it won't help them.[39] They can turn to a handbook, if they know such things exist. (Never having seen a dictionary in the MIT computer rooms, I certainly have never seen a writing handbook.) And as we all know, without some experience or training, handbooks are not that easy to use. Or, like bad spellers, they can change the words. Does this happen? Lorinda Cherry, the author of the program, in the original documentation for DICTION, says that, in its first release, between 50 and 75 percent of the recommended corrections were *[actually]* made . . . . 50 and 75 percent. Try an experiment. Show your students the preceding output and ask them to correct the sentences that need correcting. See what happens when an inexperienced person is alerted to the possibility of an error.

Admittedly, certain mistakes that DICTION catches are very likely to be mistakes themselves. Unless I write, "Oh, the might of her", 'might of' is likely to be a mistake. Maybe, in that case, it is good to alert the user to the need for change.[40] Maybe. But even in that case, the user is simply taking the computer's word for it. In a sense, that distracts the user from the error itself. Wouldn't it be better to explain the error, to say why it comes up, to show the alternatives? But only a human can do that.

The program distracts in other, more serious ways. For one thing, it brings the errors it identifies into undue prominence. How important, after all, is "construct" versus "build"? Yet when the program flags either word, other potential errors are scanted. Remember, the program doesn't exist because texts cry out for it; it exists only because it is relatively easy to create.

To see what I mean, consider what happened to me as I wrote this chapter. Because I revise frequently, I had to use DICTION many, many times, and I had to look very carefully at the sentences flagged by the DICTION program. I discovered that I often found errors in the sentences DICTION flagged. Of course, not once were those the same errors that DICTION flagged; instead, they were infelicities, repetitions, or inaccuracies that were brought to my attention because the sentences were isolated from the context. Look at the implications of this. A program that flagged sentences randomly might well produce more and better corrections than the DICTION program.[41]

The worst distraction, though, is that the program gives the user the wrong idea about error itself. There is general agreement about spelling errors; however, there's no similar agreement about diction errors. It is never a good idea to spell "which" as "witch," but it can often be a good idea to use "which" instead of "that." The very existence of the program masks this fact. Who is likely to be fooled by this mask? The same user who is likely to use "kind of" rather than "rather."[42]

All these problems, of course, would be obviated if only the real diction errors were caught, but they could only be caught if the computer responded to the meaning, not the form. Since the computer can't, the user must compensate. The forms of compensation are, as we have seen, *[quite]* subtle. First, one must fight off panic, as one discovers that one-third of the sentences have errors. Then, one must fight off the urge to change because the computer said so. Then, one must remember that the sentences probably have other, more important errors. And finally, one must decide that no matter what the computer, that is, Lorinda Cherry, says, correct diction is that *[which]* communicates. Failure to compensate means either a degradation of the product or a degradation of the user.

One way of thinking about the problem DICTION poses is to say that too much has been concluded about usage errors on flimsy statistical evidence. Usage errors are identified as such even when the probabilities that they are may be abysmally low. One way of getting around this problem is to give statistics without making any strong suggestions about what they mean. This approach is taken by the Bell Labs' STYLE program.

The STYLE program calculates statistics about style by attaching syntactic labels like 'noun' and 'verb' to each word. It then counts the occurrences of each kind of 'word', occurrences of free and clausal noun-verb sequences, and so on and so forth. Accuracy is not great, but the output, as you'll see, doesn't require accuracy.[43] The following output was obtained at the same time that the DICTION program was run:

    readability grades:
        (Kincaid) 8.6 (auto) 8.6 (Coleman-Liau) 9.6
            (Flesch) 8.7 (62.5) sentence info:
        no. sent 468 no. wds 7677
        av sent leng 16.4 av word leng 4.62
        no. questions 30 no. imperatives 3
        no. nonfunc wds 4307 56.1% av leng 6.02
        short sent (<11) 29% (135) long sent (>26) 10% (47)

> longest sent 75 wds at sent 325; shortest sent 3 wds
>   at sent 409
> sentence types:
>   simple 46% (215) complex 37% (174)
>   compound 9% (40) compound-complex 8% (39)
> word usage:
>   verb types as % of total verbs
>   tobe 39% (363) aux 24% (220) inf 10% (97)
>   passives as % of non-inf verbs 11% (92)
>   types as % of total
>   prep 9.0% (690) conj 3.1% (241) adv 6.8% (524)
>   noun 26.7% (2046) adj 13.4% (1031) pron 7.2% (555)
>   nominalizations 2% (150)
> sentence beginnings:
>   subject opener: noun (111) pron (62) pos (5) adj (39)
>   art (75) tot 62%
>   prep 9% (43) adv 9% (40)
>   verb 2% (9) sub-conj 10% (49) conj 7% (31)
>   expletives 1% (4)

This output, too, is founded on a primitive formal theory. Here the idea is that there is some correlation between syntactic facts about prose and the ability of prose to communicate meaning. If this theory had any merit whatsoever, it ought to be able to answer consistently any of the following questions, questions which a normal user would normally have. Given my purpose, audience, and style, should I increase or decrease the percentage of nominal sentence openers? Is my passive count too high or too low? My "to be" verb count? If these counts are out of line, what should I do about it? How much variation in the figures is significant? The Flesch score (Is 8.7 good or bad?) varies by as much as a grade level from draft to draft; does that mean that I'm changing my style each time?[44]

To answer these questions, one would need an extraordinarily fine-tuned idea of the relationship of statistical information to the quality of texts, adjusted, of course, for purpose, audience, and style. Not many of us are so blessed. Some versions of the program do offer a listing of "normal" ranges (compiled from Bell Labs technical documents!), but using that listing to detect errors is like cutting diamonds with a backhoe. Notice, too, that if you did have a finely tuned statistical sense, so that a difference of 1 in the Flesch score was important to you, then the program's inaccuracy would be a great problem.

The makers of the program would argue that the figures do tell a less *[sophisticated]* user something. Writers whose Flesch readability score is 15.0 (the authors of the Federalist Papers, say Cherry and Vesterman 1980, 9) or those whose average sentence length is 38.4 need to be told that their figures fall well out of normal bounds. But even here, the output is not useful. I agree that many such people need help. But they won't be helped in any fundamental way by being told to put in a bunch of periods. A sentence length of 38.4 is a symptom, not a disease, and you won't cure the disease by treating the symptom. To treat the disease, the syntactic statistics must be made meaningful in terms of the content; hapless writers have to shorten the right sentences. But in order to tell them which sentences, the program would have to be able to respond to meaning.

The objections to STYLE, then, are the same as those to DICTION. The user must compensate for the program's inability to understand meaning by interpreting the output before using the program. This output is extraordinarily difficult to interpret. Only a few people can do so, and they certainly don't need it; the people who can't shouldn't use the program. Like DICTION, STYLE could be taught, and then its use would improve. But if STYLE can be taught, so, too, can style, and time is better spent teaching the latter. STYLE, like DICTION, is a distraction.

The techniques used in STYLE and DICTION could, of course, be turned to the service of writers, but again, a different conception would be required. If the writer knows that certain usages prove personally difficult, then the writer could list those usages, and a program called MYDICTION could look for them. Similarly, if a writer is aware of certain, potentially troublesome linguistic patterns, a program called MYSTYLE could look for those. Or, if the writer has questions that are for some reason personally meaningful (for example, "How many paragraphs with more than 6 sentences and 200 words do I have?"), a STYLE program with a different interface could answer them. The picture here would be of a reasonably knowledgeable self-conscious writer (or writer and editor or student and teacher) who has questions that arise from a particular piece of prose. The picture with STYLE and DICTION is that there are standards, that the writer doesn't know them, and that the programs can be made to apply them.

One last note about existing text analysis programs. Studious application of a spelling checker (or DICTION or whatever) may really reduce the incidence of certain kinds of errors. At the same time, the existence of these programs lessens the importance of those errors.

A spelling error now is no longer a sign of the author's incompetence, but a sign of forgetfulness or of the inadequacy of the spelling checker. At the same time, the existence of text editors introduces a whole new class of errors that are, in some senses, more important. In some texts, for instance, you may well find that entire words are missing or that an entirely extraneous word has been inserted. Such errors are also signs of the way the author treats the text and thus the audience, and as more people use computers and read prose generated on computers, their significance will be more widely appreciated. Computer writing aids have given us weak ways of rectifying old errors, but they have yet to give us any way of correcting the new kinds of errors that computers have allowed us to make.

Overcoming the Limitations I:
Technical Solutions

Each kind of computer writing aid falls down because its purely syntactic theory of the task it is meant to replace is simply inaccurate. The aids can only simulate, not substitute for, the response to meaning that the task of editing requires. The aid therefore makes errors, and the user must compensate for the errors (or even the possibility that an error has been made). The extra effort (in the case of invention aids), lost flexibility (idea processors), or extra analysis step (text analyzers) is a distraction, is potentially dangerous to the naive user, and is usually not worth the effort. But, what would happen if the programs were improved? If the simulations of a response to meaning were more effective, the required compensation would be less, and the utility more.

Of course, as long as the simulation is even slightly imperfect, compensation is required, and it is having to compensate at all which is burdensome. It does seem, however, that in some cases I might be wrong. Spelling checkers are useful, even though compensation is required. What, then, about other forms of analysis? If they were very accurate, might they become useful?

Clearly, the kind of program most open to improvement is the text analysis program. Such programs work by looking up 'words' in lists. Computers are very good at list processing. Perhaps, by multiplying lists and being clever about the look-up procedures, accuracy could be improved greatly. STYLE, for instance, is not very accurate, partly because it does not actually look up the parts of speech of the words.[45] Perhaps compiling lists of parts of speech and lists of parts of speech sequences and lists of rules about the parts of speech sequences would give us a better parser.

With a better parser, not only would the STYLE and DICTION programs be improved, we might even begin to have a semiaccurate grammar checker, one that could tell us about subject-verb disagreements, errors in tense, and so on. With such a parser, moreover, better invention aids and outlining aids would also be possible. Without such a parser, a really accurate parser, mind you, little real improvement seems possible.

How difficult, then, would it be to *[construct]* a really accurate parser? Remember, this is the same question I started the book with: How easy is it to construct a formal analysis of writing? So, you know the answer; it's impossible, unless you can program in the background and knowledge of the speakers. The interesting thing about this form of the question is that considering it naively allows us to appreciate anew how deeply the Background affects our understanding of sentences.[46]

Building a parser is a big problem; why don't we cut it up? A part of the problem is the problem of parsing prepositional phrases. Part of that problem is the problem of parsing potentially ambiguous prepositional phrases, like those beginning with "in." And part of that problem is the problem of parsing a certain class of sentences, such as the following:

1. The car hit the man in the street.

In this sentence, "in the street" can identify either the man or the location of the accident. For simplicity's sake, let us assume that most English speakers automatically parse the phrase as identifying the location of the accident. I would like to look at what we would have to do in order to get the computer to do the same thing. (This problem, you'll notice, is intimately related to the problem of building good invention aids. In order to ask a question appropriate to the sentence given, the invention program must be able to parse the sentence and classify the event. After the sentence, for instance, the program must be able to ask, "Why did it hit the man there?" and not, "Why did it hit that man?") Remember, though, that our method must also allow the computer to parse similar sentences, like the following; otherwise, it's a hack.

2. The car hit the man in the side.
3. The car hit the man in the tree.
4. The car hit the man in the park.
5. The car hit the man in the play.

Our problem is to find syntactic labels (classifications) for the words in the sentence that correspond to the grammatical structure of the sentence. These labels must somehow have the same effect on the 'parsing' that the meaning of the word has on our parsing. The obvious way to do this is to start classifying the meanings of the words; each classification is a syntactic label.

Obviously, the classification should be partially motivated by what we want to do. We would like, somehow, to distinguish two different senses (formal senses) of the word "in" and have one identify the man and the other identify the location of the hitting. As a first cut, why don't we try classifying the nouns according to whether they define a location in physical space or some other kind of location. (Nonlocation nouns, for example, "The car hit the man in the noun," would just be spit out.) As legitimate classifications, we might have location in space (park, street, tree), location in the body (side), or location in an activity (play). All right, it's not perfect, but it's a start. With the classification in place, when the computer encounters a prepositional phrase beginning with 'in', it would find the noun and see what kind of location it defines. 'Nouns' which were not locations would generate a query.

'Nouns' which did define a location would then be matched with the nouns in the sentence. If it matched the subject, then it would be an adverbial phrase; if it matched the object, an adjectival. These 'matches' would be contained in another list. If the list of 'matches' were constructed correctly, then 'play' would match 'man', 'street', 'car'.

The problem, of course, is generality. We can construct a system like this that works for this sentence and these nouns, although it takes a while to do so. But we want to do something more. And already we are running into problems. "Tree," "park," and "side" match either "car" or "man." (Try it out; switch "man" and "car" in the sample sentences.) Indeed, it seems intuitively clear that we can't just use nouns; what the phrase modifies is not an artifact of nouns but of noun-verb conjunctions.

So now let us try to match noun-verb conjunctions ('events') to the objects of the preposition. The idea would be to put "car-hit-man" in a 'traffic accident' category. Since accidents occur in streets and not in parks or trees, with a little more fiddling we can work out that 'park' and 'tree' go with 'man'.[47] Notice, though, that we have to start over again and rethink all our original pairings; so the work we've done up to this point has been wasted.

And the amount of work required to compile a list of 'events' would be staggeringly large. The list would have to be so finely grained that it would distinguish among "The car hit," "The boy hit," "The car passed," and "The boy passed," since each of those produces a quite different analysis when coupled with the original five prepositional phrases. We now get the right answer for "park" and "tree." But we have some new problems with the words that had seemed easy. If we have put "car-hit-man" in a traffic accident category, "boy-hit-man" in a fight category, and "car-passed-man" in a traffic category, then we have to rethink the match between "car" and "street," and with the fight category, we have to rethink the 'play' match.

Indeed, it seems as if we actually have to match every individual location noun with an 'event'. Unfortunately, this makes our already large list even larger and more time-consuming to consult. Maybe we could have a more fine-grained classification of location nouns that matched the events. "Side" and "middle," for instance, might go together in most events where a man got hit (The robber hit the man in the [middle, side]). But even such promising simplifications run into odd problems. In the traffic accident case, "The car hit the man in the middle" means something entirely different. And, in fact, there is one further problem that we have ignored: the location nouns can be modified. In a sentence like "The car hit the man in the east side of the parking lot," "in the side" should be parsed in the same way that "in the street" would be.

Indeed, if we want to preclude failure, we must also take the context into account. If the previous sentence were, "Two men were walking side by side, one on the sidewalk and one in the street," then the phrase modifies 'man' not 'hit'. Remember, too, that if we could set up a system of classifications that would take context into account formally, we would still not be on safe ground. Each time we introduced a new system of classifications, old classifications that worked well would suddenly become unreliable. We would therefore have to go back and, at least, check and, at most, revise everything we had done before.

Such problems occur, let me remind you, because the hacks (the symbolic or formal labels we are attaching) have no natural relationship with the actual processes that are going on. We don't parse a sentence by thinking of what kind of location the park is, just as we don't understand a paragraph by checking the topic sentences. The hacks are just approximate solutions that are designed to work in a specific situation; so each time we try to generalize, they fail. And each time we fix the failure, it takes an enormous amount of work to get the new hack right. If this work is hard for "The car hit the man in the street," imagine how much work it would take to create a system that correctly parsed each sentence in this chapter.

The reason we want to develop a parser is that, ultimately, we want a computer that can take any English text and correctly detect in it a significant number of important errors. A prerequisite for that is a parser, and a prerequisite for that is a parser that parses sentences like "The X hit the Y in the Z." Yet accuracy even for that parser is almost insuperably difficult. Consider, now, how much work is left before the program can be built. We need to decide which errors we want to catch, to decide exactly what counts as an error, to calibrate the purpose and audience of documents, and to determine how purpose and audience affect the identification of errors; we also need to determine which errors are most important, to recommend how errors can be fixed, to design an interface, and to do all this in a reasonable amount of time. Each time we try to do any of this with hacks, we encounter odd, unpredictable inaccuracies, and each time we try to repair the hacks, either the system gets more jerry-rigged, or we have to start over again.

Not that this argument has prevented people from trying to implement the system I'm describing. For nine years, IBM has devoted a considerable task force to compiling the lists I've described, all in the service of a style-diction-grammar-spelling analyzer called EPIS-TLE. This chapter was originally written in the fall of 1984, just before I saw a private demonstration of this program. At that time, EPISTLE was in the experimental stage; it ran only on an IBM 370 in Kingston, New York. Even with that much computing power, the program limited the kinds of texts it analyzed, confining itself to "typical business or scientific communications."

On samples provided by IBM, the program was, according to IBM, about 75 percent accurate. That means, of course, that 25 percent of what is caught is wrong and 25 percent of what is there to be caught is missed. They did not say what the garbage ratio was. The program took about 20 minutes per page to analyze a text, and after it was finished, it worked interactively with the user, taking the user through the text and flagging each apparent error. The user then chose whether to correct the error. If the user was not sure about whether something was an error, the program could be consulted for further explanation. The program provided several different levels of explanation, ranging from a one-sentence identification of an error to several pages of explanation that resembled similar pages in textbooks.

In no sense, therefore, was the program an advance; indeed, it introduced two new forms of required compensation. It still required extensive analysis of the output, analysis which required a skill level so high that the only effective users would be those who didn't need it. It still imposed rules (of Grundian strictness, I might add) without explaining itself, demanding obedience rather than giving help. And it still was confusing and confused about the basic nature of language. Now, to all this, add the fact that you now must own an IBM 370 and wait 20 minutes per page before you can be subjected to its analysis.

At that demonstration, IBM anticipated (expected?) that the release would come in six to twelve months. At this writing, it is still alive, but it has been renamed, downgraded, and is being rewritten. If the release does come, the expense of the program means that it's likely to be used in business and technical contexts. In those contexts, it is plugged into the technology, not merely as a tool for producing text, but as an instrument for monitoring and control. Supervisors and managers would be buying it, and they would see the program as a way of gaining some more much-needed control over their subordinates' writing. There is certainly no guarantee that this control would be any less limiting than previous instances have been. The tool permits a manager to require that the Flesch score in any writing be below 9, that no sentence be longer than thirty words, and that there be no more than seven grammatical errors. The writer, then, would be forced to pay as much attention to the arbitrary limitations imposed by the program as to the very real limitations that the English language imposes. This program and others like it would then become what Joseph Weizenbaum calls "machines for manufacturing clichés."[48]

Overcoming the Limitations II:
How We Live with Them

If the programs are as weak and potentially harmful as I say, what explains the fact that people use them? Is it really that people are being ingenious? Or are the programs in fact more useful than I say? This last question gives a clue and at the same time brings the argument of this book full circle.

I have been treating these programs as things used in isolation. But to be more accurate about their use, I should also look at how their deployment functions in the organizations where they are most often used. Invention aids, for instance, are a tool for the teacher as well as the student; so are STYLE and DICTION and even spelling checkers. They permit teachers to lay off certain tasks, as we have seen, on students, and they permit teachers to exercise new kinds of objective control over the writing. In these days, where the use of the computer is still a novelty, and any such use may be written up, they also permit an objectification of what the teacher does.

There are strong reasons, therefore, for plugging these programs into the system, whether or not they work well. And in this case, the various inutilities, inconveniences, and damages caused by the use of these programs are relatively well hidden; the effects are attenuated and dispersed. The situation, indeed, mirrors what happens when writing itself is treated as a technology or as a collection of techniques.

The strategies that people have used to plug in these technologies and the dislocations of attention and values that attend those strategies might very well reflect the strategies people have used to plug in writing, and I want, therefore, to take a couple of pages to look at them. In form, the strategies have been twofold. First, people have acknowledged the limitations of these programs but claim that what I call "bugs" are actually "features." They then claim benefits for the features which are either implausible or probably attributable to some other cause. Second, they teach the users how to adapt to the limitations and claim some intrinsic virtue for that adaptation, while ignoring other potential benefits.

The first approach has often been taken by defenders of invention aids. Helen Schwartz argues, for instance, that the computer environment, in virtue of its being entirely nondirective, is likely to help weak writers overcome their fear and begin to generate responses. Schwartz adds, "Students soon realize they cannot get answers from the computer. They soon revel in the fact that *they* are doing the thinking, *not* the machine. The computer doesn't really know—or care—what the user says. This can be liberating" (Schwartz 1984, 241).

This argument ought to make us a bit nervous because its correctness does not depend on the program itself. No matter how well or badly written the invention program, the weak writer can still be helped by it. The benefit cited by this argument comes, rather, from the fact that the student is working with a computer. I think that's right; it's becoming a commonplace, now, that working on a computer is just better, though why I'm not sure. But if that's the source of the benefit, it is the teacher who should be liberated from the program; surely, there are better uses for the screen. In fact, Schwartz's program probably works because the answers are being sent by electronic mail to other students who comment on them. It is the students who are providing direction.

Schwartz's argument is similar to that advanced by Larson in favor of idea processors. The bug, remember, was that you were forced to rethink as you shifted entries around. This was a feature, Larson explained, because you could then perform "careful mental exploration of the boundaries of your . . . information" (P: 3). The program "lets you purposely shift your perspectives to gain as much information as possible." Using it "enables you to shift your view-points to bypass your current perceptions and attain additional insights." But just as with Schwartz's argument, Larson's claim would be true no matter how the program worked, just so long as it worked imperfectly. True, we get new ideas by having to update outline entries, but we would also get new ideas by contemplating our navel or by getting in our cars and driving around. There is no evidence that the former is more likely to generate productive ideas.

With text analyzers, defenders are more aware of the imperfections, but "in the right hands," they say, the programs are not harmful. In classes, the students can be taught about the imperfections; indeed, I know one class where the students are asked to analyze the computer's output, instead of vice versa. In the right hands, then, the details of the program would matter because they would be a way of teaching the student how to do those analyses better than the computer. The assumption, of course, is that, in the right hands, learning these things makes you into a better writer. Personally, I'm not sure a regimen of "construct" versus "build" makes one a better writer, but even if it did, it wouldn't be the program that did it; it would be those right hands.

A more remarkable fact about all such "fix the user" arguments is that, in the process of making them, the defenders of the programs ignore or misconstrue other potential benefits of using the programs. Surely the greatest benefit of a text analyzer like DICTION is that it gives you a new way of looking at the text. Flagging the text randomly or flagging the text on some other basis besides that of errors has the same benefit, without entering anyone into an error-catching game that's remarkable largely for its irrelevance.

When a teacher helps a student to use a tool like DICTION or an idea processor or even a word processor, something important happens. The teacher is right alongside the student, solving problems that both teacher and student experience. The teacher and student end up helping each other out. And later on, while the students are actually writing, the teacher is still there. A student can just ask any old question that happens to come up. A camaraderie develops. The teacher and student are together in front of the computer, instead of being in front of each other. And this camaraderie does more to help writing than any particular programming of the computer.

Many people have remarked on this, and a few agree with me that this relationship is more important to good writing than the tools themselves. But often enough, people fail to notice. And often they fail to exploit the chances. Helen Schwartz's experiences with electronic mail have been known for a long time. At Colorado State University, where the Writer's Workbench was first tested, the same system that has the Writer's Workbench also has excellent electronic mail. No one at Colorado State even knew that it existed (even though it's in the manual). And certainly no one thought of trying to exploit it. Indeed, this was still true two years after the experiments were over.

Several years ago, I circulated a list of questions that developers of writing tools should ask themselves before they develop a tool. Following is that list:

1. What's the special advantage of using the computer for this application? (Can it be done as well with pencil and paper?)
2. Which capacities of the computer does the application exploit? Is the program using symbol manipulation and transfer, or is it trying to simulate understanding of meaning?
3. To what extent does the accuracy of the application depend on its ability to understand the meaning of text or user responses?
4. Who, precisely, are the users; what, precisely, are the situations they'll be using your program in; and how, precisely, will the programs be useful to them?
5. How general is the application of the program? Overly general programs are likely to be useless; highly specific programs won't be easy to transfer.

In my eyes, the remarkable thing about development of computer writing aids is how little attention is paid to questions like these. I hesitate to make a big deal out of this. After all, life is full of confusions, and people who are unfamiliar with tools, but are excited by them, cannot be expected to learn everything in short order. And even after they have learned, there is plenty of room for honest disagreement with my views. You may want to see the defenses I've described as what naturally attends any new way of doing business, technology or not. But if you do, ask yourself whether the excitement, the energy, or the superficiality would be there if what were involved were a new tool that did not so nearly implicate us as human beings. Would a new kind of building technique or a new kind of television be so difficult to assess and easy to misuse?

Heidegger often presents the movement of technology as irreversible, a tide overwhelming us mortals on the beach. But I wonder whether the feints and thrusts of technology aren't more felt and reacted to by each of us, each of us coming to our own accommodation with these habits of mind. If so, then it is just as easy to make computers into tools, as it is to make us into technologies. In an appendix, I describe and evaluate some of the computer tools that will be developed if the current trends continue. I hope that I am wrong and that at least, in this area, computers are turned back into symbol processors, at the service of human beings talking to each other.

Last Notes

In this book, we have moved from coffee mills up to the life of the mind and back down to spelling. Everywhere, I have tried to point out the presence of a certain sad view of what human beings are, a view profoundly committed to the belief that human beings can know and control themselves simply by discovering rules according to which they work. We have seen this ideology in most peculiar forms: implicit in the way a man by the side of the road gives directions, exhibited in frustration over the inability of manufacturing to prevent people from hurting themselves, assumed as protective coloration by technical writers because their jobs are often not respected, advanced as the way of bringing academic studies of writing into respectability, embedded in sophisticated theories of how paragraphs work, embedded in not-so-sophisticated but automated ideas of how people organize. This is the way with ideologies: they have life because they exist within life and make sense of it.

I have been opposing to this an ideology committed to the belief that knowledge of oneself is grounded in one's situation and that knowledge itself does not consist of abstractions and rules. The struggle between these ideologies is long standing; it has not been part of my effort to find new defenses or push the enemy back in a frontal assault. The ground I have chosen to contest lies far from the main lines and has hitherto been untouched.

The peculiar interest of this territory has been that so many different kinds of endeavors have to cross the same ground. People who wish to understand how communication works in technology have chosen to come to a technological understanding of that communication. This works in one way because it permits the communication to be integrated, but it fails in another because attendant on such an integration are numerous confusions, misdirections of effort, and failures. This same technological understanding has also been turned upon writing that is not necessarily technological, writing which would not ordinarily be thought of in technological terms. This, too, has its successes, but again at the cost of a reductionism that obscures the territory around just while it apparently illuminates the path. And coming full circle, the understanding is turned back onto technology, to create technologies to serve the very technology understanding spawned.

The remarkable thing about these failures is that they occur at the margins of experience. Analysis requires careful winnowing through mountains of chaff. And once pulled out, the failures seem inconsequential. So what if Lorinda Cherry's program cannot tell whether "anticipate" or "expect" is used correctly. So what if coffee mill instructions don't tell us what we want to know, and so what if we get lost after getting apparently good directions. So what if one teacher tells students that papers should be written with outlines and another says that a student's technical writing is not objective enough. The people making these mistakes—if they are mistakes— are good-hearted enough. You know exactly why they're doing what they're doing. And in all probability, the user of the coffee mill or the outline is smart enough to get by, anyway.

The answer is simply that we can do better. We can treat the user of the coffee mill or the student as a complete human being, who brings to the coffee mill or the paper cares and interests and ideas. We can discover how communication works by studying our relationships with other human beings, not with abstract formal structures. We can build tools that work for us, not instead of us. And what we will find under our noses is something far more complex, far stranger, far more difficult to do or to understand, far more ordinary, and far more interesting and wonderful than anything we had hitherto suspected.

Appendix

The discussion of computers and writing in the previous chapter raises questions about what kinds of programs can be developed and how they can be used. The thesis of the chapter is that programs that do symbol-processing (respond to the form of the text) are likely to be useful, whereas those that attempt simulation will fail and are not likely to be as useful. The discussion is summed up in the following chart:

Application	Responds to	Accuracy/Flexibility	Utility
Communications	Form	Perfect	Great
Word Processing	Form (largely)	Near-perfect	Great
Spell Checkers	Form/Meaning	99%	Good
Text Analyzers	Meaning	Poor	Little
Idea Processors	Meaning	Inflexible	Little
Invention Aids	Meaning	Inflexible	Little

In this appendix, I present a similar chart of likely program developments:

Application	Responds to	Flexibility	Utility
Communications	Form		
a. 2-Author programs		Good	Good
b. Revision control programs		Fair	Fair
Word Processing	Form		
c. On-line editing		Good	Great
d. Formatting programs		Depends	Great
e. On-line dictionaries, etc.		Depends	Great
f. Note-taking "shells"		Fair	Fair

Spell Checkers	Form/ Meaning	99%	Good
Pedagogical Tools g. Drill programs	Form	Depends	Depends

Text Analyzers
  h. EPISTLE
  i. User-controlled
      analyzer
  j. Outliners
	Meaning	Limited
		Good
		
		Depends
			Limited
			Fair
			
			Limited

Idea Processors
  k. Improved idea
      processors
	Meaning	Some	Some

Invention Aids l. Template programs	Meaning	Some	Some

I think these will be built, not because I think they will be useful, but because programmers tend to build any program that can be built.[49] Following is a short description of each:

A. 2-Author programs.
    Word processors are only suited to one user at a time, but in modern corporate and scientific life, reports and papers are often coauthored. An environment that makes the mechanics of coauthorship easier would be a help. It might sort out drafts (see the following), make on-line editing easier (see the following), and make sharing of data easier (see the following). For these applications to work, the authors have to be in control. If they aren't (for instance, if the authors of the program already have an idea about how coauthoring ought to work), the programs will in effect be responding to meaning, and they will hamper creativity much as the idea processors do.

Utility:

Good, because currently coauthorship faces mechanical problems that can be overcome by simple mechanical symbol processing.

Expense:

Minimal, if good editing and revision-control programs are developed.

B.   Revision control programs.

Good word processing makes it easy to have many versions of a document. It's hard to keep track of them. Programmers have much the same problem; for that reason, they have developed "revision-control programs" that allow systematic labeling of revisions and a quick determination of the kinds of changes. These, coupled with good programming practices, are all that makes it possible to have five or ten programmers working on the same project. Analogous programs for writing are much more difficult to develop and use because the nature of the revisions is much harder to determine. Still, they are possible to build in principle, and they would partly help to overcome the single worst problem of using a computer for writing: it's harder to scan what you have in the same way that you do when it is all laid out on a desk.

The temptation with these programs is to make them responsive to the meaning of the changes. If this temptation is not resisted, the programs will hamper the user just as idea processors do.

Utility:

Fair, because using these requires a good deal of discipline in writing and some preparation. Many people won't want to bother.

Expense:

It will require a breakthrough to design a good one. None will be useful unless the user has a fairly big system with lots of memory. The revisions have to be put somewhere, and it will take a lot of computing power to sort through them.

C.   On-line editing.

Teachers, editors, managers, everyone sees the need for

this. As it is, there's no convenient way of adding marginal notes, making suggested revisions, or identifying editorial changes on a computer file. Two basic approaches can be taken. First, one can use current technology and develop a set of symbols that indicate various kinds of editing comments. The comments themselves can then be placed in the text or else in a separate file, with perhaps a link by way of the symbols. This approach is better for professional editing, less good for coauthors or managers, who won't learn the symbols, or for teachers, who must make extensive comments.

The other approach is to count on a technological breakthrough of some kind. One possibility is that editing takes place in a special graphics environment, where editing comments can be inserted in different fonts or on different lines or on the side, the way they are on paper. Or, the editing comments can be kept in a separate window, which is again linked to the text. Combinations, of course, are also possible.

Again, editing systems that presuppose a preferred model of editing or automatic responses to text will not work well. Some teachers, for instance, have categories of errors, and an on-line data base of descriptions of those errors. They mark the error with a category label, and the student looks in the database. This allows accounting of error-types, but otherwise it's no more effective than doing the same thing by hand, which we've been able to do for years with no discernible effect.

Utility:
On-line editing offers the same advantages that word-processing does: it's easier to change things and it's easier to move the finished documents.

Expense:
At the moment, editing symbols are technically possible, but no adequate standard has been developed. A graphics environment seems theoretically possible, but it will take years to develop and will require much computing power.

D.   Formatting programs.
These already exist, but they're not in widespread use. In most writing, formatting and design issues are important. Writers who use formatting programs can often be more

flexible and imaginative in the way they present themselves, although, without proper training, they can spend inordinate amounts of time to very little effect. Teachers of professional writing must soon begin teaching how to use the formatting capabilities that formatting and typesetting programs give.

Utility:
In the hands of a good writer, a considerable boon. Otherwise not.

E.   On-line dictionaries, thesauruses, and so forth.
These, too, already exist on some machines, though the lack of completeness sometimes makes them fairly useless. More complete programs, which include dictionary entries as well as the words themselves, must be a help, most obviously for the person working with the output of a spelling checker.

Utility:
One might think the more accessible the better, but programs available from Xerox or Borland, which beep at you as soon as they do it, recognizing the word you're typing, are probably too intrusive.

Expense:
Complete on-line dictionaries take up huge amounts of space and take enormous amounts of time to search. They will probably only be practical when everybody has 50MB storage and 3MB memory, but maybe not even then.[50]

F.   Note-taking "shells."
Environments that make assembling and planning documents (or other work) already exist for certain kinds of applications. Many companies market computerized "engineering notebooks," which allow one to record, graph, analyze, and report data in experiments with relative ease. Similar financial reporting packages also exist. The advantage of these is that they make mathematical analysis and graphing easy; they also provide a single place (a relatively safe place) to store the data. The disadvantage, of course, is that it's hard to scan or move knowledgeably from one part to another.

Xerox Corporation is now working on a more general adaptation of this idea. Called Note-Cards, the application would allow you to put any notes you want on a "card" and then label the notes with convenient key words (or whatever). The system would make it easy for you to find related cards, by checking the key words or by looking for 'similar' entries in other cards, the similarity being specified by the user.[51]

Utility:

Using something like this requires both discipline and training, but once you've learned how, it is the kind of symbol processing support one would like to have. The temptation in the design, of course, will be to try making the system responsive to the meaning of the entries. The more that's done, the more constricting the system becomes. The verdict, therefore, on such systems is still out.

Expense:

Right now, prohibitive, as the application requires enormous amounts of graphics and searching capabilities.[52]

G. Drill programs.

A trivial, but perhaps valuable, application. It is theoretically possible to construct a data base of bad examples: failed sentences or paragraphs, whose failure has some instructive value. Access to the data base can be put in the form of a drill program. A student (or professional writer) who is aware of a personal propensity for committing a certain kind of error can call up many examples of the same error (with or without explanations) and analyze and correct them. This database, of course, can contain any kind of example, and it can be built up over time. The student, for instance, can contribute personal examples and explanations.

Utility:

Depends on pedagogical context. Some teachers, like myself, who can always use more examples, would like it.

Expense:

Merely the cost of developing and maintaining the database, plus developing the interface.

H.-I. EPISTLE and user-controlled analyzers.[53]

EPISTLE could be much more useful if it were adjustable. If it could be set only to do spelling and checking for certain kinds of inadvertent errors (like subject-verb disagreement), the garbage ratio would be vastly reduced. The same is true of the other text-analysis programs. DICTION, I recently discovered, does allow you to use your own wordlist. That capability could be useful, since writers do have certain bad habits that they fall into despite precautions. Such "inadvertent" errors can be identified, and then, with DICTION, they can be checked for. (A program recently added to the Writer's Workbench checks for inadvertently doubled words, like 'the the'. The benefits of this probably outweigh the costs because the garbage ratio should be low.)[54]

J.-K. Outliners-Improved idea processors
Obviously, idea processors can be made more flexible, and the more flexible they are, the more useful they become.[55]

In an ideal world, an idea processor would exert fairly continuous control over the document as it was written. Lotus Development Corporation (makers of "Lotus 1-2-3") is soon coming out with a product that will allow you to overlay the relevant portion of the outline (and amend it) on the text. In effect, this allows one to scan backward or forward quickly, always an advantage, though scarcely a great one, but, at Lotus's prices, perhaps more a gewgaw than a tool.[56]

Better, perhaps, would be programs that 'outlined' the actual text. The outline, of course, would be only a simulation, and probably it wouldn't work. One such idea is to put in the outline the headings and the first sentence of each paragraph. Bob Berwick, a computer scientist at MIT, suggests that certain refinements can be made; an algorithm could provide, instead of the first sentence, the sentence with the greatest number of 'abstract words', which would be more likely to be illuminating.[57] Obviously, of course, it would be better for users to "outline" as they go along. Simple ways might be to have a memory-resident outliner, which the disciplined believers in outlines would fill in as they went along. Or, since the sophisticated outliners are already using an indexing program, they could present the sentences with the key, indexed words. All my general objections to outlines would apply to some extent, but the purpose of such programs is to give people a quick way of placing themselves in the document, something which is so necessary that the work of compensating for the computer's limitations might prove to be worthwhile.[58]

L. Template programs.
Certain kinds of writing assignments are apparently cook-

book. The structure of the piece is known in advance; it is even known that certain sections should contain certain items. Why not, therefore, provide the writer, particularly the student writer, with the structure in advance. Why not, for that matter, test each section to see whether certain key words (indicative of key information) are present?

To answer, we need to distinguish between a model and a template. A model shows how any element of a piece of writing works within its context. A template assumes (yet again) that the features of a text are context free, independent of the overall meaning. To provide a model is to provide a guideline for the structuring of a text; to provide a template is to provide strict rules. The one is a response to meaning; the other isn't. Template programs, therefore, ought to fail whenever some apparently extraneous factor (the failure of the experiment, some new result, an unusual approach) makes certain apparently necessary features obstructive. The overall utility of a template program, like that of drill programs, depends entirely on how well-analyzed the possible results are. In general, this analysis is so difficult and so pointless in itself that template programs are not worth the effort. Giving writers models and pointing out what makes them successful is much more likely to work.

I have tried, in the foregoing, to suggest that symbol processing applications will work well; meaning-processing applications won't. I should point out, however, that not every symbol-processing application is desirable. Consider the following, all of which are possible right now.

Monitoring Programs

Teachers or researchers can right now, today, set things up so that they can watch and record every keystroke the writer makes. If they choose, moreover, they can intervene any time they want. The advantages of this capability for certain kinds of research into the writing process are obvious. Whether the advantages ought to be taken up is a difficult question.

Productivity Measures

Monitoring programs can be adapted (perhaps by analogy with template programs) so that the quantity, and perhaps the effectiveness, of people's writing is continually measured.

Are any of the programs described in this appendix very important? No. They relieve us of no important work; like any expensive convenience, they would rapidly become inconveniences when misused. The people who use them best would be those who could get along well without them. Much, of course, depends on the implementation. In general, the more the operation of a program is given over to the user, the better the program will be. DICTION with your own wordlist is better than DICTION with Lorinda Cherry's. Where the aim of the builder is to build a tool you can use, the tool will be better. Where the aim is to do the thinking for you, it will not.

Are any programs missing from the list but crying out to be built? I have given some idea in the chapter. But before I made any final conclusion, I went around the artificial intelligence lab at MIT and asked the researchers there what kinds of tools ought to be developed as writing aids. I will let two of them have the last word. Their answers:

Better word processors
—Douglas Hofstadter

Better word processors
—Joseph Weizenbaum

Notes

1. Almost all this material is drawn from John Searle's *Speech Acts*. The relevance condition is my addition to Searle's work.

2. Notice, by the way, that we all play the speech act game, whether we consciously know the rules or not. We know, for instance, that "Is the door shut?" is defective; that's why such questions are good ways of starting fights and why one way of stopping the impending fight is to claim that you really meant the question seriously.

3. Obviously, the extent to which the reader is obligated to hear the writer out depends on what each would consider to be a reasonable amount of time to devote to the instructions. No one, by beginning to read instructions for the coffee mill, is obligated to read fifty pages.

4. This example, like the football game example and the door-shutting example, is Searle's.

5. A case that involved precisely this issue may be the source of this information. A girl was burned when her parents put a boiling-water humidifier on top of a stool and she tripped over the cord. The court ruled that there should have been a warning on the humidifier; that decision is probably the source of several of the instructions you've just read. I think that the decision was correct but badly interpreted. The warning should be there, but only because there was an unusual situation, a badly engineered lid, and a specific, boiling-water design. The error the parents made was thinking that the water would not spill. The parents would not, after all, have put an open pot of boiling water on the dresser. (*McCormack v. Hankscraft Co.* 278 Minn. 322, 154 N.W. 488, 1967.)

6. One of the members of my original audience suggested that the instructions were actually a translation from the German and that their form could be explained by the German tendency toward precision.

7. I owe this example and much of my thinking about this subject to Kevin Lynch. Lynch prefers cities that demand an intimate knowledge of them in order to orient oneself. He says those cities are more "imageable." See Lynch 1960.

8. Productively, of course. There is plenty of technical writing that makes one work for no reason.

9. Weaver is explicit about this (see Shannon and Weaver 1949, 116).

10. Those readers interested in this problem should go to Richard Rorty, *Philosophy and the Mirror of Nature* (Princeton: Princeton University Press, 1980). For an account of colors and pains, see the beginning of the book. For an account of objectivity that roughly parallels mine, see pages 303–43.

11. For more, see *Being and Time* (Heidegger 1962), especially sections 25–27. The translation of "das Man" as "the anyone" is Hubert Dreyfus's.

12. The standard objection to this account goes as follows: "In experiencing things technologically, I am not entirely taken over. There's still something human about me. As I sit on the subway seat, I rage against the dispiriting ambience." I grant the rage, but I don't think it's an objection. First of all, being human and experiencing things technologically are not at all distinct. Experiencing things technologically is one way human beings may be. Second, it's often a little hard to tell when your experience is not technological. Technology is perfectly capable of taking your "humanity" and putting it to use. Subway designers know all about my rage; it's anyone's. That's why they make tough seats and graffiti-resistant walls.

13. It's a mistake, therefore, to think of the emotional, fallible parts of ourselves as the X-factor, as what causes a technological judgment to go wrong. In technological judgments there is often uncertainty and individual variation. Technology is just good at evaluating that uncertainty and taking it into account in making the judgment or assessing its reliability.

14. I discuss this usage more in "A Teaching Tip," *Technical Communication* 32 (3): 44.

15. For the scoop on aviation, look up Ader in the Larousse.

16. It is our Background skills relating to VIPs, evaluation of friends, social status and so forth that allow us to draw that conclusion.

17. The actual audience, remember, is never a fiction.

18. A computer works just like a huge filing cabinet; the difference is that you can't just reach in and search for the files and get them out. Instead the computer has to do it.

19. Because we are taught to use outlines when writing papers, I will use the word "paper" throughout this chapter to mean any piece of writing.

20. I owe this observation to David Rodes.

21. When we're criticizing a paper or reviewing it, such metaphors are more appropriate, but even so, slightly off the mark. Criticisms of pieces of writing are largely concerned with content, the mode of life we would have in a building, not with form, the structure of the building itself.

22. This point is more controversial than it may seem; those who investigate into the writing process generally assume that the process is recoverable.

23. Let us assume, for the purposes of argument, that the FDR Drive is closed.

24. The term "horizon," which I've occasionally used before, comes from phenomenology. All the ideas and relationships we have in mind and have available, consciously or unconsciously, at any point as we have an Intentional State make up the "horizon." A landmark "focuses" that horizon. I should add that my phenomenological account is not cognitivist because it does not require that the conceptions be representational. For a cognitivist account, see Linda Flower and many others. Flower's phenomenology often resembles mine, but her ideas about mechanisms are opposed to mine. See Flower and Hayes 1977; Flower and Hayes, "Cognition of Discovery," 1980;

Flower and Hayes, "The Dynamics of Composing," 1980; Flower and Hayes, "The Pregnant Pause," 1981; Gebhardt 1982; Gregg and Steinberg 1980; Perl 1980.

25. This is, of course, a general problem—the major one with Flower's or Perl's attempts at analyzing the composing process. See also Marilyn Cooper and Michael Holzman 1983.

26. I am setting aside generic determinations of structure, of course. In any "modular" paper (one with prescribed parts, like certain technical reports), an outline entry might be a way of starting off a new module.

27. The standard terminology in the field is confused on this point. Most commentators, as I understand them, use the terms in the common speech sense, but some, like Robin Bell Markels, use "cohesion" for what I am calling coherence (Faigley and Witte 1981; Halliday and Hasan 1976; Markels 1984).

28. Familiar, of course, to the reader. This rule of thumb is one way of making your prose what Linda Flower calls "reader-based." More on Flower later.

29. Here I'm borrowing a little from Roger Schank (Schank and Abelson 1977), another influential cognitive scientist.

30. The term "shape" is Jerry Fodor's (Fodor 1981). What exactly is meant by the term is a very difficult philosophical problem, as Fodor indicates.

31. Strictly speaking, of course, it's not a computer but a word-processing program that defines a 'word' this way. A computer itself has no definition for a "word."

32. Helen Schwartz, one of the first to develop invention aids, always has her students send the answers to other students, who criticize them. The pedagogical power of this approach lies in the use of electronic mail, not invention aids (Schwartz 1985). The benefits would be approximately the same, for instance, if she had students trade first paragraphs.

33. This sequence is inspired by WANDAH, a program developed at UCLA by Michael Cohen, Lisa Gerrard, and others.

34. The programs are quite successful; ThinkTank, one of the programs, perenially appears on the software best-seller list.

35. MaxThink takes many of its ideas from LISP, an artificial intelligence programming language.

36. These and the following claims come from promotional material for MaxThink (P), from the *MaxThink Newsletter* (N), and from the MaxThink manual (M). All are published circa 1984 by the MaxThink Corporation, Piedmont, California. References for the quotations will give the letter and page number, where pages are numbered.

37. This paragraph was written before the advent of Hypercard. Obviously, Hypercard stacks are better planning tools, as I suggest. But they still have some of the limitations I mention.

38. A Swiss student once asked me to "go and bring him a cup of coffee." He didn't say "get him a cup," I found out, because he was told that "get" is not used in proper English. I know why he was told that, but look at the contortions it caused for him ever afterwards.

39. One program in the Writer's Workbench checks for sexist language.

40. The user can add or subtract words from DICTION's master list, so that one could limit the list to words like 'might of'. See the UNIX User's Manual for details, if you can understand them.

41. I was once on a panel with a teacher (who shall remain nameless) who taught DICTION. This teacher showed some sample sentences in which DICTION correctly identified errors. In each case, those sentences could have been fixed better by ignoring the advice of the program, and in each case, the teacher failed to notice that.

42. Lawrence J. Oliver voices similar objections to text analysis programs (Oliver 1984).

43. Lorinda Cherry estimates that the type of each sentence is identified accurately about 86.5% of the time. Her sample, however, was only 20 technical documents. You should, of course, be as skeptical about her claims as you are about claims for other computer programs. See L. L. Cherry and W. Vesterman. "Writing Tools—The STYLE and DICTION Programs." *The UNIX User's Guide*. Murray Hill, New Jersey: Bell Laboratories, 1980, p. 10.

44. Flesch, Coleman-Liau, and others are all measures of the readability of a piece of text. The higher the score, the longer the sentence and the more syllables per word. Theoretically, the sentence is readable by someone reading at a ninth grade reading level.

45. See Cherry and Vesterman 1980, 7.

46. As this book goes to press, I have just tested a new parser, CorrecText from Houghton Mifflin, which parses sentences much better than any previous parser, including EPISTLE. It is not, however, perfectly accurate. Its makers readily admit that it can't be for the reasons described below.

47. Actually, a lot more fiddling. See Minsky 1975, 211–77 and Dreyfus, as usual, for a criticism of Minsky.

48. Personal communication, May 15, 1984.

49. The computer industry changes quickly, so it is important to be clear about dates. The analysis contained in the chart was done in early 1984. The predictions that follow were written then, but revised in 1985. In November 1987, they were reviewed once more; to acknowledge changes, I added some footnotes, which are dated November 1987. In October 1988, the predictions were reviewed once more, and the notes about CorrecText were added. The substance of the text, however, has remained what it was in 1984–85.

50. Steven Job's NEXT computer has 250MB storage and 8MB memory and comes with an on-line dictionary and thesaurus (October 1988).

51. HyperCard, which I had not heard of when I wrote this prediction, is by far the most interesting such shell. A program which comes free with every new Macintosh, it is essentially a multidimensional note-card program that permits you to branch out with associated note cards from any notation on the original or subsequent cards (November 1987). Agenda, from Lotus Development Corporation, is a similar note-taking shell for the PC which has only recently become available. Note that both products suffer from the same kinds of limitations as MaxThink but can overcome them

better because their model of relationships among items is much more flexible (October 1988).

52. Computers have improved, and as noted above, reasonable versions of these programs are available at relatively low cost (October 1988).

53. And, as noted in chapter 9, CorrecText from Houghton Mifflin (October 1988).

54. CorrecText, too, needs to be adaptable. Too many of the errors even it catches are irrelevant or not really errors. Users need to be able to set it to catch the errors they are likely to make (October 1988).

55. Since 1985, idea processors did become more flexible, but they have largely been superseded by HyperCard-like applications (October 1988).

56. The product, Manuscript, has appeared, has not justified my invidious comment about prices, for which I apologize, and has had moderate, but not great success (October 1988).

57. Personal communication, May 2, 1984.

58. None of these applications have been written, so far as I know (October 1988).

Works Cited

Andrews, Deborah, and Margaret D. Blickle. *Technical Writing: Principles and Forms*. New York: Macmillan, 1982.

Austin, John L. *How To Do Things with Words*. Cambridge, Mass.: Harvard University Press, 1962.

Bly, Robert W., and Gary Blake. *Technical Writing: Structure, Standards, and Style*. New York: McGraw-Hill, 1982.

Britton, W. E. "What Is Technical Writing? A Redefinition." In *The Teaching of Technical Writing*, edited by D. H. Cunningham and H. A. Estrin, 23–33. Urbana, Ill.: NCTE, 1975.

Burns, Hugh. *Stimulating Rhetorical Invention in English Composition through Computer-Assisted Instruction*. Ph.D. Thesis. Austin: University of Texas, 1979.

Carter, R. "Technical Writing: A Framework for Change." *The Technical Writing Teacher* 7 (Fall 1979): 39–42.

Cooper, Marilyn, and Michael Holzman. "Talking about Protocols." *College Composition and Communication* 34 (October 1983): 284–93.

Dandridge, E. P. "Notes Toward a Definition of Technical Writing." In *The Teaching of Technical Writing*, edited by D. H. Cunningham and H. A. Estrin, 15–20. Urbana, Ill.: NCTE, 1975.

Dennett, Daniel. "Cognitive Wheels: The Frame Problem of AI." In *Minds, Machines and Evolution*, edited by C. Hookway, 129–51. Cambridge, England: Cambridge University Press, 1984.

Dewey, John. *Democracy and Education: An Introduction to the Philosophy of Education*. New York: Macmillan, 1924.

Dreyfus, H. *What Computers Can't Do*. Rev. ed. New York: Harper and Row, 1979.

Ede, Lisa. "On Audience and Composition." *College Composition and Communication* 30 (October 1979): 291–95.

Ede, Lisa, and Andrea Lunsford. "Audience Addressed/Audience Invoked: The Role of Audience in Composition Theory and Pedagogy." *College Composition and Communication* 35 (May 1984): 155–71.

Faigley, Lester, and Stephen P. Witte. "Coherence, Cohesion, and Writing Quality." *College Composition and Communication* 32 (May 1981): 190–95.

Flower, Linda, and John R. Hayes. "Problem-Solving Strategies and the Writing Process." *College English* 39 (December 1977): 499–61.

———. "The Cognition of Discovery: Defining a Rhetorical Problem." *College Composition and Communication* 31 (February 1980): 21–32.

————. "The Dynamics of Composing: Making Plans and Juggling Constraints." In *Cognitive Processes in Writing*, edited by Lee Gregg and Erwin Steinberg, 31–50. Hillside, N.J.: Erlbaum, 1980.

————. "A Cognitive Process Theory of Writing." *College Composition and Communication* 32 (December 1981): 359–82.

————. "The Pregnant Pause: An Inquiry into the Nature of Planning." *Research into the Teaching of English* 15 (October 1981): 229–43.

Fodor, Jerry. "Methodological Solipsism Considered as a Research Strategy in Cognitive Science." In *Mind Design*, edited by John Haugeland, 307–38. Cambridge, Mass.: MIT Press, 1981.

————. *The Modularity of Mind*. Cambridge, Mass.: MIT Press, 1983.

Gebhardt, Richard C. "Initial Plans and Spontaneous Composition: Toward a Comprehensive Theory of the Writing Process." *College English* 44 (October 1982): 620–27.

Gregg, Lee, and Erwin Steinberg, eds. *Cognitive Processes in Writing*. Hillside, N.J.: Erlbaum, 1980.

Hairston, Maxine. "The Winds of Change: Thomas Kuhn and the Revolution in the Teaching of Writing." *College Composition and Communication* 33 (February 1982): 76–89.

Halliday, M. A. K., and Ruqaiya Hasan, *Cohesion in English*. London: Longman, 1976.

Harris, J. S. "On Expanding the Definition of Technical Writing." *Journal of Writing and Communication* 8 (Spring 1978): 133–38.

Hays, R. "What is Technical Writing?" In *The Teaching of Technical Writing*, edited by D. H. Cunningham and H. A. Estrin, 3–8. Urbana, Ill.: NCTE, 1975.

Hays, Robert. "Model Outlines Can Make Routine Writing Easier." *Technical Communication* 29 (First Quarter 1982): 4–8.

Heidegger, Martin. *Being and Time*. New York: Harper and Row, 1962.

————. *The Question Concerning Technology*. New York: Harper and Row, 1977.

Hirsch, E. D. *Validity in Interpretation*. New Haven: Yale University Press, 1967.

Husserl, Edmund. *Experience and Judgement*. Evanston, Ill.: Northwestern University Press, 1973.

Kelley, P. M., and R. E. Masse. "A Definition of Technical Writing." *The Technical Writing Teacher* 7 (Fall 1977): 39–42.

Lannon, John. *Technical Writing*. Boston: Little, Brown, 1982.

Lynch, K. *The Image of the City*. Cambridge, Mass.: MIT Press, 1960.

MacIntosh, F. H. "Where Do We Go From Here?" *Journal of Technical Writing and Communication* 8 (Spring 1978): 139–45.

Marcuse, Herbert. *One-Dimensional Man*. Boston: Beacon Press, 1964.

Markels, Robin Bell. *A New Perspective on Cohesion in Expository Paragraphs*. Carbondale, Ill.: Southern Illinois University Press, 1984.

Miller, Carolyn. "A Humanistic Rationale for Technical Writing." *College English* 40 (February 1979): 610–17.

Minsky, Marvin. "A Framework for Representing Knowledge." In *The Psychology of Computer Vision*, edited by P. Winston, 211–17. New York: McGraw-Hill, 1975.

———. "A Framework for Representing Knowledge." In *Mind Design*, edited by John Haugeland, 95–128. Cambridge, Mass.: MIT Press, 1981.

Oliver, Lawrence J. "Monster, Not Mentor: A Comment on 'Monsters and Mentors'." *College English* 46 (April 1984): 410–14.

Paradis, James, and David Dobrin. "Writing at the EXXON Intermediates Technology Division: A Study in Organizational Communication." *Tech. Rept. 2*. Cambridge, Mass.: MIT Writing Program, 1984.

Pearsall, Thomas. *Teaching Technical Writing: Methods for College English Teachers*. New York: Society for Technical Communication, 1975.

Perl, Sondra. "Understanding Composing." *College Composition and Communication* 31 (December 1980): 363–69.

Plung, Daniel L. "The Advantages of Sentence Outlining." *Technical Communication* 29 (First Quarter 1982): 8–10.

Quine, W. V. O. "Two Dogmas of Empiricism." In *From a Logical Point of View*. Cambridge, Mass.: Harvard University Press, 1953.

———. *Word and Object*. Cambridge, Mass.: MIT Press, 1960.

Rabinovitch, M. "Technical Writing's Last Stand." *Technical Communication* 27 (Third Quarter 1980): 23–25.

Rathbone, R. *Communicating Technical Information*. Reading, Mass.: Addison-Wesley Publishing Company, 1966.

Schank, Roger C., and Robert P. Abelson. *Scripts, Plans, Goals, and Understanding: An Inquiry into Human Knowledge Structures*. Hillside, N.J.: Erlbaum, 1977.

Schwartz, Helen J. "Teaching Writing with Computer Aids." *College English* 46 (March 1984): 239–47.

Schwartz, Helen. "Critical Inquiry with Computer Programs." Paper presented to Conference on College Composition and Communication, Minneapolis, 1985.

Searle, John R. *Speech Acts*. Cambridge, England: Cambridge University Press, 1969.

———. *Expression and Meaning*. Cambridge, England: Cambridge University Press, 1979.

———. *Intentionality*. Cambridge, England: Cambridge University Press, 1983.

Shannon, Claude E., and Warren Weaver. *The Mathematical Theory of Communication*. Urbana, Ill.: University of Illinois Press, 1949. Pages 1–96 are Shannon's; the rest are Weaver's.

Sparrow, W. K. "Six Myths about Writing for Business and Government." *The Technical Writing Teacher* 3 (1976), 49–59.

Stratton, C. R. "Technical Writing: What It Is and What It Isn't." *Journal of Technical Writing and Communication* 9 (1979), 9–16.

Steiner, George. *After Babel: Aspects of Language and Translation*. London: Oxford University Press, 1975.

Walter, J. A. "Technical Writing: Species or Genus?" *Technical Communication* 24 (First Quarter 1977): 6–8.

Wittgenstein, Ludwig. *Philosophical Investigations*. New York: Macmillan, 1946.

———. *The Blue and Brown Books*. 2nd ed. London: Basil Blackwell, 1958. New York: Harper and Row, 1960.

Author

David N. Dobrin is president of Lexicom, a consulting firm in Cambridge, Massachusetts, which specializes in technical communication. His articles on subjects ranging from theory of technical communication to theory of warnings have appeared in many anthologies and such magazines as *College English*, *Computers and Composition*, and *Righting Words*. Before turning to consulting, he taught writing and literature at UCLA, Miami University, Berkeley, and MIT.

EP94